ROUTLEDGE LIBRARY EDITIONS:
COMMUNICATION STUDIES

Volume 8

THE ART OF LISTENING

THE ART OF LISTENING

Edited by
GRAHAM MCGREGOR AND R.S. WHITE

Routledge
Taylor & Francis Group
LONDON AND NEW YORK

First published in 1986 by Croom Helm

This edition first published in 2016
by Routledge
2 Park Square, Milton Park, Abingdon, Oxon OX14 4RN

and by Routledge
711 Third Avenue, New York, NY 10017

Routledge is an imprint of the Taylor & Francis Group, an informa business

British Library Cataloguing in Publication Data
A catalogue record for this book is available from the British Library

ISBN: 978-1-138-93903-5 (Set)
ISBN: 978-1-315-67052-2 (Set) (ebk)
ISBN: 978-1-138-94153-3 (Volume 8) (hbk)
ISBN: 978-1-138-95953-8 (Volume 8) (pbk)
ISBN: 978-1-315-67046-1 (Volume 8) (ebk)

Publisher's Note
The publisher has gone to great lengths to ensure the quality of this reprint but points out that some imperfections in the original copies may be apparent.

Disclaimer
The publisher has made every effort to trace copyright holders and would welcome correspondence from those they have been unable to trace.

THE ART OF LISTENING

Edited by
Graham McGregor
R.S. White

CROOM HELM
London • Sydney • Dover, New Hampshire

Croom Helm Ltd, Provident House, Burrell Row,
Beckenham, Kent, BR3 1AT

Croom Helm Australia Pty Ltd, Suite 4, 6th Floor,
64-76 Kippax Street, Surry Hills, NSW 2010, Australia

British Library Cataloguing in Publication Data

The Art of listening.
1. Psycholinguistics 2. Comprehension
3. Listening
I. McGregor, Graham II. White, Robert
401'.9 BF455

ISBN 0-7099-4654-6

Croom Helm, 27 South Main Street
Wolfeboro, New Hampshire 03894-2069 USA

Library of Congress Cataloging-in-Publication Data

The Art of listening.

Bibliography: p.
1. Listening. 2. Communication. I. McGregor,
Graham. II. White, R.S., 1948-
P95.46.A78 1986 001.54'2 86-11658
ISBN 0-7099-4654-6

Printed and bound in Great Britain by Mackays of Chatham Ltd, Kent

CONTENTS

Contents

NOTES ON CONTRIBUTORS

LINDA ANDERSON, after taking her PhD at Aberdeen, was James Knott Fellow at the University of Newcastle upon Tyne, where she is now a Lecturer in English Literature. She is author of _Bennett, Wells and Conrad: Narrative in Transition_ , Macmillan, 1986. She was a co-founder and is now co-editor of _Writing Women_ and is at present working on a book on women and autobiography.

DESMOND GRAHAM is Senior Lecturer in English Literature at the University of Newcastle upon Tyne. He has taught in Tubingen, Mannheim and Munich universities; biographer and editor of Keith Douglas; recent publications include _The Truth of War: Owen, Blunden and Rosenberg_ (1984) and _Keith Douglas: A Prose Miscellany_ (1985).

REBECCA HISCOCK is writing her PhD on the novels of Dorothy Richardson for the University of Newcastle upon Tyne where she took her first degree. She has contributed to _Writing Women_, has worked in the theatre and is at present writing a screenplay. She lives at Corbridge, Northumberland.

CLAIRE HUMPHREYS-JONES lives in the Isle of Man and is completing a PhD, for the University of Newcastle Upon Tyne. She also took her first degree at Newcastle. Her thesis is titled _An Investigation of the Structure and Types of Misunderstanding_. Two other articles based on her research are to be published in edited volumes due out this year.

R. A. LUMSDEN, poet and teacher of literature, took degrees at Sussex and East Anglia. He has taught at the National University of Singapore, where he published his latest essay in _Tropic Crucible_ (1984). He is now living in his birthplace in Australia, writing and seeking publishers for his poems.

Notes on Contributors

GRAHAM McGREGOR originally trained as a school teacher before undertaking postgraduate studies at the University of Newcastle upon Tyne. Following work in schools and as an English language tutor, he was appointed to his current position of Lecturer in English Language. He has published several articles on listener oriented approaches to the study of discourse and apart from this volume, has also edited *Language for Hearers* (Pergamon Press) which is due to appear later this year.

LESLEY MILROY is Lecturer in Speech at the University of Newcastle upon Tyne. She was previously Principal Lecturer in Linguistics at Ulster Polytechnic and Senior Simon Research Fellow at the University of Manchester. She is author of *Language and Social Networks* (Blackwell, 1980) and is co-author of *Authority in Language*, (Routledge & Kegan Paul, 1985).

NORBERT H. PLATZ is Professor of English Literature at Mannheim University. His publications include translations of *Tess of the D'Urbervilles* and *Twelfth Night*; works on Ben Jonson, English Dramatic Theories and Contemporary British Drama. *Writing with a Purpose: The Reader in Nineteenth Century Fiction* will appear in 1986.

NEIL SAMMELLS, after taking his PhD at London University was Lecturer in English Literature at the University of Newcastle upon Tyne, and he is now lecturing at Bath College of Higher Education. He has published articles on modern drama and his book on Tom Stoppard is being published by Macmillan.

TRUDE SCHWAB was educated at Mannheim University and has lived and worked in Heidelberg and Frankfurt. She is currently a freelance translator in Newcastle upon Tyne and is preparing a translation of short stories by Ingeborg Bachman for Carcanet Press.

JOHN PELLOWE has taught linguistics at Universities in England, Libya and Singapore. He is well known for his scholarly contributions to Sociolinguistics, the latest of which is the essay 'For Ourselves We Are Silent' in *Tropic Crucible* (University of Singapore, 1984). At present he is renovating a cottage in Italy.

MICHAEL PICKERING is Senior Lecturer in Communication Studies at Sunderland Polytechnic. He is author of *Village Song and Culture* (London, Croom Helm 1982), which won the 1982 Katherine Briggs Memorial Prize. He teaches cultural and mass media studies, and has also published in the area of working class writing, documentary and music hall culture. His major area of current research is on the topic of autobiography.

R. S. WHITE grew up in Sydney and was educated at Adelaide (Law and Arts) and Balliol College Oxford. He is Lecturer in English Literature at Newcastle upon Tyne and has been Visiting Research Fellow at the Australian National University. He has published many articles and three books on Shakespeare, the latest of which is *Innocent Victims: Poetic Injustice in Shakespearean Tragedy* (Athlone, 1986). *Keats as a Reader of Shakespeare* will appear in 1986.

INTRODUCTION

This collection of essays represents an idea applied to various bodies of material. The idea is that the active and creative abilities of listeners and readers deserve as much if not more attention than the skills of speakers and writers[1]. Behind the essays lies a belief that knowledge should not be compartmentalised. Although the expertise of one individual may be limited to a subject area, knowledge can be a unity at the level of guiding ideas. The authority of methodologies and ideologies which rest upon assumptions based on the 'power' or dominance of initiators, speakers, texts and the production of 'meaning' is directly challenged by a mode of analysis which takes as its centre the creativity of recipients, the activity of those who, in the past, have been regarded as passive.

Recent research into the physiology of listening establishes that we do not simply 'hear' all the sounds generated by others because of the complexity of the auditory system which is always selecting, sifting, making sense of and interpreting a wide variety of acoustic signals.[2] This finding, applied to fields of linguistics, literature and popular culture, forms the basis of the book. The first essay, ranging over literary and linguistic concerns, sets out the theoretical argument that listeners and readers alike have 'intentions', and as a consequence they govern the direction of conversation, social behaviour, and the 'meaning' of a work of imaginative literature.[3] Something of what can happen to these signals in the interactional context of everyday language use is considered in the following essay which examines the nature of communicative breakdown between speakers from different dialect backgrounds. This exercise in 'applied sociolinguistics' enables the author to address the major theoretical issue of how hearers use linguistic and contextual knowledge to interpret utterances in context. The range of possible outcomes to communication attempts is shaped by the evolving dynamism of verbal exchange but cannot be directly investigated. A study of what has gone wrong when communication breaks down or where there have been 'misunderstandings' provides one way of overcoming this problem. What happens when we fail to 'get the message across' and how we go about resolving misunderstandings is the subject of a separate essay. Another approach to investigating what is going on in verbal exchange is to look at the listening behaviour of individuals who are outside the participation framework. The 3rd. person listener judge and the kinds of interpretive work that s/he might undertake is explored in a subsequent paper.

In the study of written communication, particularly in the field of literary works, the reader is equivalent to the active listener. Reception Theory and Reader-Response Theory[4] are recent developments which concentrate not upon how a text is produced nor upon the 'author's' part in the process, but upon how it is received, and one essay surveys a branch of such investigation, the psychology of the reader. Other essays examine similar questions from different points of view in considering the active participation of the reader (or, analogously, the audience in a theatre) in the creation of poetry, the novel or drama. Gender is a factor which can be seen to affect profoundly the relation of reader to text, and essays on the woman as reader and women's diaries consider some implications of this fact. Even in the quasi-scientific field of translation there is, as one essay demonstrates, a significant and even determining exercise of the listening function in operation, a process which can be traced vividly when two translators collaborate. In the related field of socially significant music, whether 'pop' or 'folk', questions may be asked about what constitutes an 'authentic' response, and indeed whether such a notion can be logically sustained. We did not require our contributors to accept a specific stance, and some essays are indeed critical of undiscriminating 'Response' theories, but all concentrate upon the activity of the listener and reader and maintain the originality and complexity of a fresh approach to communication in all its dynamic aspects.

Such is the fundamental nature of an idea that recipients are creative, that we believe a completely different collection of essays and approaches could have been made. The role of the listener whether as judge, juror or witness has important ramifications for our legal system, for example.[5] 'Classical' music should be and sometimes is, analysed from the point of view of what is heard by an individual rather than from the sounds that are produced by instruments in concert. The work of Ernst Gombrich[6] in the field of art history stresses the importance of visual conventions which affect the artist and more interestingly the viewer. In film studies the investigation of semiotics - the science of signals - has demonstrated that the watcher is affected by many codes provided by a film, but there is little to prevent an analyst approaching such a subject from an interest in how the viewer is in fact involved not in perceiving patterns but in creating or 'projecting' them, interpreting actively by bringing to bear individual experience and expectations. Just as we hear what we are predisposed to hear, so there is evidence that we see what we want to. The idea could well be applied in almost any field of knowledge - politics could be studied from the point of view of how power is perceived rather than how it is exercised; history from an analysis of how events are the cumulative creation of many participants at all levels rather than the imposition of constitutional changes by institutions and 'great men'; psychology could concentrate not upon dominance and 'repression' but upon the creativity of vulnerability. We had hoped to include an essay on co-counselling, an area in which active listening as a prelude to sensitive responsiveness is not provocative but axiomatic. Analogies can be made in scientific fields such as quantum physics, crystallography, relativity and uncertainty theory (to name only a few), where the active participation of the apparently 'passive' experimenter is crucial to what is observed.

However, to list 'fields of knowledge' is contrary to our intention, which is to break down the mystifying charisma of 'experts' and 'specialisms', to put the truthfully innocent responses of ordinary people at the centre of communication where they belong. The comprehensiveness of the methodology illustrated in the various essays here (from 'specialists' in their respective fields) is more important than the specific findings, and it is designed to lead away from subject boundaries. Beneath prevailing analyses of the acquisition of knowledge itself have lurked assumptions about power, the creativity of initiators and the insignificance of functions which are conventionally characterised as passive. These assumptions need to be questioned, challenged, and eventually swept away.

We acknowledge Academic Press for giving us permission to reproduce Lesley Milroy's essay, 'Comprehension and Context: Successful Communication and Communicative Breakdown' which was first published in Applied Linguistics edited by P. Trudgill (1984, Academic Press, Florida). We are grateful to Alison Gallagher for her typing skills. Dr. Hermann Moisl helped us demystify the word-processor in the School of English at the University of Newcastle upon Tyne.

NOTES

1. We owe this information to Dr. Gary Green of the Department of Physiological Science in the University of Newcastle upon Tyne. It is regrettable that his essay commissioned for this volume did not arrive for inclusion. The editors have found useful the analysis and bibliography in W. A. Ainsworth, Mechanisms of Speech Recognition (1976, Pergamon, Press, Oxford). Although this book does not stress the creative nature of listening, much of the evidence implicitly supports our thesis; e.g. 'When a listener hears a sound for a relatively long period its loudness appears to decrease' (p. 29), and the so-called 'cocktail-party effect' whereby 'it is normally possible to follow a selected conversation even though the total loudness of the other conversations seems greater' (p. 102). There are many other examples, but these seem the most elegant.

2. The fact that modern language study has tended to ignore the skills and achievements of 'listeners' is taken up in McGregor, G. (ed.) (In Press) Language for Hearers, Pergamon Press, Oxford. The volume includes work in theoretical linguistics, phonetics, sociolinguistics, social psychology and discourse analysis and aims to illustrate the theoretical and methodological implications of looking at language from the hearer's point of view.

3. It is no accident that the current volume should emanate from the School of English at the University of Newcastle upon Tyne, since the Tyneside Linguistic Survey under the direction of the late Professor Barbara Strang, and John Pellowe, from 1966 to 1979 was based on an evolving model of the centrality of the auditor. However, whilst many of the papers have been produced by individuals currently working at Newcastle, none of the contributors, with the exception of John Pellowe, have been engaged in the work of the Survey, nor necessarily influenced by its aims or methods.

4. See, for example, Robert C. Holub, Reception Theory: A Critical Introduction (1984) Methuen, London, with its extensive bibliography.

5. Milroy, J. (1984) 'Sociolinguistic Methodology and the Identification of Speakers' Voices in Legal Proceedings' in P. Trudgill (ed.) Applied Sociolinguistics, Academic Press, London, pp. 51-72 provides a very good example of what might be at issue in this respect.

6. Ernst Gombrich, Art and Illusion: A Study in the Psychology of Pictorial Representation (1959 first ed.), Phaidon Press, Oxford, and the author's many other studies.

ONE

HEARERS´ INTENTIONS[1]

John Pellowe

> ´You will find that whenever people are together, they´re making an effort to be listened to, and <u>are</u> very seldom listened to because the person they are trying to get to listen to them is waiting desperately and impatiently for a chance to be listened to himself or herself´[2] (Harvey Jackins, in Personal Counselors Inc. 1982, p. 49).

> ´Jean Barker. Wife of minor Party Official. Aged thirty-four. Small, dark, plump. Rather plain. Husband patronises her. She wears, permanently, a look of strained, enquiring good-nature. Comes around collecting Party dues. A born talker, never stops talking, but the most interesting kind of talker there is, she never knows what she is going to say until it is out of her mouth, so that she is continually blushing, catching herself up short, explaining just what it is she meant, or laughing nervously. Or she stops with a puzzled frown in the middle of a sentence, as if to say: "Surely I don´t think that?" So while she talks she has the appearance of someone listening ... Because of her verbal incontinence, which shocks people, or makes them laugh, she is developing the personality of a clown, or a licensed humorist. She has no sense of humour at all. But when she hears some remark that she makes that surprises her, she knows from experience that people will laugh, or be upset, so she laughs herself, in a puzzled nervous way, then hurries on´ (Lessing, 1973, p. 176).

> ´He opens his mouth and lets the wind blow his tongue about.´ (Tyneside idiom for a compulsive talker [locally, ´gobshite´]).

Hearers' Intentions

In a preface whose spirit should be a condition of employment for teachers and a guarantee to students, Doris Lessing muses upon the variability of response which she receives from her readers, wondering at the way in which one and the same book can be perceived so differently:

> ... naturally these incidents bring up again questions of what people see when they read a book, and why one person sees one pattern and nothing at all of another pattern ... And from this kind of thought has emerged a new conclusion: which is that it is not only childish of a writer to want readers to see what he sees ... - his wanting this means that he has not understood a most fundamental point. Which is that the book is alive and potent and fructifying and able to promote thought and discussion _only_ when its plan and shape and intention are not understood, because that moment of seeing the shape and plan and intention is also the moment when there isn't anything more to be got out of it ... then perhaps it is time to throw the book aside, as having had its day, and start again on something new (Lessing, 1973, p.22).

I imagine that Lessing's new conclusion applies no less to these words than to her own; that what a reader, any reader, carries into and through the praxis of interpreting (in the form of motive, mood, memory and unconscious) has very significant components which are both individual as to distribution, and immanent as to expressibility. Much of what is exciting and useful in reading and listening (and writing and speaking) is what Wittgenstein would enjoin us to pass over in silence. Regrettably such expressive imperatives are made to do ideological service in shoring up a spurious empiricism and to curtail the useful rhetoric of conjecture - the dialectic of imagining. By conjuring and conjoining images and thoughts from other selves (my own and others') and other times, I am feeling my way into, but maybe not all the way through, a largely chimerical maze known as intention. This is a maze which many linguists and philosophers who are intent upon catching and taming the unicorn of meaning have mistakenly apprehended as a net to achieve their ends.

Anyone who is engaged in creating meaning from the chaos all around understands the complexity of the experience. The chaos clearly, centrally, includes those recurrent problems known as 'utterances' and 'writings' (Pellowe, 1984, p. 41). And literary critics, whether they must suffer categorisation as 'post-structuralist' or not, have shown that the process of creating meanings - like seeing something clearly at dusk precisely by _not_ looking directly at it - can only be approached by distancing, by drawing the gyre tangentially.

The creating of meaning cannot be analysed, but can only be modelled in further creatings, the metaphoric, the ludic, the indeterminate, the mimetic. (The sort of writings with which I have created such meanings for myself are: Derrida, 1978, 1982; Young, 1981.) Here, then, there will be no progress (rather a dynamic stasis), and there will be no data (since with meaning there are no data - no giving, no repeating).

Ask yourself - naively/naifly of course - what the source is for the meanings which arise from the process of reading. There seem, on the edge of it, to be three possible guesses available to me. First, absolving myself and the text of all responsiblity in the matter, I simply say that the meaning 'I' get is the meaning which the writer intended me to get. Since understanding the meaning of the text is tantamount to knowing what the intention of the writer was, meaning is intention. In this view the text is a passive vehicle, a pellucid representation of the writer's intention, and I am a passive transformer, a machine unhampered in its capacity to be triggered by text and to transform that text back into intention (the writer's). In this view, clearly, the writer knows his/her intentions thoroughly and minutely.[3] And, in addition, the text comprises neither more nor less than just the expression of these (no doubt complex) intentions. Since if it did comprise either more or less it could not be an expression of this intention, these intentions.

Secondly, treating persons penumbrally, I imagine that the meanings which arise in reading are in the text; some of them reside there very visibly, some no doubt in code, but they are all there as components and concomitants of the sounds on the page, of the scribblings in the air. On this account we do not expect the writer to know very clearly, if at all, what he or she has done in doing what he or she has done. In this possible world we would presumably come to expect that a writer could be believingly delighted with meanings in the text of which he or she was cognitively or memorially incapable. It acknowledges an unbridgeable gap between intention (if any) and the expression of that intention. (I return to the nature of this chasm, briefly, later.) The text takes on a kind of life of its own, independent of the writer's efforts and beliefs; it may be thought of as 'writing itself' to some extent. (Flann O'Brien's At Swim-Two-Birds.) The other human in the shadows, the reader, is equally ineffectual, effaced. The text will always contain more, stand for more, than a single person (of howsoever many selves) can discover, even delving for a whole life.[4]

Thirdly, the eyes above the printed page are, to use a construal from an earlier age, the very source of light. The 'text' is no slave, no carrier, has no portage, is, rather, plastic, empty, awaiting charge, invisible before enfilling. It may have colour, but neither shape nor contents. (Or, like the objects in eternity, so obligingly conjured by the First and Second Policemen, it is horrifying because it lacks an essential quality possessed by all known objects.[5]) If the falling tree in the forest has no witness, it makes no sound. If the text is unread, it can have no meaning (leaving out of account the currency of its code, or the creation of its context). In this picture, the writer is no less fictively empty than the text; a hazy succession of increasingly dim mirrors waiting for the reflection/reflectiveness and light of a reader's vision.

It is not simply that readers, by their work of applying their unique knowledge of their language, make the pages of a text mean whatever they make them mean. (Let us here [will you?] agree, despite the difficulty and the beggared questions, that each individual reader of a language has a unique grammar and a unique lexicon of that language. See it, if you will [volition, invitation, persuasion], as a necessary reflection of that unique, incommunicable experience known as 'language acquisition'.) But in addition, a reader creates the internal and the external contexts of and for these meanings. The distinction is an arbitrary mark on a continuum, but may serve to make us skip. In reading I create <u>internal</u> contexts for the meanings I simultaneously make. How and to what extent am I investing my own recollections, imaginings, hopes, desires (both convergent and divergent) around those meanings? The <u>external</u> context which I create for my reading consists of my world - all that is the case, for me - before and after my reading. (The 'after' can only ever be guessed at.) <u>Both</u> of these sorts of contexts seem to be new for each reading.

According to this view, the implication of Lessing's remark (<u>the</u> 'plan and shape and intention' of a book [1973, p. 22]) or that of Hesse's ('the author is not the right authority to decide on where the reader ceases to understand and the misunderstanding begins'; 'moreover, misunderstandings may be fruitful under certain circumstances'; 'I neither can nor intend to tell my readers how they ought to understand my tale. May everyone find in it what strikes a chord in him ... But ...' [1965, pp. 5-6]) would have to be denied. The implication in each case is that there <u>is</u> one appropriate understanding (or a cluster of closely related understandings) of a text.[6]

Quick cartoons of three relations between writer, text, reader. (Though some might have made their readings lampoons.) Each of these sketches of the sources of literary meanings may seem not believable but they have each been believed in one form or another, at some time or another.[7] Competing models in the absence of any agreed criterion for their resolution ...

But, in my view, a revolution of sensibility concerning literary meanings, and hence, by Nietzschian implication, <u>all</u> meanings, has quietly come about. (I was not 'trained' as a literary critic or as a textual scholar, but as a linguist (sensu linguistics). But, as many readings of any newspaper seem to show, avowals or disavowals of ´interest´ are, at best, irrelevant, and at worst have complicated inverse implications.) The revolution is of the same order as that which moved static, atomistic, Newtonian physics, into dynamic, wholistic (sic), post-Einsteinian, quantum physics.[8] By comparison, for reasons set out by Sampson (1980), the revolution associated with Chomsky´s work is no revolution at all.

Like other ideational revolutions, deconstruction seems difficult, generates high feelings, is impossible to summarise, to translate, to explain. (How many educated people, more than fifty years later, can create a meaning for Einstein´s theory of relativity, or Heisenberg´s principle of uncertainty? And yet these ideas have transformed the world we live and feel in.) Any attempt to make a system of meanings assumes one of four things: that the meaning of something is equivalent to the idea of that something in a mind; that the meaning of something is equivalent to that something itself; that the meaning of something is equivalent to the behaviour of a person in respect of the expression of that meaning; that the meaning of something is equivalent to the use of the expression containing it. Respectively, ideational, referential, behavioural, and functional systems of meaning.

A six year old child, playing alone, constantly shows us the following: that a sign is neither the same as ´its´ signification, not the same as a thing signified; that a signification is neither the same as a sign for it, nor the same as the thing signified, that a thing signified need be neither a sign nor a signification. That there need not be, but that there may be, relations of transitivity, and symmetry between each component of any pair of these three, and that, in either case, every occasion is, literally, unique, guarantees the failure of the equivalences in the previous paragraph. In other words (as Adrienne Rich says of truth) meaning is not a system at all, but a constantly expanding and changing complexity for each individual (Rich, 1980, p. 187).

From such and similar considerings the following conjectures, amongst many, may be pondered:

(1) For a given expression, there is no singular, transcendent, canonical meaning;

(2) The ´information in´ an expression and a ´meaning of´ that expression, are totally different accounts of that expression;

(3) There are no grounds whatever for the/an authoritative attribution of meaning to a given expression;

(4) No reading of a given expression which is arrived at in good faith can be wrong;[9]

(5) The author (writer/speaker) of an expression is not the author of its meaning, but only of its expression;

(6) Meaning is created by an individual´s sense of his or her connections to a space-time percept.[10]

The theoretical richness of the quantum semantics known as deconstruction is not restricted to literary texts at all (or indeed to language). Its dialectic will, no doubt, eventually dissolve our paltry ethics, greedy economics, and jejune politics in a new lotion for the rebirth of peace, proportion, and gentleness. Its dialectic works by neutralizing the three accounts of the source of written meanings, by integrating their differences in the constantly shifting dynamic between sign-signification-signified.

In the remainder of these marginalia I shall only try to think a little more about ´intention´ in terms of the sorts of space shadowed above.

....

In what they seem to believe is a new method for demystifying meaning and understanding, several linguists and philosophers have returned to intentionalism. (Wimsatt said somewhere that ´the design or intention of the author is neither available nor desirable as a standard for judging the meaning or the value of [a work of art]´. I can think of no reason why ´speaker´ should not be substituted for ´author´, nor ´utterance´ for ´work of art´.)

Grice (1969), for instance, suggests that the meaning of an utterer´s remark is reducible or equatable to the intention of the utterer in making that remark. The role of the hearer is then to determine what that intention was. Success or failure in such a determination is then attributable to the hearer, who may fail to determine any intention (does not under-stand), or may determine a wrong intention (mis-understands), or does determine the utterer´s intention (understands). Grice´s framework is yet one more example of ours being a speaker´s civilization: one in which the skill of a speaker is praised, but the skill of a listener is not even noticed (Parker-Rhodes, 1978). Grice assumes (1969, 1975) that speakers and hearers are rational, but even this assumption does not restrict the remarks of speakers sufficiently narrowly such that hearers will always be able to recover intentions from ´literal´ or ´normal´ uses of remarks. Given the nature of the world, for example, there may be circumstances under which it is rational to take four times as long to say something as would be necessary in a closely similar possible non-actual world; it may sometimes be rational to tell lies; it may sometimes be rational to give more information than is strictly necessary for the realisation of some intention.

Because of these problems, Grice (1975) introduces various conversational maxims which constrain the possibilities of the speaker in precisely such a way that the hearer will be more likely to be able to recover the speaker´s intentions. As more such restrictions are introduced, the types of intention the speaker can have move closer to uses of language which have to do with the transmission of information. Put another way the remarks of speakers who are constrained by these maxims will tend to be remarks which one can more easily imagine fitting in with the idea that speakers say things in order to change the beliefs or knowledge-structures of hearers.

Apart from Occamesque arguments (that the assumption of rationality requires more monster barring equipment than its maintenance merits), there seem to me to be three arguments against trying to handle understanding (and meaning) through the detailed intentions of the speaker.

(1) In wondrous ´ordinary´ daily life, people often do not know why they say what they say. I do not mean those cases of social extrication in which A says something which upsets B in some way and says, by way of recognition and pacification of the problem, that s/he didn´t know what made her/him say such a [negative value term] thing. No, I mean that the experience of Jean Barker, so well caught by Lessing (the second epigraph above), is by no means a rare one. People often speak without having recoverable or specific intentions, other than those indicated by the first and third epigraphs above. The first (Personal Counselors Inc. 1982, p. 49) suggests that a person says whatever that person says with the intention of being listened to. The third, from the point of view of a somewhat laconic hearer, suggests that hearers are well aware of the phenomenon of speakers who have no readily specifiable or recoverable intentions other than that of being heard and/or being listened to. Such general intentions as these are of no use whatever for the apparatus which Grice fiddles with.

(A further example. At a certain stage of their work, postgraduate students are often grappling with a lot of ideas at once in an effort to reach some conceptual breakthrough. They talk and talk, but on being asked ´I don´t understand, what are you trying to get at?´ [by e.g. their supervisor], they say ´I don´t know, I was hoping you could tell me´- That is, ´Please supply me with a retrospective intention´.)

If these cases are as normal as I believe them to be, then the folk, as opposed to the professional, linguistic view, is that hearers are more powerful than speakers (Pellowe, 1984). This is precisely because a person who is able to listen, but who does not need to speak, suffers fewer doubts (does not need to trade vulnerability for confirmation) than one who needs to speak but is unable to listen (cf.

Jackins´ epigraph).

Each moment, were it unpolluted by power and imposition, would hear many more praises for the good listener than for the good speaker. The good listener confirms the unique, the good and the universal in each of us, despite our pain. The ´good´ speaker, as likely as not, will engender in us feelings not from our experience, acts not consonant with our thinking, hopes not compatible with our good.

A good listener is not one who passively construes a speaker´s intentions, but one who attends the speaker´s vulnerability, ´attends´ in the senses of ´elicits´, ´waits for´, ´assists´, ´holds´.

(2) The second argument against trying to equate meanings with speakers´ intentions is that hearers are not passive transformers. Hearers may also have intentions. If hearers can have intentions in respect of speakers and/or the remarks which speakers turn out to make, then, clearly, the detailed intention which a speaker may have in uttering a certain remark cannot be guaranteed to be recovered by the hearer, <u>however the speaker expresses her/himself</u>.

What sort of intentions can hearers have? In general, the nature and degree of attention which the hearer gives to the speaker´s remarks is determined by the hearer. Within and around this generality, a hearer may intend, before or during the speaker´s utterance, to ensilentise, to deauthorise, to disrupt, to deflect, to appropriate, to enjoke, to conspiratise, to enmonologue, to embarrass, to anger, to enmoralise, to feel with/for, to confuse ... the speaker. And for each of these intentions there are various techniques.

A hearer´s intention, if s/he has one, is or may be independent of what a speaker says. A speaker, because s/he does not know what this intention is, cannot make allowance for it in her/his utterances. A speaker may not have any detailed intention. A hearer may entertain more than one intention at the same time, which in some cases may encourage the simultaneous creation of two meanings for the same remark. Under these conditions there is no guarantee that the meaning a hearer creates for a remark will reflect the speaker´s intention in uttering that remark.

(3) The third argument against Grice´s position is a more general one which relates to what I called quantum semantics above: this is a general attack on intentionalism through holism, through Eastern philosophy (Loy, n.d.)

Any intention leads to bifurcation, dualities, polarities. In the first place an intention has a source (mind) and an agent (body); the mind sets a goal (then) in the present (now); the body (agent) generates behaviour (means) (act), to achieve the goal (end). All of the dualities present/future, body/mind, means/end, agent/act, <u>require</u>

us to invent a fictive self to bridge the gaps which they embody. Free from ´intention´ our daily activities may be realised as non-dual. Without the activities of naming and intending the self evaporates. Such are the goals of meditation.

....

We are constantly being informed that there has been an ´information explosion´, a huge, exponential increase in the number of facts. But as William James said, facts are not of themselves true or not-true. Only because individual experience starts and terminates amongst facts, in the generation of individual beliefs, so those facts have an aura of reflected truth. Truth is made. By individuals.

There is no ´meaning explosion´. Meaning arises from the sense of connections which is sustained by individuals. Meanings are not outside of people, and should not be objectified. Just as time is not outside of people and should not be objectified. It is no good one asking X what the meaning of Y´s remark is. Meaning is not ´out there´. (If I do ask X what the meaning of Y´s remark is, the meaning (which I give to X´s reply) will be a connection between me and X, not between me and Y. The peculiarity of such a question (´what is the meaning of Y´s remark´) guarantees that its answer cannot be given the meaning which, on the surface, it seems to require.) The hearer is responsible for the nature of the connection which s/he creates.

On the other hand, meanings are not ´in here´ either. They are not distinct from one, or many, of my selves. At one level of duality, meaning cannot be separated from its representation, any more than mind can be from its body. That is, the meaning/form duality is as misleading as the mind/body one.

At another level of duality, the meaning/person duality is as misleading as the person/time one. The meanings which I create are not independent of my self (my selves). It is ridiculous to imagine taking an other on a psycho-physical tour of one´s selves and saying: ´Please meet this one of my selves and here is the pile of meanings it/he/she/this one produced last week.´ (I imagine that part of what Beckett is dissecting in Krapp´s Last Tape is his own [and Descartes´s] uncertain assumptions about the continuity of ´the self´.)

It is, precisely, the way in which we recognise different ones of our selves, that they are associated with the different meanings which have been made by us. ´Are associated with´ hides a further duality. It says ´there are selves´ and ´there are meanings´ - separate. What can we say to dissolve this?

Just as my selves are what they eat and drink; just as my selves are time; just as my selves are space; just as my Being is what energy-time-space is doing in this force-moment-place, so the meanings I make constitute me.[11] If I am fully to partake of my eternity (i.e. humanity, <u>not</u> immortality) I must deny the force of intentions (whether speaker´s or hearer´s) over my capacity to make meanings. Intention of any sort disappears in the significance-energy-time-space which is centred now. My ´I´ is, then, a pattern of a meaning-force-moment-place which continuously recreates a significance-energy-time-space. And since force-moment-place and energy-space-time are amongst the meanings which I make, this is equivalent to: my being is the meanings I create, the meanings I create are me.

To say that meaning arises in any other way than <u>as</u> me, is to deny my existence. To say that meaning arises in any other way than <u>as</u> you [dear reader], is to deny your existence.

Not knowing the myriad meanings you have made which <u>are</u> you, how can I determine the meanings you make of/for this?

It is always now.

NOTES

1. Continuing thanks to Bob Lumsden for continuing to listen with his customary generosity and subtlety - his hearerly intentions are always delicate - and to all the good, wholesome, zestful, intelligent, cooperative, listeners inside and outside re-evaluation co-counselling. Graham McGregor asked me to write what turns out to be this for another book. Bob White and Pauline Graham, have sustained me with their hearts as well as their minds, patience, humour, commitment.
2. All emphases in quotation are in the original unless otherwise stated.
3. This would be a less idiotically simple position if I glossed ´knows´ by ´consciously/unconsciously´. However, ´unconsciously knowing an intention´ seems to be a collocation which evaporates any residual sense of ´intention´. The contradiction merits further analysis, but not here.
4. Stevens´ poem <u>Of Mere Being</u> (Stevens, 1972, p. 398) corrects the banality of the account I´m giving by being emblematic of all three positions but if I were a poet I wouldn´t need to be a poets´ parasite.

> The palm at the end of the mind,
> Beyond the last thought, rises
> In the bronze decor,

A gold-feathered bird
Sings in the palm, without human meaning,
Without human feeling, a foreign song.

You know then that it is not the reason
That makes us happy or unhappy.
The bird sings. Its feathers shine.

The palm stands on the edge of space.
The wind moves slowly in the branches.
The bird´s fire-fangled feathers dangle down.

5. Cf. O´Brien, F. (1974) The Third Policeman , Picador, London, pp. 116-17. It seems both obvious and paradoxical that we cannot specify this missing quality.
6. I am grateful to Bob White for mentioning the existence of Hesse´s (1961) Authorial Note in this edition of Steppenwolf.
7. ´Everything possible to be believed is an image of truth´, as one of hell´s proverbs has it, but note that such beliefs themselves must pass through the mystery of meaning creation - ´Truth can never be told so as to be understood, and not be believed.´ (Blake)
8. The revolution is associated with the names ´deconstruction´, ´Jacques Derrida´, ´post-structuralism´... Its quietness has nothing to do with its force, the irrefutability of its theoretical synthesis, but rather stems from the indolent silence of the literary, linguistic, and philosophical establishment.
9. I mean ´good faith´ in the existential sense(s); though I am aware of the problem of definition, I think it both impossible and foolish to seek a solution. I would want to say that a commitedly ludic reading was in good faith, a cynically derivative (cribbed) one in bad faith. There is less a line, than a rainbow of distinction ...
10. ´Meaning is discovered in what connects, and cannot exist without development; ... without an unfolding, there is no meaning; ... meaning is a response, not only to the known, but also to the unknown: meaning and mystery are inseparable and neither can exist without the passing of time.´ (Berger and Mohr, 1982, p. 89)
11. I thank David Loy for all our conversations, in which he taught me a tiny fraction of his understanding of Eastern philosophy - however different our paths may be, the Path is the same.

REFERENCES

Bateson, G. (1979) Mind and Nature: A Necessary Unity, Wildwood House, London.

Berger, J. and Mohr, J. (1982) Another Way of Feeling, Writers and Readers Publishing Co-op, London.

Derrida, J. (1978), Writing and Difference, Chicago University Press, Chicago.

Derrida, J. (1982), Margins of Philosophy (transl. with additional notes by Alan Bass), Chicago University Press, Chicago.

Grice, H.P. (1969) ´Utterer´s Meaning and Intentions´, Philosophical Review, 78, pp. 147-77.

Grice, H.P. (1975), ´Logic and Conversation´ in P. Cole and J.L. Morgan (eds.), Syntax and Semantics Vol. 3 Speech Acts, Academic Press, London, pp. 41ff.

Hesse, H. (1965) Steppenwolf (transl. Basil Creighton; rev. Walter Sorell), Penguin, Harmondsworth.

Lessing, D. (1973) The Golden Notebook, Granada, London.

Loy, D. (n.d.) The Mahayana deconstruction of time (mimeo: 3-20-8 Omachi Kamakura 248 Japan).

Parker-Rhodes, F. (1978) Inferential Semantics, Harvester, Sussex.

Pellowe, J. (1984) ´For Our Selves we are Silent´ in C. Nicholson and R. Chatterji (eds) Tropic Crucible, Singapore University Press, Singapore.

Personal Counsellors Inc. (1982) Fundamentals of Co-counselling Manual, Rational Island Publishers, Seattle, Washington.

Rich, A. (1980) On Lies, Secrets and Silence: Selected Prose, 1966-78, Virago, London.

Sampson, G. (1980) Making Sense, Oxford University Press, London.

Stevens, H. (1972) The Palm at the end of the Mind. Selected Poems and a Play (ed. Holly Stevens), Vintage Books, New York.

Young, R. (1981) (ed.) Untying the Text. A Post-structuralist Reader, Routledge and Kegan Paul, London.

TWO

COMPREHENSION AND CONTEXT: SUCCESSFUL COMMUNICATION AND COMMUNICATIVE BREAKDOWN[1]

Lesley Milroy

INTRODUCTION

The major theoretical issue to which this paper addresses itself is the manner in which hearers use a combination of linguistic knowledge, knowledge of a heterogeneous range of factors which broadly might be called 'contextual', and various perceptual strategies when they interpret utterances in context. This issue is approached using methods familiar in sociolinguistics; that is, the data base is real utterances as they are spoken in their social context rather than constructed data intuitively interpreted. It seems likely that _both_ intuitive _and_ empirical approaches are necessary (and a combination of the two) if we wish to advance our knowledge of how speakers comprehend what they hear in everyday situations. The problem is tackled initially by looking at a number of communications which have gone wrong; as Gumperz and Tannen (1979) point out: 'by studying what has gone wrong when communication breaks down, we seek to understand a process that goes unnoticed when it is successful' (p. 308). A similar approach to speech production may be found in Fromkin (1973 and 1981).

Most of the miscommunications examined here are between people from different dialect backgrounds: that is people whose internal grammars are different in some specifiable way. This limitation is important methodologically as it helps us to assess the role of specifically _linguistic_ knowledge in comprehension, and it seems likely that conclusions on this wider matter can be extended to communications between people with the _same_ dialect background.

Although it may be seen as a contribution to a major theoretical issue, this chapter is primarily intended as an exercise in applied sociolinguistics; the insights of sociolinguistics are used to analyse the manner in which _communicative breakdown_ occurs between speakers in everyday situations and the consequences of this breakdown are considered. These two issues, the theoretical and the applied, will be considered in parallel throughout the discussion.

A miscommunication may be said to take place when there is a mismatch between the speaker's intention and the hearer's interpretation. When two persons <u>do</u> communicate successfully, it is clear that much more is involved than the mapping of internal structures (or linguistic rules) on to external sequences, or conversely (from the listener's point of view), mapping external sequences on to internal structures (Bever, 1970, p. 286). A number of perceptual strategies or 'short-cuts' appear to be implemented by a listener in decoding utterances, and it is probably most sensible to adopt for the moment Aitchison's notion of a person's grammar as a 'linguistic archive', available and ready for consultation in interpreting utterances, but not necessarily consulted. Thus, a sentence like the following is difficult to comprehend, although it is perfectly grammatical:

The pig pushed in front of the piglets ate all the food.

This is because the perceptual strategies adopted by the listener are to

> assume that the first noun will go with the first verb in an NP-VP (actor-action) sequence as part of the main clause . . . So he understandably makes the wrong guess when he hears the words <u>the pig pushed</u> . . . especially as his knowledge of the world tells him that pigs are not usually pushed they generally do the pushing (Aitchison, 1976, p. 203).

Thus, the relation between internal grammars and comprehension is indirect, especially since comprehension in natural settings (as opposed to the experimental settings from which much of the psycholinguistic work discussed by Aitchison derives) is often assisted by such factors as the following:

I. Natural language contains a great deal of redundancy (see Lyons, 1977, p. 44 for discussion of this).

II. 'Context' and 'shared background knowledge' assist interlocutors in interpreting utterances (Smith and Wilson, 1979). I refer to both linguistic and extra-linguistic context here, and will return to a discussion of it shortly.

III. Interlocutors in unplanned discourse have a range of strategies for monitoring comprehension, for clarifying and for repairing mistakes and misunderstandings as they follow the facial, gestural and interjectional cues which accompany interactions. Constant repetition and repair are important components of communication in context and are themselves highly systematic (Schegloff _et al._, 1977; Givon, 1979, p. 230).

IV. It appears that out of consideration for each other's and their own 'face', speakers often make remarks whose ambiguity has a clear social motivation (Brown and Levinson, 1978, p. 74). Speakers also appear to be willing to allow a great deal of vagueness and ambiguity to pass, on the assumption that meanings will become clear as the talk proceeds (Cicourel, 1973, p. 54).

Thus, when miscommunication _does_ take place, a whole range of factors may be responsible. It is probably the indirectness of the relationship between 'linguistic knowledge' (in Chomsky's sense) and language use which accounts for the fact that speakers with partly different grammars understand each other much of the time in natural settings; they rely on a wide and varied range of comprehension strategies. However, when comprehension between such speakers is tested experimentally (i.e. when factors I to IV above are controlled), they appear to be unable to associate sentences not generated by their own grammar with an appropriate semantic structure (see Labov, 1972a; Trudgill, 1981). Generally speaking, arguments for a 'polylectal grammar' as a reflection of a speaker's pan-dialectal competence have not been supported by experiments such as Labov's or Trudgill's which require subjects either to select a paraphrase for sentences generated by other dialect grammars, or to judge whether such sentences are 'possible' English sentences (see also Ross, 1979 for a different, but related, approach). The gap between these experimental results and results of the observational research reported in this paper is sometimes quite large, and will be discussed below. Meantime, it is perhaps worth noting Plutchik's comments on the value of observational (as opposed to experimental) research in a field where knowledge is limited (Plutchik, 1976, p. 23).

While then it is certainly true that speakers with markedly different grammars are frequently able to understand each other in context, it does not seem quite justifiable to adopt uncritically the common view cited by (for example) Smith and Wilson that differences between the grammars of dialects are essentially trivial, and that potential misunderstandings can be resolved by the implementation of perceptual strategies, or by context (Smith and Wilson, 1979, p. 197). One purpose of this chapter will be to try and isolate the conditions under which differences in speakers' grammars may produce misunderstandings in natural settings; that is when the various comprehension strategies available to a speaker have failed to work and he is forced to consult his

´linguistic archive´ to assist him in interpreting utterances.

Since Labov´s initial demonstration of the ´limits´ of individual grammars, it has been generally accepted (at least by sociolinguists) that pandialectal competence, active or passive, is extremely sharply constrained. However, there is an implicit tendency to assume that it is competence in non-standard grammars which is limited. It is significant, for example, and quite characteristic of work in this area, that all the sentences discussed in Trudgill´s 1981 paper are designed to test knowledge of non-standard grammars. In an earlier publication, Trudgill expressed the view more explicitly that non-standard speakers had at least a passive competence in standard English (Trudgill, 1979) and Trudgill´s view does not seem at all uncommon.

In relation to this issue, it is worth noting Lyons´ observation (made generally, rather than with reference to cross-dialectal communication) that misunderstandings are probably rather frequent during communicative acts, and that this likelihood should be allowed for in any theoretical model of communication (Lyons, 1977, p. 33). It is only rarely that speakers are provided with feedback in any consistent way, and when this does happen (as when students write down in examinations what they think has been said to them) the level of misunderstanding is frequently revealed to be quite horrifying (Aitchison, 1976, p. 197). If we take comments such as those of Lyons and Aitchison into account, as well as the complex of knowledge and strategies underlying comprehension, I think we have to treat the idea that non-standard speakers ´understand´ standard English as a not very clearly defined and quite unsupported assumption, rather than a self-evident truth (in fact, some data will be discussed below which suggests that the assumption requires some modification). A more interesting question may well be concerned with the extent to which miscommunications are associated with cross-dialectal communication.

The approach taken in this chapter will be to examine and analyse instances of miscommunication against the extremely complicated but still by no means comprehensive background which has been outlined so far; an attempt will be made to bring together material from a number of relevant academic perspectives. The main focus of interest will be in identifying as precisely as possible the linguistic and contextual factors contributing to miscommunication, but there will also be some brief discussion of the consequences of miscommunication. This will be both in terms of speakers´ responses, and in more general social terms. However, preliminary to analysis of data two of the issues already raised are looked at in a little more detail. These are, first, the relationship between standard and non-standard English (this will be a brief section), and next the generalized notion of ´context´ to which linguists frequently appeal when they are attempting an explanation of how speakers comprehend utterances in real situations.

STANDARD AND NON-STANDARD ENGLISH

It is important to remember in a study like this one, which looks primarily at cross-dialectal communication, that any account of a language-system like English is extremely idealized and abstract and inevitably based on the standard form of the language (a form routinely used, it should be noted, by only a small minority of speakers). Although the notion of a standard is notoriously complicated and hard to pin down, it is useful here to ignore the social dimensions of standardization and adopt Lyons' view of it as one kind of idealization of the data in which the linguist ignores differences within a system and 'discounts all but the major systematic variations in the language behaviour of the community' (Lyons, 1977, p. 587). Standard English then is the form of the language from which most linguists cite their examples, and it is usually believed that structural differences between standard and non-standard varieties are relatively superficial and can be accounted for in terms of rule addition or rule loss. Some examples of syntactic differences within British English are cited by Hughes and Trudgill (1979) which include differences in tense and aspectual systems, and in the formal distribution of individual verbs such as _have_ and _do_.

The question of genuine communication problems arising from structural differences of this kind is not often seriously discussed, the assumption generally being that non-standard speakers can 'understand' standard English presumably in the sense that in some hypothetical context-free situation they are able to assign the same semantic structure as a standard speaker to a given phonetic string. The reason for this assumption (which is noted here mainly to encourage readers to consider whether they themselves hold it) is probably the constant dissemination of spoken and written standard English through the news media and the educational system. The possibility that some speakers do not 'understand' standard English appears for the most part to be mooted only when their systems are so divergent that they may, like West Indian creole-speakers in England, or Black English-speakers in the United States, be thought of in some unsatisfactorily specified way as not being English speakers at all (Edwards, 1979; Nelson and McRoskey, 1978). However, in a recent extensive study of the Hiberno-English perfect (associated with a larger study of non-standard English) John Harris refers to frequent misinterpretations by Hiberno-English speakers of such standard English utterances as

How long are you staying here?

This type of structure is often interpreted as being equivalent to standard English

How long have you been staying here?

Harris goes on to argue convincingly that there is no semantic isomorphism between any given set of Hiberno-English and standard-English sentences which exemplify the range of perfect constructions. For example, the three sentences

(a) Joe has sold the boat.
(b) Joe has just sold the boat.
(c) Has Joe sold the boat?

exemplify the simple perfect tense-aspect form in Standard English. However, they are all quite anomalous in even educated Hiberno-English and would be ´translated´ as follows:

(a) Joe has the boat sold
(b) Joe is just after selling the boat
(c) Did Joe sell the boat?

The non-isomorphism is semantic as well as formal, since, for example Hiberno-English (c) is not only a translation of standard-English (c) but is also equivalent to the same standard-English string. Thus, Hiberno-English cannot distinguish between ´Has Joe sold the boat?´ and ´Did Joe sell the boat?´ However, an action completed in the <u>recent</u> past is expressed by a construction of the (b) type. Cross-dialectal miscommunications are very commonly reported which seem to be located in the disparity between the two versions of sentence (b) and these may be seen as symptomatic of a deep structure disparity between the grammars of the two dialects. The two dialects cannot be related satisfactorily simply by applying slightly different transformational rules to derive them from the same deep structure (Harris, 1982). This suggests that dialect grammars may sometimes be more different than is commonly supposed, and justifies a somewhat closer examination of how far the communicative competence of a non-standard speaker includes the capacity to assign the same semantic structure as a standard speaker to a given phonetic string.

THE NOTION OF CONTEXT

We have already noted that comprehension involves very much more than knowledge of phonological, syntactic and semantic rules. So much redundant information is introduced into communicative situations by a combination of linguistic and real world knowledge that it is often possible to produce an appropriate response to an utterance without any knowledge at all of the structural rules underlying its production. For example, during a recent visit to a rural area of Austria, I was able to comprehend a request (from a shopkeeper) to shut the door even though I was quite unable (despite my knowledge of standard German) to recognize in the utterance any familiar syntactic patterns or even a single lexical item. A combination of cold weather, gestural cues, and limitations on the kind of message likely to be transmitted in a service encounter of that kind facilitated successful communication; that is, an appropriate response was produced to the utterance. It is of course a truism to assert that actual utterances are always interpreted in context, and instances like this one seem to have encouraged linguists to exaggerate the capacity of context to resolve ambiguity, while at the same time not defining particularly closely what is meant by context. It is still commonplace to find the term used freely without any more careful examination of its scope. Yet, context-boundedness is an important inherent characteristic of all natural languages and arguably should be accounted for explicitly in any comprehensive linguistic theory, rather than being used as a 'terminological immunization' (Klein and Dittmar, 1979, p. 4) to cover up problems of fitting data to theory.

That linguists are in general aware of this problem is evidenced by the major and long-running controversy within generative semantics as to whether the illocutionary potential of an utterance should in some way be incorporated into a formal grammar (Ross, 1975) or whether the interpretation of utterances in context should be accounted for by separate sets of conversational rules (Sperber and Wilson, forthcoming; Smith and Wilson, 1979; Gordon and Lakoff, 1971). More recently, attempts have been made to resolve empirically the issue of how far the social and situational context affects understanding and judgement (Ervin-Tripp, n.d.). Preliminary findings suggest that some, but not all, listeners rely heavily on routine non-linguistic knowledge, and on what might be described as 'pragmatic intelligence'. Stimulus utterances are decoded by applying lingustic rules only if something unusual or discordant occurs (cf. the notion of the 'linguistic archive', discussed above).

It is useful here to note Lyons' distinction between the layman's intuitive, pre-theoretical concept of context to which speakers frequently make appeal when they discuss interpretations of utterances, and on the other hand context as a theoretical construct which has been analysed from various points of view by different traditions of scholarship. Lyons' working definition of context (in the second sense) is as follows:

> a theoretical construct in the postulation of which the linguist abstracts from the actual situation and establishes as contextual all the factors which, by

> virtue of their influence upon the participants in a language event, systematically determine [my italics] the form, the appropriacy and the meaning of utterances (Lyons, 1977, p. 572).

We look now at two different approaches to the systematization of context, both of which are relevant to the discussion here.

Hymes' discussion of the nature of 'communicative competence' attempts to provide a theoretical framework for describing components of context which have just the kind of systematic effect referred to by Lyons on the production and comprehension of particular phonological, syntactic and lexical options within the language system (Hymes, 1972). They are manifold and complex, and the reader is referred to Hymes' own paper for a comprehensive account and to Coulthard (1977, p. 30) for a brief but useful discussion. Examples of the kind of knowledge which forms part of communicative competence in any real society are knowledge of status systems and social roles, and of the language appropriate to various settings and topics. Many linguists regard communicative competence as part of a speaker's linguistic knowledge in just the same way as his knowledge of syntactic and semantic rules. For example, Lyons suggests that a French speaker's knowledge of when to select the intimate or the polite second person pronoun is as much part of his linguistic competence as his knowledge of the French language-system (Lyons, 1980, p. 248); others would argue that this is an example of encyclopaedic, rather than strictly linguistic, knowledge.

A different approach to the systematization of context follows the traditions of Searle (1975) and Grice (1975). Scholars working along these lines are generally concerned with specifying those contextual cues, logical processes and other conditions which enable interlocutors to interpret utterances in context appropriately. Particularly interesting attempts to apply analyses of this kind to real speech events have been made by Labov and Fanshel (1977) and Gumperz and Tannen (1979). But on the whole, the most sophisticated analyses of utterances in context are applied to isolated pieces of constructed data, and have not yet been challenged by being tested in real conversations. In the sections which follow, an attempt will be made to assess the relative importance of these various systematic components of context, of perceptual strategies, and of internal grammars in enabling successful communication. Particular attention will be paid to those instances where a miscommunication seems to be located in a mismatch between the grammars of the speaker and the hearer.

SOME MISCOMMUNICATIONS: AN ANALYSIS

First, a brief note of some terminological and methodological points. For reasons which will become clear, it is important to try and maintain a distinction between two different kinds of miscommunication. What will be described as <u>misunderstandings</u> involve simple disparity between the speaker's and the hearer's semantic analysis of a given utterance. However, misunderstandings are not perceived as interrupting communicative efficiency, and it is probable that many more misunderstandings take place than are ever discovered. <u>Communicative breakdown</u> on the other hand occurs when one or more participants perceive that something has gone wrong. This 'something' may or may not be analysed as linguistic; if it is, the breakdown may or may not be repaired.

All the data discussed below are taken from real conversations. Only (1) is tape-recorded, having cropped up by a happy chance during a long conversation between myself and an inner-city informant in Belfast. The rest of the data were recorded in notebooks by myself and colleagues, and the researchers were usually able to report their own reaction to a miscommunication. By its nature, material on miscommunications is hard to collect in any systematic way, since unlike some of the classic linguistic variables described in the quantitative literature they occur unpredictably and sometimes infrequently. I tackled this problem simply by searching out, over a period of time, analysable examples of miscommunication which seemed to be located in disparate individual grammars. These were transcribed on the spot, and where necessary contextual factors were noted in as much detail as seemed appropriate. An analysis was then carried out to try and locate the source of the miscommunication.

This <u>post hoc</u> type of procedure is very similar to that of Gumperz (see especially Gumperz and Tannen, 1979) who deals with those miscommunications which result from disparities in the inferences drawn by conversational participants from utterances in context. Both pieces of research follow the principles of careful observation in the tradition of social anthropology pioneered by Evans-Pritchard, and more recently in linguistic research recommended by Ferguson (1977) for dealing with phenomena about which little is known. Careful observation of this kind is of course an essential preliminary to the development of a predictive and testable theory.

Youse wash the dishes

This heading is part of a narrative told to me during a fieldwork session by a Belfast working-class woman. The rest of it, which may serve as an illustration of vernacular second person pronoun usage, is as follows:

> (1) /So I says to our Trish and our Sandra/youse wash the dishes/and I might as well have said you wash the dishes/for our Trish just got up/and put her coat on and walked out/

In much of Scotland and Ireland the second person pronoun can be marked for number as illustrated here, giving the plural form _youse_. This extract is quoted here because it shows clearly that the speaker considers _you_ an inappropriate choice for a plural referent. This fact is relevant to analysis of subsequent miscommunications between myself and some Belfast vernacular speakers.

An examination of the sociolinguistic distribution of _youse_ in Belfast reveals rather more complexity than might at first be assumed. First of all, as we might expect, many relatively standardized speakers have categorical _you_ for both singular and plural pronouns. For these speakers, the _youse_ form is highly stigmatized (despite the obvious usefulness of the distinction), and is often singled out for overt criticism. As a consequence of this stigma many speakers who do have the _you/youse_ distinction in their grammars alternate between the marked and the unmarked form of the plural pronoun according to various contextual (and possibly syntactic) constraints. For example, one local post-graduate student was observed to address the class as _you_ while giving a seminar paper, but to revert to _youse_ as the class broke up and the topic changed. Thus the pronoun appears to be a classic social and stylistic variable rather similar to, for example, the double negative. It has of course quite a different sociolinguistic distribution from the T and V pronouns studied by Brown and Gilman.

The really surprising fact to emerge during a lengthy and systematic study of the language of several very low-status social groups in Belfast was that many speakers _categorically_ distinguished _you_ (singular) and _youse_ (plural); that is evidence began to build up which suggested that they never alternated between the marked and the unmarked form of the pronoun.

This sociolinguistic distribution might be diagrammed as in Table I, with three different groups of speakers distinguished, which are likely to correspond to hierarchical social stratifications. What is of interest here is the communicative consequence when a Group I speaker and a Group III speaker interact. Do categorical differences in this portion of their grammars result in communicative difficulties? Or do Group III speakers have the kind of passive competence in standard English which is often assumed to exist? In fact, the speaker of (1) was almost certainly a Group III speaker and the addressee (myself, as the listener to the narrative) a Group I speaker. It is perhaps worth emphasizing that the social context in which speakers from these two socially distant groups interact are likely to be quite limited, and to be in situations where Group I speakers have a measure of control over the proceedings and may be interacting on a one-to-one or one-to-many basis. Examples are classroom, legal, medical and bureaucratic situations. In other words, as a consequence of the social norms governing cross-group communications, occasions on which the categorical nature of the mismatch between the two grammars might emerge are likely to be quite limited.

Table 1. The sociolinguistic distribution of ´youse´.

	singular	plural
Group I	you	you
Group II	you	you/youse
Group III	you	youse

It has been suggested by James Miller (personal communication), correctly I think, that as speakers grow older and become more firmly established in educationally and occupationally determined statuses, they interact less and less on a symmetrical basis with socially distant persons. This constitutes a social problem which vitiates systematic knowledge of non-standard dialects and gives rise to unsupported claims which tend to exaggerate not only the similarities between the grammars of these dialects and of standard English but also the knowledge which non-standard speakers have of standard English. Thus, evidence of how efficiently people from socially distant groups decode each others´ utterances is extremely difficult to collect. The fieldwork situation which involved a Group I speaker in prolonged and relatively relaxed conversation with Group III speakers is rare, and so is a valuable source of data. The evidence and conclusions which emerged are as follows.

First, it is fairly clear from (1) that the speaker takes the you/youse distinction for granted to the extent that she comments on its communicative importance to a socially distant addressee without any apparent awareness of the stigma attached to it, or that the addressee might not use such a distinction. Secondly, one consequence of this categorical distinction was that during the field-work period I consistently encountered problems when I used the unmarked form of the plural. For example a conventional greeting such has ´How are you?´, addressed to two or more persons usually elicited a zero response (silence) and an exchange of puzzled glances. Since I found it hard to believe that the youse rule was responsible for these breakdowns, they initially went unrepaired. However, the sequence 'How are youse doing?' always elicited an appropriate response such as 'Not too bad, what about yourself?' Further examples can be cited to illustrate the categorical nature of the distinction for some speakers, the most spectacular of which is a letter to two researchers who are consistently addressed as youse. Other examples of youse in formal written communication have been reported. It seems that the communicative competence of these speakers is limited to a knowledge of the choice appropriate within their own social group. The same can probably be said of more standardized speakers.

It is also clear that the usage exemplified in (1) bears strongly on the issue discussed above, that is the kind of linguistic knowledge which non-standard speakers may be said to have of standard English. At the very least we may conclude that there is a great deal which we simply do not know about this matter. Although the assumption (made usually by Group I speakers) that all speakers have at least a passive competence in standard English seems on the face of it perfectly reasonable, the youse evidence suggests that this may be correct for Group II speakers but not for the more socially distant Group III speakers. In a similar vein, Miller shows that Scottish speakers who do not use the will/shall distinction have it in their passive competence only in the limited sense that they recognize it as belonging to some variety of English. When pressed to state the basis of the distinction, they either confess to bafflement or manufacture 'rules' which bear little relation to linguistic reality such as 'Shall is more polite than will' (Miller, 1981, p. 87). All in all, Labov's argument that linguists derive many of their facts about low-status vernaculars from upwardly mobile and relatively standardized speakers with whom they have a measure of social affinity seems to be depressingly near the mark (Labov, 1972(a), p. 287).

In view of our general ignorance both of non-standard grammars and of the limits of communicative competence, I do not think that we can afford to dismiss the breakdowns located in the you/youse disjunction as isolated and unrepresentative of cross-dialectal interactions; the extent to which breakdown located in other sociolinguistically distributed grammatical elements might occur is at the moment simply a matter of speculation.

Whenever he came in he hit me

The set of data discussed in this section has a sociolinguistic distribution quite different from that of the youse variable. The temporal conjunctions whenever and when do not contrast even in educated varieties of Hiberno-English. Thus, Hiberno-English whenever has a meaning quite different from the whenever of standard British English, and need not be interpreted as indefinite or as referring to more than one occasion in the past (Milroy, 1978).[2] The following utterances are taken from four separate conversations:

(2) Whenever I saw her I fell for her.
(3) Whenever he came in he hit me.
(4) My husband died whenever I was living on the New Lodge Road.
(5) Whenever Chomsky wrote Syntactic Structures there was a revolution in linguistics.

It is clear that Irish and English listeners are likely to map these utterances on to different grammars, and so produce different interpretations. However, (2) and (3) differ from (4) and (5) in that (2) and (3) are semantically acceptable for both sets of speakers. But, for the standard English speaker, (4) and (5) simply do not make sense, because the interpretation suggested by his grammar conflicts with real world knowledge. What appears to happen then in real situations (but not under experimental conditions, as we shall see shortly) is that he concludes correctly that Hiberno-English whenever is equivalent to standard English when probably because this is the easiest way of extracting relevance from the utterance. This feature of Hiberno-English grammar is in fact quite frequently the subject of overt comment by standard English speakers, and where an interpretation is impossible for them in accordance with their own grammars does not appear to be a source of miscommunication.

The same cannot be said of utterances like (2) and (3). While the temporal clause in (2) was misinterpreted by a standard English speaker as referring to several different occasions, the misunderstanding did not have the effect of producing communication problems and was not noticed by either of the interlocutors. Only direct questioning after the exchange revealed the disparate interpretations, and it is very likely that a great many unimportant misunderstandings of this kind go both unresolved and unnoticed. A similar case is documented by Berdan (1977, p. 15), where in cross-dialectal communication speakers may communicate successfully with each other despite the fact that both are mapping quite different grammars on to utterances containing got as a verb of possession. In the terms which we have adopted here, the ambiguity of (2) resulted in misunderstanding but not in communicative breakdown.

The misunderstanding resulting from (3), which passed unnoticed at the time, was potentially more serious simply because of the propositional content of the utterance. The addressee was myself, and the topic of conversation was the unreasonable behaviour of the speaker's husband. Being at that time unfamiliar with this part of the Hiberno-English system, I interpreted the reference of the utterance as a large number of assaults upon the speaker. Only many weeks later did it become apparent, on reflection, that I had drawn an entirely wrong series of inferences from the miscommunication.

If these observations on examples (2) to (5) are taken together, we can begin to isolate some structural and pragmatic conditions which appear to be necessary before syntactically located cross-dialectal miscommunications take place. First, the utterance must be semantically acceptable to both speakers; otherwise it is simply odd, like (4) and (5) rather than ambiguous (but see further below). Second (and this is a matter of social norms) the reference must be of some 'real world' importance. Otherwise, as with (2), the interaction will proceed without the interlocutors necessarily being aware of the misunderstanding. In contrast, the misunderstanding following utterance (3), although not noticed at the time, was identified retrospectively because in our society a man who repeatedly beats his wife attracts more notice than one who repeatedly falls in love with the same woman. Thus, it appears that successful cross-dialectal communication in context depends on a fairly complicated combination of structural and pragmatic factors.

It is worth drawing attention here to an experimental study by Trudgill where subjects are asked to select an interpretation of a range of sentences generated by non-standard English dialect grammars (Trudgill, 1981). The whenever sentence selected (whenever it was born I felt ill) is semantically acceptable only if whenever is interpreted as equivalent to when, and so is of the same type as utterances (4) and (5) above. Contrary to what appears to happen in real contexts, where such utterances do not seem to result in communication problems, Trudgill found that 'the grammatical constraints of their own dialects forced a majority of subjects to select [an] anticommonsense interpretation'. Subjects often regarded the sentence as complete nonsense or, in some cases, attempted a contextualization of their semantically odd interpretation. This disparity between experimental and observational results is instructive, and is probably best viewed as showing the unwillingness of speakers in real social situations to regard any utterance as complete nonsense. Relevance will always be assumed (in Grice's sense) and a likely interpretation will be sought, while a subject in an experiment (a constructed situation) will not be under the same social pressures to locate the speaker's intention. Additionally, he may not assume that the stimulus sentence is relevant.

An interesting parallel to this mismatch between experimental results and the results of naturalistic observation may be found in recent psycholinguistic work on the basis of linguistic intuitions (Carroll *et al.*, 1981). Here, the authors describe the manner in which judgments of 'borderline' sentences as acceptable vary in quite a systematic way, as the judges' mental states are manipulated towards either 'objective self-awareness' or 'subjective self-awareness'. These states may well be parallel to states in experimental as opposed to real life situations.

How long are youse here?

This utterance is the opening sequence of (6). A is a native of South West Donegal; B and C are both standard English speakers (and linguists).

(6) A: (i) How long are youse here?
B: Till after Easter
(A looks puzzled; a pause of two seconds follows)
C: We came on Sunday
A: (ii) Ah, Youse're here a while then.

The miscommunication here is located in an extremely complicated difference between the aspect systems of standard English and Hiberno-English, which may for the present purposes be outlined as follows (but see also p. 22 above).

A standard English speaker will usually interpret an utterance like A (i) as equivalent to *How long will you be here for*? Hiberno-English generally avoids the use of the *have* auxiliary as a marker of the perfect, and has a range of structures, including the A (i) type, which appear to be equivalent to the standard English perfect (see Harris, 1982 for further discussion). Utterance B was therefore an inappropriate response to A (i), and speaker A was quite unable to interpret it. For him, A (i) and B simply constituted an ill-formed exchange. The breakdown was, after a time lag, noticed and repaired. It is by no means certain that a linguistically unsophisticated speaker such as A (both B and C were linguists) could have located the breakdown and effected the repair).

This is an extremely clear example of a cross-dialectal breakdown which can be located specifically in a disparity between the grammars of speaker and hearer. The difference between the two semantic structures associated with A (i) involves the existence of a state in time *either* up to a certain point, *or* from a certain point. The somewhat intangible nature of this difference, together with the absence of further relevant contextual cues, appear to rule out comprehension strategies which involve contextual factors or real world knowledge. The claim made by, for example, Smith and Wilson (1979, p. 197) that perceptual strategies of various kinds facilitate cross-dialectal communication, to the extent that differences in internal grammars are communicatively unimportant, seems to be contradicted by this example. Moreover, the fact that speakers B and C knew (in the encyclopedic rather than the linguistic sense) of the disparity between this portion of the two grammars was not enough to prevent the breakdown in the first place, although it was eventually noticed. It may be concluded then that there are specifiable situations where grammars (as opposed to strategies) are crucial to effective communication between speakers of different dialects.

Finally, it is worth noting the reaction of the participants to the breakdown. During the two-second pause, B and C at least had an extremely unpleasant sense of simply not knowing what was going on and being quite unable to analyse it; this is very reminiscent of the reactions of puzzlement and frustration reported by Gumperz (1976) when breakdown involving differences in the kind of conversational inferences drawn by speaker and hearer takes place. Thus, the possibility that breakdowns of this kind may not be analysed as linguistic at all is another reason for caution in assuming that they are rare.

The communicative breakdown exemplified in (6) may be compared with (7), a successful communication between an Ulsterman and an Englishman working as a temporary lecturer in Northern Ireland.

(7) A: How long are you here?
B: Just this term.

Here the misunderstanding was not noticed (although the same Englishman had experienced problems in understanding similar constructions) apparently because the response can be construed as 'length of time during which', i.e. unlike 6B it does not contain a temporal item referring to either future or past. Alternatively we may assume ellipsis, and restructure 7B as either 8 or 9:

(8) Just (until the end of) this term.
(9) Just (since the beginning of) this term.

Since neither past nor future time were overtly marked in the response by a temporal conjunction, each speaker was able to associate the response with a different underlying semantic structure. A comparison with (6) and (7) suggests that _ellipsis_ may play a part in masking miscommunications.

A somewhat surprising insight into the role of _linguistic_ context in successful cross-dialectal communication is provided in an important experimental study by Berdan (1977). (In view of the facts reported above, we should be cautious however of drawing over-general conclusions about comprehension-in-context from experimental studies.) Berdan presented to two groups of American students (one black and one white) a number of potentially ambiguous sentences and, as a means of determining their interpretation of these sentences, asked them to construct tag questions for them. The rule of copula deletion in Black English was the locus of the ambiguity.

Where contracted is appears on the surface, it is often phonetically indistinguishable from the plural morpheme. Thus, the sequence [frɛnz] in (10), with contracted is, is indistinguishable from plural friends in (11), although each is derived from a different underlying sentence:

(10) Her best friend is playing jump rope.
(11) Her best friends are playing jump rope.

On hearing the resulting identical phonetic sequence, speakers of a dialect which does not allow copula deletion would allow, Berdan considered, only the interpretation shown in (10) while speakers of a dialect which does allow copula deletion would find both (10) and (11) possible interpretations.

In fact, for the sequence Her best [frɛnz] playing jump rope, all of the white and all but two of the black students provided a singular tag, showing that they understood the sentence as (10). However, Berdan noted that it appeared to be possible to change semantic and other contextual cues in an ambiguous sentence to make one reading at first sight more plausible than another without making either reading ungrammatical. He suggested, for example, that a superlative like best seemed to facilitate a singular interpretation, although plurals with best, such as (12) clearly do occur:

(12) They are my best friends.

He also suggested that a singular possessive pronoun like her might facilitate a singular reading, while a plural pronoun like their might increase the possibility of a plural reading. To explore the effects of these contextual cues, the sequences (13) to (16) were included among the test items:

(13) Her best [frɛnz] playing jump rope.
(14) Her [frɛnz] playing jump rope.
(15) Their best [frɛnz] playing jump rope.
(16) Their [frɛnz] playing jump rope.

As predicted, singular interpretation frequencies decreased progressively from (13) through to (16), most spectacularly among black students. However, one unexpected finding was a significant number of plural readings of (15) and (16) even among the white students whose grammars were thought not to allow the deletion rule.

Berdan's results confirm the extremely indirect relationship between comprehension and grammatical rules. They add to our knowledge of comprehension strategies in that they show that for some white informants, logically irrelevant linguistic cues are sufficient to override interpretations suggested by the application of grammatical rules. However, the magnitude of the contextual conditioning was smaller for the white than for the black students; therefore it seems that the capacity of contextual cues to encourage persons to employ particular perceptual strategies is greater when the cues do not conflict with linguistic rules, than when they do conflict with them.

Although Berdan's findings confirm the importance of perceptual strategies in skewing the interpretation of ambiguous sentences, it appears that quite simple lexical changes such as those which he manipulates may influence comprehension one way or another. However, these cues do not operate independently of a speaker's internal grammar or, as has sometimes been suggested, take precedence over it. Rather, grammatical rules and perceptual strategies operate in conjunction with each other (and, as we have seen, with extra-linguistic contextual factors) in an orderly way in influencing the interpretation of utterances.

Conversational inferences

Since much reference has been made in this chapter to contextual and pragmatic cues, it is appropriate to note that the locus of a miscommunication may be specifically 'pragmatic' rather than 'structural'. By this I mean that it is located in a disparity between the inferences which conversational participants draw from a given utterance, rather than in a disparity of the kind discussed here so far between the semantic structures from which they derive that utterance. This section relies heavily on the work of Gumperz and his associates on cross-cultural communicative breakdowns (Gumperz, 1976, 1977(a), 1977(b); Gumperz *et al.*, 1979; Gumperz and Tannen, 1979).

Fundamentally, Gumperz argues that difficulties in inter-ethnic communication arise not only as a result of generalized prejudice, but through differences in various kinds of shared knowledge and in culture-specific communicative preferences. These differences affect the kind of inferences drawn in conversation to interpret a given utterance. For example, ethnic groups differ in the uses which they make of a given prosodic pattern: the tune appropriate for polite questions in one culture may signal an emphatic statement in another. Many miscommunications are documented which may be located specifically in disparate interpretations of prosodic cues (Gumperz, 1977(b); Gumperz and Tannen, 1979, Gumperz *et al.*, 1979). The culture-specific nature of different levels of loudness and different proxemic behaviours in a given situation has been shown elsewhere to be the source of miscommunication (Watson and Graves, 1966; Hall, 1963; see also Brown and Levinson, 1978, p. 258). Similarly, culture-specific differences in 'the distribution of required and preferred silence' (Hymes, 1972) have been documented as a source of miscommunication (Philips, 1976; Milroy, 1980). In Milroy (1980) the differences were between norms appropriate to different status groups rather than different ethnic groups in the usual sense.

A source of miscommunication which may be labelled as more specifically pragmatic may be located in disparate interpretations of the illocutionary force of indirect speech acts. For example, an utterance such as (17) can in some situations be interpreted as a directive, and in others as a simple comment with no particular illocutionary force, while (18) might be interpreted either as a request for information, or a request for action:

(17) It's dinner time and I'm hungry.
(18) Can you play the Moonlight Sonata?

In the absence of clear prosodic cues, the speaker's communicative intent is interpreted in relation to certain presuppositions which are influenced by aspects of the (extra-linguistic) context such as setting, topic, the speakers' knowledge of each other and of their mutual rights and obligations. Currently there is a great deal of interest in the presuppositions and logical processes which underlie the interpretation of such indirect speech acts; but as Gumperz points out, what is meant by context and the manner in which it enters into the interpretation process has been discussed only in general terms (Gumperz, 1976; but see Labov and Fanshel, 1977 for an attempt at a more precise formulation). More seriously, it seems to be commonly assumed, though not explicitly stated, that conversational participants generally share a kind of pragmatic competence which enables them to interpret contextual factors in much the same way (Gumperz, 1976, p. 281). This assumption is particularly clear in an early article by Lakoff (1971), and more recently Smith and Wilson (1979) refer to utterances-in-context as containing 'items of non-linguistic knowledge shared by speaker and hearer, and a set of shared inference rules' (p. 174). Leaving aside for a moment the question of how much relevant non-linguistic knowledge persons with different cultural norms might be said to share, it is clear that the 'shared inference rules' are often insufficient to prevent misinterpretation of the illocutionary force of indirect speech acts even between persons who know each other well; sometimes these mis-interpretations are repaired. Many examples of exchanges such as the following could no doubt be provided by the reader:

(19) Wife: Will you be home early today?
Husband: When do you need the car?
Wife: I don't, I just wondered if you'd be home early.

It may in fact be more accurate to talk of 'inferential preferences' of a probabilistic nature, rather than 'inference rules', so as to allow for the fact that such misinterpretations are quite frequent (cf. the comments of Lyons and Aitchison above, and see Klein and Dittmar, 1979 for a good discussion of probabilistic models). Tannen (1981) has recently made a very similar suggestion, viz. that in explaining how persons interpret indirect speech acts, the notion of _patterns of interpretation_ is more appropriate than that of _rules of discourse_. These patterns of interpretation depend, in a complex way, on 'context, individual and social differences and interpersonal dynamics' (p. 484).

While taking the non-categorical nature of the inference process into account, Gumperz suggests tentatively, on the basis of a number of documented conversations and direct questions put to judges, that a predisposition to interpret contextual cues in a given manner may vary _systematically_ between speech communities. For example, he considers that American speakers are more likely than British speakers to interpret interrogatives of a pragmatically ambiguous kind (such as (18)) as requests for information. Interestingly, the miscommunication between himself and an American salesman reported by Trudgill (1981) seems to support this view. More recently, Gumperz and Tannen have examined in some detail a number of miscommunications, some but not all of which may be located in the systematically different types of inference likely to be drawn by a number of American ethnic groups. Further, Tannen reports that in a study of cross-cultural differences in inferential preferences, more Greeks than Americans, when presented with a sample of conversation, interpreted _why_ utterances (such as _Why are you here?_) as indirect speech acts (Tannen, 1981).

One point made by Gumperz repeatedly is that communicative breakdowns are seldom analysed as _linguistic_. Speakers typically react with a sense of frustration and hostility; frequently each participant accuses the other of perverse and wilfully difficult behaviour, and if confronted with a re-run of the conversation, claims that his own interpretation of a given prosodic pattern, or a given utterance, is the only reasonable one. In the case of cross-ethnic communication, this kind of breakdown appears to contribute to hostile stereotyping, and one concern of Gumperz has been to devise training programmes for those whose work involves them in communicating with other ethnic groups. This would appear to be an important application of any theory of communication which could account elegantly and systematically for the frequent miscommunications which do undoubtedly take place. It seems likely, moreover, that the kind of culturally distributed problems and reactions to these problems which Gumperz describes are not limited to inter-ethnic communication. They almost certainly occur in a similarly systematic manner in conversations between, for example, Englishmen who, like the Group I and Group III speakers discussed in relation to youse wash the dishes, are socially distant from each other.

SUMMARY AND CONCLUSION

By focussing on miscommunications, the purpose of this chapter has been to explore the manner in which people communicate successfully. Comprehension is a complicated matter, requiring a multidisciplinary approach; it seems that the perspective offered by sociolinguistics, concerned as it is with the analysis of speech events in their social context, might be a helpful one. Analysis of a number of miscommunications has shown that, despite the complex range of strategies involved in comprehension, it is possible to locate some problems specifically in the mismatch between the dialect grammars of speaker and hearer.

The first of the miscommunications examined (altogether three relevant areas of Hiberno-English grammar were isolated) was located in a syntactic disparity which also had a clear sociolinguistic distribution; that is, the you/youse contrast. Analysis suggested that the non-standard speaker's general communicative competence, as well as his passive competence in standard English, might be more limited than is commonly supposed.

The analysis focussing on Hiberno-English whenever suggested that structurally located miscommunications were likely to occur and be noticed under specifiable conditions: the ambiguous utterance had to be semantically acceptable to both speaker and hearer; and the ambiguity had to be located in a message which was of 'real world' importance to the hearer. However, it was noted that under experimental conditions, subjects appeared to misinterpret even semantically unacceptable sentences. This may be because experimental subjects do not search out relevance in 'odd' sentences whereas conversationalists do. In other words, Grice's maxim of relevance may not apply in test conditions. A further analysis which focussed on the Hiberno-English perfect suggested that, probably because of the abstract nature of the reference, non-linguistic context was often of little use in helping conversationalists avoid breakdowns. However, ellipted responses sometimes concealed misunderstandings. The question of how specifically linguistic context influenced comprehension was pursued further, and some experimental results were discussed which suggested that in cross-dialectal communication perceptual strategies worked together with linguistic rules in an orderly manner when persons interpreted ambiguous sentences.

Since consideration of all the data suggests that it is possible to specify conditions under which syntactic mismatches are likely to produce miscommunications, we may consider these observations as a modest contribution towards a more explicit and testable theory of communication.

Finally, some breakdowns located in disparate <u>inferential strategies</u> were briefly discussed, and it was suggested that the notion of <u>inferential preferences</u> of a probabilistic kind might be easier to work with than that of <u>inference rules</u>, so as to allow theoretically for frequently occuring miscommunications.

One particularly interesting (if negative) conclusion is that there is much about cross-dialectal communication which we simply do not know, although the general assumption in standard linguistics textbooks is that there is very little worth knowing. I do not think that we can afford to dismiss the instances discussed here as 'marginal' in the sense that Hiberno-English has an unusually exotic grammar. There are many subtle differences between even Anglo-English dialects and standard English (such as those associated with the temporal conjunction <u>while</u> in Northern England) which might, if investigated, be found to be the locus of communicative problems.

Linguists who consider themselves to be socially responsible may also feel that the possibilities of applying work of this kind to situations where cross-dialectal communicative problems have unpleasant social consequences are considerable. Preliminary attention has already been given to the analysis of problems which are known to arise in language-testing situations (see for example, Labov, 1972(a); Taylor, 1977; Milroy and Milroy, forthcoming). It is hoped that this chapter will stimulate readers to consider further specific applications of a detailed, dispassionate and accountable analysis of cross-dialectal communication problems. These are problems which are of practical concern to many, but only a linguist is capable of carrying out such an analysis; if linguists do not do the job, it will be done, but less well, by others.

NOTES

1. Much of the work reported in this chapter was carried out in the course of research projects HR 3771 and HR 5777, funded by the Social Science Research Council. This support is gratefully acknowledged here.

I also acknowledge the contribution of my co-workers, James Milroy, John Harris, and Linda Policansky, all of whom have been struggling to cope with the vagaries of non-standard syntax which sometimes seems to defy analysis. Thanks are due particularly to James Milroy for his initial insights into the very great differences between Hiberno-English and standard English syntax. The following have been of great help in providing data or commenting on earlier drafts, and I thank them: Greg Brooks, Alison Davis, Michael McTear, John Harris, James Milroy, James Miller and Michael Stubbs and Margaret Deuchar.

2. It is also distinct, semantically, from Scottish *whenever* which is equivalent to 'as soon as'.

REFERENCES

Aitchison, J. (1976) *The Articulate Mammal: An Introduction to Psycholinguistics*, Hutchinson, London.

Berdan, R. (1977) 'Polylectal Comprehension and the Polylectal Grammar' in Fasold and Shuy (eds.) pp. 12-29.

Bever, T. G. (1970) 'The Cognitive Basis for Linguistic Structures in *Cognition and the Development of Language*, J. R. Hayes (ed.), Wiley, New York.

Brown, P. and Levinson, S. C. (1978) 'Universals in Language Usage: Politeness Phenomena' in E. Goody (ed.), pp. 56-289.

Carroll, J. M., Bever, T. G. and Pollack, C. R. (1981) 'The Non-uniqueness of Linguistic Intuitions', *Language*, 57, 368-381.

Cicourel, A. (1973) *Cognitive Sociology*, Penguin, Harmondsworth.

Coulthard, M. (1977) *An Introduction to Discourse Analysis*, Longmans, London.

Edwards, V. K. (1979) *The West-Indian Language Issue in British Schools: Challenges and responses*, Routledge, London.

Ervin-Tripp, S. (n.d) 'Structures of Control', Mimeo, Department of Psychology, Berkeley.

Fasold, R. W. and Shuy, R. W. (1977), *Studies in Language Variation*, Georgetown University Press, Georgetown, Washington D.C.

Ferguson, C. A. (1977) 'Linguistics as Anthropology' in Saville-Troike (ed.), pp. 1-12.

Fillmore, J., Kempler, D. and Wang, S. Y. (1979) *Individual Differences in Language Ability and Language Behaviour*, Academic Press, London and New York.

Fromkin, V. (ed.) (1973) *Speech Errors as Linguistic Evidence*, Mouton, The Hague.

Fromkin, V. (ed.) (1981) *Errors in Linguistic Performance*, Academic Press, London and New York.

Givon, T. (1979) *On Understanding Grammar*, Academic Press, London and New York.

Goody, E. N. (ed.) (1978) Questions and Politeness, Cambridge University Press, Cambridge.
Gordon, D. and Lakoff, G. (1971) 'Conversational Postulates' in Papers from the Seventh Regional Meeting of the Chicago Linguistic Society, CLS, Chicago.
Grice, H. P. (1975). 'Logic and Conversation' in Syntax and Semantics: Speech Acts, P. Cole and J. Morgan (eds.), Academic Press, London and New York.
Gumperz, J. J. (1976) 'Language, Communication and Public Negotiation' in P. Sanday (ed.) Anthropology and the Public Interest: Fieldwork and Theory, Academic Press, New York and London.
Gumperz, J. J. (1977a) 'The Conversational Analysis of Interethnic Communication', Mimeo: University of Berkeley.
Gumperz, J. J. (1977b) 'Sociocultural Knowledge in Conversational Inferences' in Saville-Troike (ed.), pp. 191-211.
Gumperz, J. J., Tupp, T. C. and Roberts, C. (1979) Cross-talk: A Study of Cross-cultural Communication, National Centre for Industrial Language Training, Southall.
Gumperz, J. J. and Tannen, D. (1979) 'Individual and Social Differences in Language Use' in Fillmore et al. (eds.), pp. 305-326.
Gumperz, J. J. and Hymes, D. (1972) Directions in Socio-linguistics, Holt, Rinehart & Winston, New York.
Hall, E. T. (1963) 'A System for the Notation of Proxemic Behavior', American Anthropologist, 65, 1003-26.
Harris, J. (1982) 'The Hiberno-English Verb Phrase: Variation, Change and Dialect Maintenance', Belfast Working Papers in Language and Linguistics, 6.
Hughes, A. and Trudgill, P. (1979) English Accents and Dialects, Arnold, London.
Hymes, D. (1972) 'Models of the Interaction of Language and Social Life' in J.J. Gumperz and D. Hymes (eds.), pp. 35-71.
Klein, W. and Dittmar, N. (1979) Developing Grammars, Springer, Berlin.
Labov, W. (1972a) 'Where do Grammars Stop?' in R.W. Shuy (ed.),Socio-linguistics: Current Trends and Prospects, Georgetown University Press, Washington D.C.
Labov, W. (1972b) Language in the Inner City, Pennsylvania University Press, Philadelphia.
Labov, W. and Fanshel, D. (1977) Therapeutic Discourse, Academic Press, New York and London.
Lakoff, G. (1971) 'Presupposition and Relative Well-formedness' in D. Steinberg and D. Jacobovits (eds.), Semantics, Cambridge University Press, Cambridge.
Lyons, J. (1977) Semantics (2 vols). Cambridge University Press, Cambridge.
Lyons, J. (1980) 'Pronouns of Address in Anna Karenina: The

Stylistics of Bilingualism and the Impossibility of Translation' in S. Greenbaum, G. Leech and J. Svartvik, (eds.), Studies in English Linguistics, Longmans, London.

Miller, J. (1981) Spoken Language, Written Language and Competence, Mimeo, Department of Linguistics, University of Edinburgh.

Milroy, J. (1978) 'Stability and Change in Non-standard English in Belfast', Journal of the Northern Ireland Speech and Language Forum, 72-82.

Milroy, L. (1980) Language and Social Networks, Blackwell, Oxford.

Milroy, L. and Milroy J. (forthcoming) Authority in Language: a Sociolinguistic Study of Prescriptivism, Routledge and Kegan Paul, London.

Nelson, N. W. and McRoskey, R. L. (1978) 'Comprehension of Standard English at Varied Speaking Rates by Children whose Major Dialect is Black English', Journal of Communication Disorders, 11, 37-50.

Philips, S. (1976) 'Some Sources of Cultural Variability in the Regulation of Talk', Language in Society, 5, 81-95.

Plutchik, R. (1976) (2nd ed.) Foundations of Experimental Research, Harper & Row, New York.

Ross, J. R. (1975) 'Where to do things with words' in P. Cole and J. Morgan (eds.) Syntax and Semantics 3: Speech Acts, Academic Press, New York and London.

Ross, J. R. (1979) 'Where's English?' in Fillmore et al. (eds.), pp. 127 - 164.

Saville-Troike, M. (ed.) (1977) Linguistics and Anthropology, Georgetown University Press, Washington D.C.

Schegloff, E. A., Jefferson, G. and Sacks, H. (1977) 'The Preference for Self-correction in the Organisation of Repair in Conversation', Language, 53, 361-382.

Searle, J. (1975) 'Indirect Speech Acts' in P. Cole and J.L. Morgan (eds.), Syntax and Semantics 3: Speech Acts, Academic Press, New York and London.

Smith, N. and Wilson, D. (1979) Modern Linguistics, Penguin, Harmondsworth.

Sperber, D. and Wilson, D. (forthcoming) Language and Relevance: Foundations of Pragmatic Theory, Blackwell, Oxford.

Tannen, D. (1981) 'Review of Therapeutic Discourse by W. Labov and D. Fanshel, Language, 57, 2, 481-486.

Taylor, O. (1977) 'The Sociolinquistic Dimension in Standardized Testing' in Saville-Troike (ed.), pp. 257-266.

Trudgill, P. J. (1979) 'Standard and Non-standard Dialects of English in the United Kingdom: Problems and Policies', International Journal of the Sociology of Language, 21, 9-24.

Trudgill, P. J. (1981) 'On the Limits of Passive "Competence": Sociolinguistics and the Polylectal

Grammar Controversy', in D. Crystal (ed.), Linguistic Controversies: Festschrift for F. R. Palmer, Arnold, London.
Watson, O. M. and Graves, T. D. (1966) 'Quantitative Research in Proxemic Behavior', American Anthropologist, 68, 971-985.

THREE

RESOLVING MISUNDERSTANDINGS[1]

Claire Humphreys-Jones

INTRODUCTION

Communication is an activity in which the majority of us are engaged for much of the time. We talk to people and listen to what they have to say and we expend considerable effort in 'getting the message across'. How we do this and what it means to 'get the message across' are the concerns of this paper.

Communication involves the interaction between (a) a speaker who produces an utterance in order to express a proposition and (b) a hearer who listens to that utterance and duly processes it to reach an understanding of that proposition. This understanding should optimally correspond with the proposition which the speaker intended to express in order for successful communication to take place. The relationship between what the speaker intends and what the hearer understands essentially determines the outcome of a communication attempt. If what the hearer understands to have been expressed differs from what the speaker intended to express, that speaker's communication attempt has not been successful: a misunderstanding has occurred. The speaker's communication attempt need not irredeemably fail because the hearer has misunderstood his utterance. Conversations consist of exchanges of utterances and consequently the speaker can endeavour to correct the hearer's understanding of his utterance, providing that he is aware that the misunderstanding has occurred. Thus the speaker's communication attempt might ultimately be successful although initially it was unsuccessful.

This paper aims (a) to illustrate the range of possible outcomes to communication attempts, paying particular attention to those outcomes which involve misunderstandings, and (b) to suggest criteria for what counts as successful communication. Discussion of the relationship between speaker's intention and hearer's understanding is made possible by utilizing a model of communication put forward by

Lyons (1977, p. 36). The model, which is outlined below, is based on research presented in Humphreys-Jones (forthcoming), from which the illustrative data used in this paper is largely drawn.[2]

A MODEL OF COMMUNICATION

Lyons' model of communication is based on the following exchange sequence:

> The message originated by X is encoded by the transmitter into a signal. The signal is sent over a particular communication channel to the receiver. The receiver decodes the signal into a message and passes the message on to Y (Lyons, 1977, p.37).

In spoken communication X is both message originator and transmitter while Y is both receiver and message recipient. The signal is an utterance sent in the channel of speech.[3] The message is a 'proposition' which may be a statement, command or question involving descriptive, expressive or social information (see Lyons, 1977, p.141 ff. for a fuller discussion of the various uses to which the term 'proposition' has been put). As I use it here, the term 'proposition' refers to any utterance which expresses whatever the speaker intends to communicate.

When a speaker communicates a proposition to a hearer I suggest that there are three possible outcomes to the communication attempt, namely, the hearer can (i) correctly understand the proposition that has been communicated, (ii) fail to understand the proposition at all, or (iii) misunderstand the proposition. The following model of communication details how these possible outcomes might derive in spoken communication.

The proposition, p, is expressed in the utterance, x, by the speaker, S. It is S's responsibility to ensure that the construction of x is an apt expression of p. Optimally, x expresses p as clearly as possible, complying with the grammar of the language in which it is produced, with the semantic conventions of that language and with the various pragmatic constraints which pertain at the time the utterance is produced. If S expresses p in an apt x in such a way that it can clearly be heard, the success of the communication then depends on how the hearer, H, receives both x and p, that is, how he hears and decodes x and what p he understands it to express. It is possible to receive x correctly yet fail to receive p correctly and _vice versa_.

H's reception of x, that is, what H hears and decodes, is xr. H's reception of p, that is, what H believes to have been expressed, is pr. xr and pr are unlikely to match p exactly. The received utterance, xr, is an approximation of x and the received proposition, pr, is an approximation of p. Close approximation counts as equivalence: if xr is equivalent to x, then H has heard and decoded x correctly; if pr is equivalent to p, then H has understood pr correctly.

The three possible outcomes suggested above can now be modelled as follows:

S expresses p in x:

For H: (a) understanding

(i)	(ii)	(iii)
$xr = x$	$xr \neq x$	$xr = 0$
$pr = p$	$pr = p$	$pr = p$

(b) non-understanding

(iv)	(v)	(vi)
$xr = x$	$xr \neq x$	$xr = 0$
$pr = 0$	$pr = 0$	$pr = 0$

(c) misunderstanding

(vii)	(viii)	(ix)
$xr = x$	$xr \neq x$	$xr = 0$
$pr \neq p$	$pr \neq p$	$pr \neq p$

I shall discuss and illustrate each of these outcomes in turn.

COMMUNICATION OUTCOMES

(a) Understanding

When the outcome of communication is understanding, H receives the proposition which S has intended to express. In the first instance of understanding, (i) xr = x, pr = p, xr is equivalent to x and pr is equivalent to p. H correctly hears and decodes the utterance produced by S and correctly understands the proposition which S intended to express.

The majority of communication attempts probably have this successful outcome but it should be noted that a successful outcome may be restricted to the participant H to whom the utterance is addressed. The outcome may not be successful for other hearers as the following example illustrates:

(1) S: Why have you stopped?
/pause/
(2) H: It's all right, it was only a bus

S and H are playing tennis in the road and H has suddenly stopped playing. S and H have no difficulty in understanding each other's utterances but it is doubtful if any other hearer would be able to understand (2) without being privy to additional information. Whenever a car turns into the road in which they are playing they stop their game until the car has gone. H, hearing the sound of a vehicle, stops, which prompts S's question in (1). H then continues to play, explaining to H that the sound that he heard was that of a bus; buses do not go down the road but stop at the top of it and therefore there is no need to stop playing. The background knowledge shared by S and H plays a major part in ensuring the success of their communication attempt.

In (ii), $xr \neq x$, $pr = p$, H fails either to hear or to decode correctly the utterance which S has produced but he correctly understands the proposition intended by S. The faulty reception of x can be due to mishearing or to an incorrect interpretation of the grammatical constituents of the utterance. One often encounters the claim 'I don't follow what you are saying but I know what you mean'. Neither mishearing nor utterance interpretation error need preclude correct understanding of the proposition expressed in the utterance. H can, however, seek guidance as to how x should have been received.

In (iii), $xr = 0$, $pr = p$, H does not receive any utterance at all but nevertheless correctly understands the proposition. In a crowded bar, for example, one might not hear what is being said but one can correctly understand that one is being offered a drink. One could, if one wished, ask for a repeat of x, to make sure that pr is correct.

(b) Non-understanding

When the outcome of communication is non-understanding H does not receive any proposition at all.

In the first instance of non-understanding, (iv) $xr = x$, $pr = 0$, the utterance is received correctly but no proposition is received. Examples of such non-understanding are common in teaching sessions where a pupil correctly hears what the teacher has said and decodes that utterance correctly but has no understanding of it whatsoever. The following mathematical joke frequently results in non-understanding: Question: If two Witches of Agnesi revolved around their asymptotes and then lay beside a hyperboloid in one sheet, would there be a perfect union? Answer: It depends on their eccentricities.[4] In such a case of non-understanding one would probably seek an explanation although it is quite possible that non-understanding might persist after receiving the following explanation: the joke involves a number of geometric terms - a Witch of Agnesi is a type of curve, an asymptote is a type of line which a curve approaches, a hyperboloid in one sheet is a three dimensional shape and eccentricity describes the characteristics of certain curves.

In (v), $xr \neq x$, $pr = 0$, the utterance is incorrectly heard or decoded and because of the mishearing or incorrect decoding no proposition is received. H might receive 'Have you got white shoes?' as 'View got why choose' and be unable to understand this. Again, H can ask for an explanation of either x or p or both.

In (vi), $xr = 0$, $pr = 0$, no utterance is received and no proposition is received. In a crowded bar, for example, this could be an offer of a drink by S which H cannot hear and cannot understand. S could repeat x of his own volition or in response to a request once H is in earshot if H has realized that he had been addressed.

(c) <u>Misunderstanding</u>
When the outcome of communication is misunderstanding H receives a proposition which is not the proposition which S intended to express.

In the first instance of misunderstanding, (vii) xr = x, pr ≠ p, the utterance is correctly received but the proposition which H receives is incorrect. The following example illustrates this outcome:

(1) S: Nice, aren´t they?
(2) H: Well they´re useful
(3) S: I meant the glasses
(4) H: Oh yes

S is watching H put drip mats under wine glasses and she comments on the glasses. H believes that S is referring to the drip mats and comments on the drip mats. H has thus received the utterance correctly but because she attributes the wrong referent to it she receives an incorrect proposition. S realizes what has happened and explains what she meant.

In (viii), xr ≠ x, pr ≠ p, neither utterance nor proposition are correctly received. H hears or decodes x incorrectly and as a consequence of this has an incorrect understanding of p, as in the following example:

(1) S: Are you Manx?
(2) H: No, eh, I´m divorced actually
(3.1) S: / laugh /
.2) : Not MARRIED
.3) : I asked you are you Manx

´Manx´ in (1) is misheard as ´married´ and therefore the proposition is misunderstood. Again, the answer to the question gives evidence of the misunderstanding and enables S to correct it.

In (ix), xr = O, pr ≠ p, no utterance is received and the proposition which is received is incorrect. In other words, one does not hear the utterance but one nevertheless makes an assumption about what it expressed. In a crowded bar, for instance, this could be the understanding of an utterance which H has not heard as an offer of a drink when actually S is telling H that he is leaving.

The communicative outcomes given above are in respect of single utterances but the roles of S and H are exchanged when H responds to S´s utterance. There must therefore be a communicative outcome to H´s utterance, and then one to S´s and so on to the end of the conversation. In the example above in respect of (vii), the drip mats versus wine glasses example, S receives both utterance (2), and proposition correctly and is able to realize that (1) has been misunderstood; because she is aware that a misunderstanding has occurred she is able to resolve it by explaining what she meant. She thus changes the communicative outcome of (1) from pr = p to pr = p. Similarly, in the example relating to (viii), the mishearing of 'Manx' as 'married', H's response is correctly received by S who is then able to resolve the miunderstanding. After a laugh which signals the misunderstanding, S refutes H's xr and explains what x was. In this example, the outcome of (1) changes from $xr \neq x$ to $xr = x$ and as a consequence of this $pr \neq p$ changes to $pr = p$. In other words, once H has received the utterance correctly she is able to amend her pr, that is, change her understanding of the proposition, so that it becomes equivalent to p, so that correct understanding and therefore successful communication is achieved.

It is apparent from these examples that speakers and hearers have the wherewithal to facilitate successful communication. Provided that they realize that a misunderstanding has occurred they can take steps to resolve that misunderstanding and ensure that pr = p. The following example illustrates the detailed work which speaker-hearers can do in order to be sure that communication is successful; the example also illustrates the consequences of failure to do this:

(1)	S:	Can I borrow (O) for a few minutes
(2)	H:	Yeah sure
(3)	S:	I'll not be a tick
(4.1)	O:	What?
.2)	:	What?
.3)	:	Oh you were talking to (H) then were you?
(5)	S:	No I was just broaching the subject
(6)	H:	A question of ownership
(7)	S:	That's right, yeah
(8)	O:	But you were saying to (H) can I just borrow (O) for a minute
(9)	H:	There's nothing wrong with that
(10)	S:	You weren't paying any attention
(11.1)	O:	I misinterpreted that
.2)	:	Can I just borrow (O) for a minute
.3)	:	I thought you were going to go on
.4)	:	Can I just borrow (O) for a minute such and such is what I thought you were going to do so you eh eh
(12)	S:	I thought that it would be in the department and strolled out of the library for a copy of the relevant
(13)	O:	That's right, you've got you you you've got the

		necessary yeah you´ve got the
(14)	S:	You´re just so used to me having dysphasic
(15)	O:	No the tonicity tonicity was wrong
(16)	S:	Dysphasic syntax
(17.1)	O:	Can I just BORrow
.2)	:	You had the tonic on borrow, right?
.3)	:	You should have had the tonic on (O̲)
(18.1)	S:	Can I just BORrow (O) for a minute
.2)	:	That´s what I said
.3)	:	Can I just BORrow (O) for a minute
(19.1)	O:	Yeah right
.2)	:	What you should have said was can I just borrow (O̲) for a minute
(20)	S:	Did you understand it?
(21)	H:	No not a word
(22.1)	S:	That´s right that´s why you said yes
.2)	:	Great
(23.1)	O:	Well that´s just total rot
.2)	:	/ laugh /
.3)	:	But he´s just been teaching at school for a year or two
(24)	S:	It hasn´t left its mark yet
(25)	O:	It has if you say yes to anything

The conversation begins with a request by S who has just entered O´s room interrupting a conversation between O and H. In (4.1, .2, .3) O signals his misunderstanding and also resolves it by determining that S was talking to H and not to O as O had thought. They discuss O´s understanding of (1) in considerable detail. S and O are linguists and they use terminology with which H, a non-linguist, is unfamiliar. O makes it clear that the reason he misunderstood (1) was because of the intonational patterns used by S, which he suggests were incorrect. The consequence of the discussion from (4.1) to (19.2) is that all three know what O´s xr and pr were on hearing (1), why they were that and what they have become on further consideration of (1). It might seem that communication has been successful due to the efforts made by the participants.

At this point in the conversation, however, another misunderstanding occurs. In (20) S asks H if he "understood it". He intends to ask B if he understood the request addressed to him in (1). H did understand this request; evidence of his correct understanding of the request is displayed in his response "Yeah sure" in (2) and in his observation in (6), "A question of ownership". H, however, understands S to be asking in (20) if he understood the discussion on S´s tonicity in the request; he did not understand this discussion and he answers accordingly. S fails to realize that H has misunderstood (20) and consequently comments on the fact that H had answered appropriately to something which he now claims not to have understood, that is, (1). S, in failing to realize that H has misunderstood (20) himself misunderstands (21). Judging by (22.1) S has assumed that H understood the question in (1) and he anticipates the answer 'yes' to his question in (1), since he points out that H has already given evidence of having understood 'it' by responding to the original question with 'yes'. It seems likely that S asked H if he 'understood it' because he wished to defend his initial utterance and the manner in which he produced it. The person to whom (1) was addressed, H, understood it and therefore the lengthy discussion which deliberates on what was wrong with the way in which it was produced reflects on O's abilities as a hearer rather than on S's as a speaker. Rather than vindicate S, however, the exchange leaves the participants with the impression that S has used incorrect tonicity and that H 'says yes to anything'. The failure to communicate successfully thus results in frustration for S and puzzlement for H and O (cf. the hostility raised by undetected misunderstandings discussed by Gumperz & Tannen, 1979; Milroy, 1984).

It is easy to suggest ways in which the participants could have achieved successful communication. H has not understood the discussion on tonicity and because he has not said 'yes' to any part of it he ought to realize that he has misunderstood the referent of 'Did you understand it?'. S, instead of commenting on H's answering 'yes', could have pressed him further by asking a question such as 'Why did you answer yes if you didn't understand it?' which might have prompted discussion of what B said 'yes' to and what he had failed to understand.

It is apparent from this example that ensuring that pr = p is by no means a straightforward task (see Humphreys-Jones, forthcoming, for a discussion of the various methods used by participants to detect and resolve misunderstandings). In order to communicate successfully one must be aware when one is not communicating successfully. If one fails to pick up the cues that signal this lack of success, communication continues with participants having different beliefs about what is being or has been expressed and, most importantly, not knowing that their beliefs differ. In the case of non-understandings, it is usually easy for the hearer to know that he has no understanding of what has been said to him, although initiating explanations is not always easy (Brown & Levinson's (1978) problem of 'face').

In the model of communication S expresses p in x. In the examples of misunderstandings discussed above H fails to understand correctly a single proposition expressed in a single utterance and although in the last example the misunderstanding was compounded in that S's failure to realize that the misunderstanding had occurred led to a further misunderstanding, each misunderstanding was of one proposition at a time. Linguists have established that one can say one thing while meaning another and this phenomenon is usually referred to as an 'indirect speech act' (Searle, 1975). An example is the statement, 'It's cold in here', which is a statement describing the temperature of a room but which is usually produced with the intention of its being a request for someone to close a window or a door. For communication to be successful in respect of an indirect speech act, H must understand the intended request as well as the descriptive statement.

In the following example S wishes to know if H is going to a seminar in A.I. (Artificial Intelligence), which is shortly due to start. H and O usually attend this seminar but S has never been before and H has offered to take him to it. Both S and H attend a different seminar, Andy Durrant's, which is held the following day:

(1) S: Are you going to the seminar?
(2.1) H: No it's tomorrow
.2) : Today is Tuesday
(3) O: The A.I. seminar
(4) H: No he means Andy Durrant's seminar
(5.1) S: No the artificial intelligence one
.2) : It's at four today
(6.1) H: Oh
.2) : Yes
.3) : Are you?
(7.1) S: Yes
.2) : Are you going now?
(8) H: Oh of course, I said I'd take you there didn't I?

H's misunderstanding of (1) is twofold. In the first instance she misunderstands the referent of 'seminar', believing that S refers to Andy Durrant's seminar, whereas he is referring to the A.I. seminar. This misunderstanding is resolved by O's explanation of which seminar S is referring to and also H's refutation of this together with an explanation of her pr in the guise of an explanation of S's p; knowledge of H's pr enables S to refute it and to explain his p, thus resolving the misunderstanding.

The communication attempt is not yet successful, however, because although S has asked a question of H in (1) to which H duly provides an answer, S's intention is to remind H that she is going to take him to the seminar; it is both a reminder and a request for her to do so. When H asks S if he is going he answers affirmatively and then asks H if she is going at that moment. His persistence in asking the question, virtually a repeat of (1), makes H aware that S is wanting to know more than whether or not she is going to the seminar (a question to which he knows the answer) and she therefore remembers that she has volunteered to take him with her. S's communication attempt is ultimately successful and S, H and O leave together for the seminar.

The fact that utterances can be the products of multiple intentions makes the process of communication highly complex. What one seeks to express may not be clear from one's utterance but negotiation of the type illustrated in the above example can reveal the speaker's intended proposition. For communication to be successful pr must be equivalent to p. xr need not be equivalent to x and in fact can be O but only if pr is equivalent to p has communication been successful. In the case of indirect speech acts pr must be equivalent to p in respect of the underlying intention, that is, the proposition which S intends to express, irrespective of the proposition which the utterance expresses. In order to achieve successful communication p should be expressed clearly, conventionally and appropriately in x; many indirect speech acts take a conventional form so that the underlying propositions can be recovered without difficulty (see Grice, 1975 for a discussion of conversational maxims which aim to promote the correct understanding of indirect speech acts). In the event of success not being forthcoming, participants must be able to detect that H's pr is not equivalent to p. If they assume that correct understanding obtains their communication attempts cannot succeed.

From this specification of what constitutes successful communication it could be claimed that a good listener is one who is able to receive a correct xr and pr regardless of difficulties. However, when four people were informally asked what they felt a good listener was, the ability to understand correctly did not appear:

1. 'Listens to what people say, listens to their point of view without putting their own, listens without interfering';
2. 'Doesn't interrupt, absorbs what's being said before making a considered reply, patient; if he knows it all and interrupts he's not a good listener';
3. 'Listens and pays attention and can say something relevant if need be, someone who really listens rather than going blank, and doesn't interrupt';
4. 'Doesn't interrupt, listens to what you say, replies so as to further or develop what you say'.

All four feel that a good listener does not interrupt and that a good listener heeds what is being said. The art of good listening is thus a question of manner; the listener's approach to what is being said and to the speaker is of paramount importance. Presumably all four assume that in order to listen, and in the case of (2) and (4) to reply constructively, the good listener does understand correctly what is being said. Understanding, however, is not cited.

The behaviour and attitude of the listener is vital to the success of communication. It appears that a speaker believes he needs to have a good listener in order to be able to express himself clearly.

Thus it may not be sufficient to claim that communication is successful only if pr is equivalent to p. Communication may be considered fully successful only when the attitudes of speaker and hearer are in accord, when the speaker believes that his proposition will be heeded and will be received sympathetically. In successful communication one does not simply hear and process what is said, one listens to it and one reaches a correct understanding in the light of this listening. The hearer must act positively in order that the speaker may ´get his message across´.

NOTES

1. I am grateful to Graham McGregor for comments on earlier drafts of this paper.

2. The data were collected by the ´diary´ method. The corpus is presented in full in Humphreys-Jones (forthcoming).

3. The signal can also be a paralinguistic feature such as a laugh, or an extralinguistic feature such as a gesture.

4. I am indebted to R.M. McHarrie who devised this mathematical joke.

REFERENCES

Brown, P. and Levinson, S. (1978) 'Universals in Language Use: Politeness Phenomena' in E. Goody (ed.) Questions and Politeness: Strategies in Social Interaction, Cambridge University Press, Cambridge, pp. 56-311.

Grice, H. P. (1975) 'Logic and Conversation' in P. Cole, and J. Morgan, (eds.) Syntax and Semantics Vol. 3: Speech Acts, Academic Press, London, pp. 41-58.

Gumperz, J. and Tannen, D. (1979) 'Individual and Social Differences in Language Use' in J. Fillmore, D. Kempler, and S.Y. Wang (eds.) Individual Differences in Language Ability and Language Behavior , Academic Press, New York, pp. 305-325.

Humphreys-Jones, C. (forthcoming) An Investigation of the Types and Structure of Misunderstandings, Thesis to be submitted for PhD, University of Newcastle Upon Tyne.

Lyons, J. (1977) Semantics (2 Volumes), Cambridge University Press, Cambridge.

Milroy, L. (1984) 'Comprehension and Context: Successful Communication and Communicative Breakdown' in P. Trudgill, (ed.) Applied Sociolinguistics, Academic Press, London, pp. 7-31.

Searle, J. (1975) 'Indirect Speech Acts' in P. Cole and J. Morgan (eds.) Syntax and Semantics Vol.3: Speech Acts, Academic Press, London, pp.59-82.

FOUR

LISTENING OUTSIDE THE PARTICIPATION FRAMEWORK[1]

Graham McGregor

INTRODUCTION

The investigation of naturally occuring talk has increased exponentially in the last fifteen years or so, to the extent that the study of discourse has virtually achieved the status of an independently recognized discipline. Witness to this fact is borne out by the range of similarly titled works that have appeared in print since the beginning of the decade (compare, for example, Coulthard and Montgomery, 1981; Edmonson, 1981; Gumperz 1982a; Brown and Yule, 1983; Hoey, 1983; Stubbs, 1983; Wardhaugh, 1985).

Yet rich as the literature on conversational discourse has become, it reflects in Grimshaw's (1982, p. 15) terms continuing difficulties for the would be analyst with some fundamental methodological (and practical and ethical) and theoretical problems'. Two central problems Grimshaw raises are (1) the difficulty of undertaking 'comprehensive discourse analysis' of the kind proposed by Labov and Fanshel (1977) and (2) the problem of collecting adequate data. In this paper, I would like to address a third problem which I believe has the same kind of centrality. The problem is essentially one of 'perception' and is usefully raised by Stubbs (1983, pp. 238-246) who asks 'What is the researcher to do when confronted with what has been called the "bloomin', buzzin', confusion" of any normal social setting?' (p. 238).

By recognizing that 'Too much happens too fast for the researcher to take account of it and describe it directly' (1983, p. 239), Stubbs clearly appreciates the analytical bind of discourse analysis, 'how can we learn to notice what we normally take for granted?'. Since the data of everyday language use is enormously rich and correspondingly complex, Stubbs goes on to argue that 'one needs a way of focussing on the features of communication which are relevant'. But relevant for who and in what way?

Current models of interpersonal communication have tended to neglect the interactional dynamic of contexts that help to determine the nature of the variables and the kinds of variation that everyday language use involves. From a linguistic point of view, for example, the orientation of such models has largely been geared to the study of written and spoken discourse and the elucidation of its content and structure within a variety of different discourse types (see, for instance, Coulthard and Montgomery, 1981; Edmonson, 1981; Brown and Yule, 1983; Hoey, 1983; Stubbs, 1983).

Since successful communication has to depend on the contingent satisfaction of a variety of enforceable conditions on particular occasions of use, we suggest that models of this type provide but one possible approach to the study of what is going on in interactional contexts. By focussing on possible discourse patterns in spoken and written texts what such models tend to ignore are the kinds of communicative effects that result as a consequence of speaker-listener interaction. The problem for the analyst of talk is how to go about studying such effects when s/he has no direct access to what may be of communicative significance or value for the participants. Labov and Fanshel (1977, p. 350) summarize this difficulty thus:

> Working with real conversations of real speakers poses a profound and perhaps insoluble problem for the external observer, and we may refer to this as 'the problem of correct interpretation'.

Whilst Labov and Fanshel acknowledge that the 'problem of correct interpretation' can never be resolved entirely because 'we can never hope to have all the knowledge that the participants shared themselves' (p. 351), they suggest that an approximate solution to the problem can be offered by developing strategies that take into account as much of the available evidence as possible. In order to get at this evidence, Stubbs (1983, p. 239) suggests, that the analyst requires some kind of 'estrangement device to enable him to step back and observe what is going on in situations of face-to-face verbal communication'. The form this estrangement device might take is clearly of some theoretical and methodological importance as its nature will largely determine the kinds of claim that the analyst makes about the data in question. According to Widdowson (1979, p. 70-71), the analyst can pursue two basic lines of enquiry:

> One can on the one hand, deal with instances of discourse from the point of view of the third person analyst; that is to say, one can treat discourse in detachment from its instantiation, after the event as a product. On the other hand, one can deal with discourse from the point of view of the participants caught, as it were, in the act, that is to say as a process.

What is at issue for the analyst, however, is that the perceived significance and/or communicative effectiveness of verbal exchange can only be studied as 'an EMERGENT phenomenon, explicitly specifiable in retrospect (and then by way of simplifying procedures that may well distort the participants' experience)' (Dore and McDermott, 1982, p. 386). In other words, from an analytical point of view, we can only gain access to what is going on in the talk of others indirectly, that is, by listening between the lines of the speech communication process. As Widdowson neatly puts it 'what the analyst observes is not necessarily what the participant experiences'. The question thus arises as to how we overcome this difficulty for analytic method without falsifying or simplifying the complexity of processes that everyday communicative interaction is based upon?

One approach is to investigate discourse where there are perceived difficulties of communication as evidenced, for example, in 'misunderstandings' (see, Grimshaw (1982) and the papers by Milroy and Humphreys-Jones in this volume). Another is to query the participants themselves about what they thought was going on, or what they were doing and it is this approach that is of primary concern in this paper.[2] Indeed, Grimshaw (1982, p. 37) notes increasing numbers of investigators are employing such practices (cf. Gumperz and Tannen, 1979; Kreckel, 1981; Gumperz, 1982a, 1982b, for example.) But what does such an approach entail and what can it add to our understanding of the interactive process?

LISTENING IN THE THIRD PERSON

Since presumably participants in various different kinds of verbal exchange may be supposed to know what is going on, we might reasonably expect that individuals from the same speech community possess the ability to describe or 'make sense' of what has gone on, if only from their own point of view. This ability would seem to be linked to the capacity of human beings to describe or 'make sense' of anything at all as de Beaugrande (1980, p. 30) argues; 'the question of how people know what is going on in a text is a special case of the question of how people know what is going on in the world at all'.

Given the ability of individuals to say what is going on in the talk of others, we suggest that this ability is researchable. Indeed, this ability is often assumed by the professional analyst of talk who undertakes to 'interpret' the conversations others as a matter of course. But such interpretive work involves a different kind of 'listening' as Lyons (1977) clearly recognized in making the distinction between a 'receiver' (a person who receives and interprets the message) and an 'addressee' (a person who is an intended receiver of the message). Thus as Leech (1983, p. 13) points out, it is as a 'receiver' rather than an 'addressee' that the analyst of pragmatic meaning, for example, undertakes his or her work; 'the analyst of pragmatic meaning is best thought of as a receiver: a proverbial "fly on the wall" who tries to make sense of the content of a discourse according to whatever contextual evidence is available' (cf. Labov and Fanshel's (1977) approach to therapeutic discourse). This kind of approach has in fact received increasing attention from linguists and linguistic philosophers as part of their attempts to describe speaker 'intent' by identifying those grammatical and lexical factors that can affect the interpretation of particular utterances or the connections between utterances (Brown and Yule, 1983; Leech, 1983; Levinson, 1983). However, as Goody (1978, p. 10) remarks, 'linguistic philosophers have been too ready to ignore the problem of "knowing how we know" the intention of a speaker'.

DEVELOPING AN INTERPRETIVE SOCIOLINGUISTIC APPROACH

It is in response to this problem that Gumperz (1982a, 1982b) has developed a descriptive framework for 'conversational inferencing', that is, 'the situated or context bound process...by means of which participants in an exchange assess others' intentions, and on which they base their responses'.

Gumperz uses this notion of inferencing in conversational contexts to show how social knowledge is used in situated interpretation. The question Gumperz addresses, then, is

> How do we analyse such exchanges so as to account for both linguistic and the social knowledge that participants rely on in interpreting what went on? (Gumperz, 1982a, p. 30).

His answer to this question is to try to deal systematically with participants' co-occurrence judgements in interpreting the discourse and to this end he specifies that the analyst's task must be

> . . . to make an in depth study of selected instances of verbal interaction, observe whether or not actors understand each other, elicit participants' judgements of what goes on, and then (a) determine the social assumptions that speakers must have made in order to act as they do, and (b) determine empirically how linguistic signs communicate in the interpersonal process (Gumperz, 1982a, p. 36).

Whilst Gumperz recognizes that members' judgements appear to be 'elusive', (something of the difficulties facing the analyst who wishes to make use of such judgements is presented in McGregor (1985)), we would suggest that this approach warrants further investigation. But such investigation requires that we extend Gumperz's notion of 'conversational inferencing' for reasons that we will need to consider in some detail.

In the first place, we must recognize that there are different kinds of listeners to talk as Goffman (1976, p. 260) suggests by distinguishing between:

> . . . those who overhear whether or not their unratified participation is inadvertant and whether or not it has been encouraged; those who are ratified participants but (in the case of more than two person-talk) are not specifically addressed by the speaker; and those ratified participants who are addressed that is, oriented to the speaker in a manner to suggest that his words are particularly for them, and that some answer is therefore, anticipated from them, more so than for other ratified participants.

In conversational contexts where we are ratified participants ('addressees' in Lyons (1977) terms), we presumably listen to talk because we expect to make use of it in some way; let's say for purposes of comprehension and recall. However, it is clear that in circumstances where we are 'overhearers' or 'receivers', our motivation for listening must be different. In such circumstances, the listening we undertake might be best thought of as 'critical' or 'evaluatory' listening; we listen in order to make judgements about 'what has gone on' in the talk of others. What actually motivates us to listen is clearly crucial, since I take it that the interpretive work of the professional analyst, for example, is stimulated by a very different kind of 'design' from that of the lay judge (Bell [1984] gives a brilliant account of how this design affects speaker style).

We therefore suggest that Gumperz's notion of 'conversational inferencing' must at least recognize the following listener types. The relevant distinctions are presented in Figure 1 which is adapted from Bell (1984, p. 159). Bell identifies four audience roles and to these we need to add the roles of those individuals who have been specifically invited to overhear and comment on the tape-recorded conversations of others, and also those overhearers who undertake such listening as part of their professional work. Thus we include two other categories of 3rd person listener, that is, 3rd person participant eavesdropper judges (individuals who have listened to an interaction in which they have actually participated) and 3rd person non-participant eavesdropper judges (individuals who have not participated in the interaction in question). It is within this second category of eavesdropper that we need to distinguish between professional analysts and lay observers.

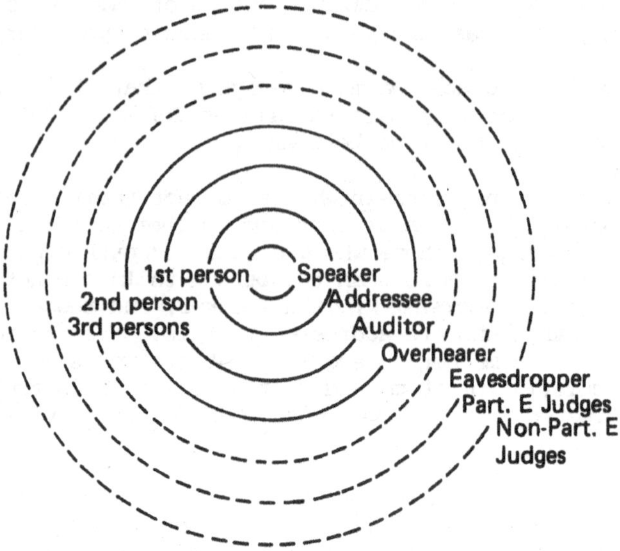

Figure 1: Types of listener to talk.

The need to examine the inferential skills of both analysts and lay observers is important for two reasons. Firstly, analysts of talk ought to provide frameworks for inferencing that go beyond their own subjective platforms. Kreckel (1981), for example, maintains that one of the main objectives of any study of face-to-face interaction ought to include the conceptualization of the interaction not only by the analyst, but also by both outside observers and the participants themselves. The use of judges of this type would seem to come some way to meeting the kind of criticisms that have been levelled at the ethnomethodologists for example. Whilst the ethnomethodologists claim to make inferences about discourse processes they invariably deal with products of the interaction without attempting 'to conduct experiments that might yield information about how the participants see the discourse at a particular point in its development' (Widdowson, 1979, p. 71). Secondly, in the absence of an adequate conceptualization of 'what has gone on', analysts always run the risk of falsifying, or at the very least, simplifying the data. A similar point is made by Brown and Yule (1983, p. 269) who suggest that 'until we can develop experimental techniques which allow us to draw conclusions about how people process naturally occurring discourse in 'real life' contexts, we shall continue to overindulge our simplistic analytic metaphors'. Indeed, they go on to suggest that 'this applies not only to the notion of inference but also to the more general concept of comprehension itself'.

In this respect, we contend that Hoenigswald's (1966) plea to encourage the exploration of the lay-person's folk-linguistic knowledge of everyday interactions has attracted less attention than it deserves. Hoeniqswald (1966, p. 20) argues in particular that 'our main concern should be to match the informant's own description with the linguistic analysis of the data'. He notes, 'we should not only be interested in (a) what goes on (language), but also in (b) how people react to what goes on (they are persuaded, they are put off etc.) and (c) what people say goes on (talk concerning language)'.

As well as specifying different types of listener and explaining their motivation for undertaking the kinds of interpretive work that they do, we also need to consider the nature of the interpretive processes which may lead informants to make particular judgements. Since it is apparent that other kinds of information, as well as 'intent' are conveyed in verbal exchange, we suggest that this information ought to be incorporated in any sociolinguistic account of 'conversational inferencing'.

Laver (1972, p. 189) for example, informs us that

> As actors in a social world, we interact with people by virtue of an exchange of information on many different levels...Any given utterance contains not only a great deal of linguistic information but also a great deal of information for the listener about the characteristics of the speaker himself.

(cf. Abercrombie (1967) who refers to the features in speech which convey this information as 'indexical' features).

In his discussion of the transmission of 'semantic' as opposed to 'signal' information, Lyons (1977) also argues the need to include 'social and expressive information' in his model of communication since he recognises that language not only functions to express speaker 'intent' for the purposes of signalling factual or propositional information, but also serves to (a) establish and maintain social relationships, and (b) express our attitudes and personality.

From an interpretive sociolinguistic point of view, then, any attempt to provide a formal model of conversational inferencing ought to incorporate <u>both</u> linguistic and non-linguistic information. In order to meet this aim, it is necessary to develop methods for eliciting the widest range of judgements that we can. Consequently, I propose to use the term 'conversational inference' in a broad sense to include whatever kinds of connections that eavesdroppers make when attempting to describe or reach an interpretation of some extract of talk which they have been asked to listen to.

This is not to argue that these connections will necessarily match or relate to the experience of individual judges as actual speaker-hearers. What eavesdroppers have to say may reveal only peripheral aspects of underlying complex processes as Dore and McDermott (1982) point out. We do suggest, however, that an examination of eavesdropping behaviour promises to be at least as interesting as theoretical introspection about the nature of communicative interactivity viewed as part of the discourse process.

It is also important to point out that in investigating the 'inferential' skills of eavesdroppers, 'we do not and need not treat the psychological issue of what an individual has in mind' (Gumperz, 1982b, p. 17). What we do need to provide as analysts is evidence for our claims and the use of both participant and non-participant eavesdropper judges may contribute significantly towards this end.

The research which is presented below is the first stage in my own work towards providing a generalised model of conversational inferencing. This research attempts to not only account for the ability of lay observers to interpret or make judgements about the verbal behaviour of others, but also to investigate the necessary forms of knowledge that such inferences as are made may be based upon.

THIRD PERSON JUDGES AND THE INFERENTIAL PROCESS

In order to begin to account for these abilities and forms of knowledge, I have undertaken a series of pilot studies using 3rd. person participant and non-participant eavesdropper judges who were asked to listen to and comment on various different tape-recorded extracts of talk. Something of the results of these studies are variously reported in McGregor (1983; 1984; 1985). Essentially, three major projects were undertaken using different judges (singly and in pairs) to try to elicit as wide a range of responses as possible. In these studies, the instructions which eavesdroppers were given were made as general as possible in order to try to avoid directing and/or prejudicing what eavesdroppers would say about the data they listened to. Consequently, judges were always informed that whilst I would not specify what I wished them to listen for, beyond inviting them to comment on the extracts in question, <u>any</u> comments they made would be welcome since one could not predict the significance of particular kinds of information, for particular individuals, in advance.

All comments which judges offered were noted and it is with the nature of these comments that I shall deal in the remainder of this paper.

EAVESDROPPERS' COMMENTS

In the work reported in McGregor (1983), four broad categories of description were delimited on the basis of what eavesdroppers had to say about the opening five minutes of an

exchange between two male participants. These included:
(a) descriptions of the kind of exchange that was said to be going on,
(b) descriptions of the kind of participants who were said to be involved,
(c) descriptions of the interactional behaviour of the participants and
(d) assessments or evaluations of characteristics of the exchange described in (a) to (c) above.
Closer inspection of these comments, however, has revealed that these categories can be refined by using a binary features matrix to account for the frequency and types of descriptive statement that judges made. Although a number of comments were made about the quality of the recordings and auditory difficulty due to (a) the occurrence of various different kinds of non-linguistic noise and (ii) the volume and style of speech used by the participants, these comments will not be discussed on this occasion. We would point out, however, that what eavesdroppers had to say must have been constrained in part by what they could actually hear. Excluding comments of this type, then, two basic kinds of descriptive statement can be identified: (a) 'observations' and (b) 'inferences'.

In order to help define these terms, we need to distinguish between descriptive statements that can be checked against some record of what was actually said on the one hand, and descriptive statements that could only be based on guess work, after hearing the recordings, on the other. We shall discuss each of these types in turn with exemplification from the comments elicited in the context of the study reported in McGregor (1983).

(a) Observations

Observations are defined to include descriptive statements that can be verified in the sense in which they can be checked against a transcribed record of the exchange to which they refer. Hence, they are presumably based upon eavesdroppers' knowledge of language in use. In the research I have undertaken to date, four sub-categories of observation have been identified. These include, in the order in which they were most frequently cited:
(i) Observations about sequential organization. Two different kinds of descriptive statement were offered about the sequential organization of the exchanges. These were:
(a) within-turn observations used to describe various different verbal phenomena perceived to be characteristic of the speech used by the participants:
'There is lots of hesitancy, "uhm", "uh" and so on'; 'There are plenty of "uhms", "I means" and "you knows"'; '"Uhms", "yeahs" and "wells" add to the informality'; 'They seem to say "yes" and "uhm" to everything', 'He was very hesitant', and

(b) dialogic observations used to describe various different discourse phenomena perceived to be characteristic of the exchange:
'There are a number of pauses'; 'There are gaps'; 'There is some overspeaking'; 'They move on to different things'; 'It's interspersed with them talking over each other'; 'They switch from topic to topic'; 'There are lulls in the conversation, gaps when nobody has anything to say'; 'Gaps come when they didn't know what to say'.
(ii) Observations about subject matter. This category of observation includes descriptive statements that indicate eavesdroppers' ability to recover and specify what some exchange was about. Hence, eavesdroppers offered observations such as:
'They talk about a range of topics - black holes, how to teach, how to get money'; 'They talk about a kid's language. They also talk about money and life as a student'; 'Student-teacher relations are discussed'; 'Two people talked about three subjects - painting, black holes and teaching. They talk about previous events'.
(iii) Observations about lexis. Descriptive statements of this kind relate to the participants use of particular words or phrases. Thus we get observations of the following kind:
'They use words like "bona fide" and "relationship" and hip language like "rip-offs"'; 'Words like "rip-offs" are used'; 'Words such as "junk" and "rip-offs" are used'.
(iv) Observations about prosody.
Within this category eavesdroppers offered descriptive statements about a range of perceived prosodic and paralinguistic phenomena as follows:
'A lot of it was mumbly'; 'He was a bit low and mumbly at times'; 'There is humour when they talk about tax'; 'One is louder than the other'.
The extent to which different non-participant eavesdroppers offered observations in each of these categories, as a result of the research reported in McGregor (1983), is charted in the table which follows overleaf.

A total number of 55 observational statements were offered by eavesdroppers and proportionally the largest number of these were about sequential organization. Indeed, we can see from the matrix that twelve of the sixteen judges made observations of this type. Of the three other types of observation, there is little difference between the number of eavesdroppers who offered descriptive statements about subject matter, lexis and prosody. A possible explanation for this apparent focus on dialogic characteristics of the exchange would appear to be closely tied to inferences eavesdroppers made about patterns of discourse control which, in this instance, many of them seemed to be very sensitive to.

For purposes of comparison we shall now consider the types and frequency of inferences in the same way.

OBSERVATIONS

Eavesdropper	Sequential Organization	Subject Matter	Lexis	Prosody
1	+	−	−	−
2	+	−	−	+
3	+	−	−	−
4	+	+	−	−
5	+	+	−	−
6	+	−	+	−
7	−	+	+	−
8	−	−	+	−
9	+	−	+	+
10	−	+	+	+
11	+	+	−	−
12	+	+	+	−
13	+	+	−	−
14	+	−	−	+
15	−	−	−	+
16	+	+	−	−
Total	12	8	6	5

(b) Inferences

Inferences are defined to include descriptive statements that refer to characteristics of the exchanges which eavesdroppers can only deduce or guess at after listening to the recordings.

We may compare in this respect an ′observation′ such as, ′Words such as "junk" and "rip-offs" are used′, with an ′inference′ like, ′They don′t know each other very well. They′re not on intimate terms, not bosom pals′. The inference here, about the interpersonal relationship between the participants, cannot be verified by reference to some transcript of the exchange. We can only check its validity by questioning the participants and that only after they themselves have heard a recording of the exchange. Thus inferential statements must be the consequence of processes that are impossed on the exchanges in question and which are based, presumably, upon different kinds of social knowledge which eavesdroppers have developed as a result of their own interactional experience. This experience may be actually remembered, derived from acquired stereotype, or simply invented in response to the informant role in which different individuals have been placed. Although we have no way of ascertaining exactly what has prompted some particular comment, it is possible to begin to identify the kinds of social knowledge that may have been employed by different eavesdroppers by working backwards, as it were, from the descriptive statements they have provided. Such a procedure obviously entails a higher level of inferencing based on the kinds of professional knowledge that the analyst brings to bear in handling the data (cf. the approach of Agar (1980), which although primarily ethnographic in orientation, recognizes that different schemata may be employed depending on one of several different analytic ends. These ends are discussed in order to tackle the question of how much of a text is made sensible by analysts and their audiences). For our present purposes, however, we shall deal only with 3rd. person inferencing of the lay kind.

Inferences made by eavesdroppers are classified into three major sub-types which are adapted from Hymes's (1972) analysis of communicative events. They include:

(ii) Inferences about the participants.

Inferences of this type appear to provide answers to the question, 'Who are the participants and what are they like?' They include essentially two types of information:

(i) inferred indexical information about individuals in terms of their identity, age, sex, region of origin, educational/cultural background, speech style, affective states and attitudes, and personality. Thus the participants were described in terms of either being recognized, for example, 'The first person was Ian, I recognize his manner', or by named social stereotypes such as the following: 'The other guy is a southerner, R.P.'; 'One of the speakers sounded eager but hesitant. It came from the way he said things maybe his tone'; 'They sounded cultured, well-educated'. Clearly, knowledge of the participants would affect the kinds of inferences that eavesdroppers might make in this case. The participants were also characterized in terms of named person prototypes. For example, one of the participants was connected with the person prototype of being 'a student' whilst his interlocutor was connected with the prototype of being conversationally dominating - 'one guy is slightly paternal'; 'he had control all along'; 'the one who initiates all the questions seems more dominant'.

(ii) information about the interpersonal relationship of the participants, that is, their knowledge/liking of each other as well as their roles within the discourse and social power or status. One of the participants, for example, said 'It was very much like a student-supervisor chat. I felt that somebody else was in command. It wasn't like talking to a close friend. I had to be more formal. The formality came from the words I was using from the demeanour of the situation'. We may compare this statement with those offered by non-participant judges:

'They don't know each other very well. They're not on intimate terms, not bosom pals. There is a distance, yet they know each other'; 'The speakers are feeling their way around there is a sense in which they don't know each other'; 'One had control all along. The other speaker sounded eager but hesitant. I'm conscious that he was being put at ease'; 'They are colleagues, not intimate but relaxed. They sound as if they know each other'; 'They seem to have a lot in common and know each other quite well'; 'The one who initiates all the questions seems more dominant'; 'One man is entertaining another to coffee. He plays the role of host and asks all the questions'.

(ii) Inferences about the text.

Inferences of this kind relate to what the participants are perceived to be doing from a communicative point of view and the statements offered by eavesdroppers are indicative not only of their ability to recover situation from text, in terms of specifying the kind of 'activity' that is going on, but also to undertake interpretive work on various chunks of text by glossing the communicative 'function/goal', 'key' or 'effect' of some utterance or sequence of utterances.

In naming the 'speech activity' or 'event' (Levinson, 1979) that is inferred to have taken place, eavesdroppers used descriptive phrases such as:
'It's a normal conversation'; 'It's easy chatty conversation'; 'It sounded like a beginning of term interview'; 'It's a coffee interim conversation'. Again the validity of such statements can only be compared against the comments of the participants. In the exchange in question, one of the participants described the event as 'a student-supervisor chat' whilst the other simply described it as 'two blokes talking'.

In undertaking interpretive work on some utterance or sequence of utterances, eavesdroppers provided descriptive statements involving three different but clearly interrelated kinds of information: (i) the inferred communicative function and/or interaction goals of individual participants in remarks such as: 'He wants to do something but isn't sure how to go about it. He was sounding out'; 'There is an active attempt to converge in style and attitude'; 'One of the speakers was probing for advice, feeling his way along'; 'The speakers are feeling their way around, trying to establish a rapport'; (ii) the inferred communicative key (that is, the 'tone, manner or spirit') in which an act or event is performed). Compare, for example, '"Really" is ambiguous. It's not convincing. It had shades in it'; 'When he said "it sounds good", there is approval'; 'He introduces the thing by saying "tell me about your life". It's non-involved'; 'There is humour when they talk about tax': (iii) the inferred communicative effect of particular message sequences. For instance, '"Yeah, yeah" all the time is a kind of prompting. It is meant to give encouragement'; '"Yes" marks understanding rather than agreement'; 'He encourages him by saying "uhm yes" all the time; "So you're not broke anyway" is trying to relax the situation, trying to establish a confidentiality'.

(iii) Inferences about the situation.

Descriptive statements of this kind are indicative of

eavesdroppers' willingness to locate some fragment of discourse in time and space. They include guesses that have a referential function and would appear to answer the questions 'Where, when and in what circumstances did the exchange take place?' Compare the comments of one of the participants, 'It was mid-way through my career. I wanted to reprocess my application as a research student. I was trying to explain why I wanted to come back to University. It was a student-supervisor chat. We were not meeting as mates. I was conscious of the situation', with the following inferences made by non-participant judges:
'It's a casual encounter. He's just called by. The business is to come after'; 'It's a coffee making interim conversation. The preliminaries before getting down to the real thing'; 'Sounded like a school common room with teachers discussing things. It's a discussion between colleagues not intimate but relaxed. It's an occasion to go for coffee and talk while you are making it'. 'It's in their tea break. They are in an office or at home'; 'They are people who know each other, filling in time because they happen to be there. It wasn't for a purpose'; 'One man is entertaining another to coffee'.

The number of eavesdroppers offering inferential statements is charted in the following table.

	INFERENCES		
Eavesdropper	Participants	Text	Situation
1	+	+	+
2	+	+	+
3	+	+	+
4	+	+	+
5	+	+	+
6	+	+	+
7	+	+	+
8	+	+	+
9	+	+	+
10	+	+	+
11	+	+	+
12	+	+	+
13	+	+	+
14	+	+	+
15	+	–	–
16	+	+	+
Total	16	15	15

In comparison to the number of eavesdroppers offering observations, it is remarkable that every judge but one made some kind of inference in all three types that have been identified. The exception in this case was an individual who in fact made only two statements about the exchange; one observation and one inference respectively. For the remainder, their willingness to make inferences as opposed to observations is perhaps indicative of their lay status. In other words, judges of this kind appear to be less interested in the surface features and/or organization of the dialogue, or at least less prepared to make statements about them in this instance, whilst being readily prepared to make inferences. A total of 188 inferential statements were provided by eavesdroppers which is more than three times the number of observations.

Interestingly, this pattern was reversed in the two other pilot studies that were undertaken in which eavesdroppers were given much shorter fragments of talk to listen to. This reversal of pattern presumably occurred as a result of constraining the amount of talk that was played making it more difficult for eavesdroppers to construct a context for what was going on. In the absence of being able to guess at or deduce such a context, eavesdroppers´ comments indicate that they focussed much more on what was actually said.

SUMMARY AND CONCLUDING REMARKS

Figure 2, is an attempt to summarize the kinds of input and judgmental factors that have been identified in the context of the reported research. It is important to note, however, that the diagram has no psychological reality and is not intended to describe the actual decision processes which eavesdroppers may have invoked in offering the comments they did.

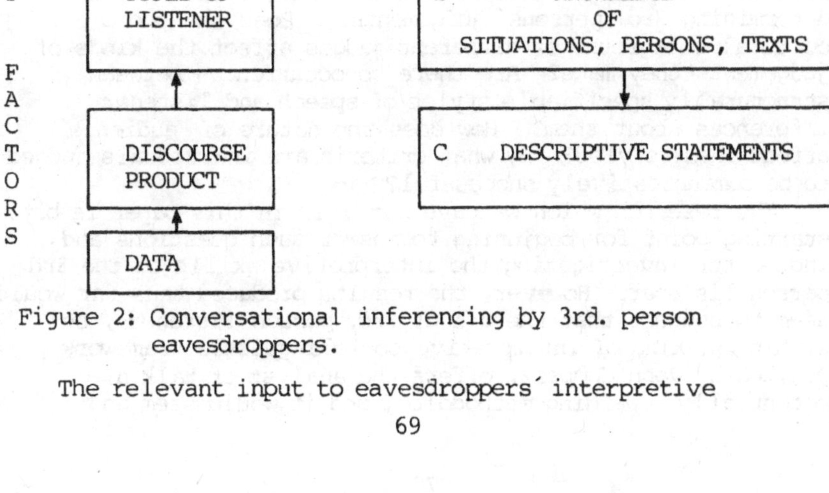

Figure 2: Conversational inferencing by 3rd. person eavesdroppers.

The relevant input to eavesdroppers´ interpretive

processes are presented in terms of the flow chart. Rectangle A represents all possible interpretive processes that 3rd. persons might employ. Whether real or imagined, these possibilities can be thought of as providing a 'frame of reference' within which eavesdroppers can create a context for establishing who the participants in some exchange are and what they are perceived to be doing from their own point of view. The nature of the kinds of connections that eavesdroppers can make within this frame are clearly going to be constrained by the kinds of knowledge they have available and three major types are identified in Rectangle B, that is, knowledge of situations, persons and texts. We can infer this knowledge exists by working back from the kinds of descriptive statements described in this paper, Rectangle C.

Given the two basic categories of statement that we have identified, namely 'observations' and 'inferences', we can begin to explore something of the kinds of connections that such statements are based upon. Whilst 'observations' can be checked against a transcribed record of what was actually said, 'inferences' are not verifiable in the same way. However, by determining possible links between observation and inference, one can potentially develop a series of hypotheses about the nature of such links which could be formally tested in some controlled experimental environment. Thus, for example, one could begin to investigate in some more systematic way the fact that information is sometimes differentially processed by different eavesdroppers (see, for example, McGregor, 1985).

Whilst Gumperz (1982a, 1982b) has focussed on the importance of contextualization cues for recovering speaker 'intent', it is clear that this work needs to be extended in ways we hope to have illustrated. There are a number of possible avenues for future research and questions of the following kind are indicative of where such research might lead. What role might interactional phenomena such as politeness strategies (Brown and Levinson, 1978) play in determining 3rd. persons' judgements? Does the socio-cultural background of different judges affect the kinds of judgements they make? Are there co-occurrences between structurally specifiable styles of speech and listener inferences about them? How does the nature of 'audience' affect these styles? By what criteria are individuals judged to be communicatively successful?

The research which we have outlined in this paper is but a starting point for beginning to answer such questions and indeed for investigating the interpretive skills of the 3rd. person listener. However, the results produced thus far would seem to suggest that the use of 3rd. person listeners, set within the kind of interpretive sociolinguistic framework posited by John Gumperz, offers the analyst of talk a potentially rewarding methodology and it would seem an extremely rich data source for exploring the nature and complexities of everyday verbal interaction. We suggest, in conclusion, that listeners' creativity outside the participation framework deserves a great deal more of our attention whatever our disciplinary motivation.

NOTES

1. Lesley Milroy's helpful comments and advice on the research which I have undertaken is gratefully acknowledged. Needless to say, I am singularly responsible for any inadequacies that remain.

2. We must bear in mind of course that 'Since conversation is a multifaceted and complex human activity, it is plain that there will be many approaches to an understanding of it.' (Labov and Fanshel (1977, p.349). Indeed, as Labov and Fanshel go on to warn, 'No _one_ technique could say very much of what could be said about conversation' (my underlining).

REFERENCES

Abercrombie, D. (1967) _Elements of General Phonetics_, Edinburgh University Press, Edinburgh.

Agar, M. (1980) 'Stories, Background Knowledge and Themes: Problems in the Life History Narrative, _American Ethnologist_, 7, 223-39.

Bell, A. (1984) 'Language Style as Audience Design', _Language in Society_, 13, 145-204.

Brown, G. and Yule, G. (1983) _Discourse Analysis_, Cambridge University Press, Cambridge.

Brown, P. and Levinson, S. (1978) 'Universals in Language Usage: Politeness Phenomena' in E.N. Goody (ed.) _Questions and Politeness_, Cambridge University Press, Cambridge, pp.56-289.

Coulthard, M. and Montgomery, M. (1981) (eds.) _Studies in Discourse Analysis_, Longman, London.

de Beaugrande, R. (1980) _Text, Discourse and Process_, Longman, London.

Dore, J. and McDermott, R.P. (1982) 'Linguistic Indeterminacy and Social Context in Utterance Interpretation', _Language_, 58, 347-398.

Edmonson, W. (1981) _Spoken Discourse_, Longman, London.

Goffman, E. (1976) 'Replies and responses', _Language in Society_, 5, 257-313.

Goody, N. (1978) (ed.) _Questions and Politeness_, Cambridge University Press, Cambridge.

Grimshaw, A.D. (1982) 'Comprehensive Discourse Analysis: An Instance of Professional Peer Interaction', _Language in Society_, 11, 15-47.

Gumperz, J.J. (1982a) Discourse Strategies, Cambridge University Press, Cambridge.
Gumperz, J.J. (1982b) (ed.) Language and Social Identity, Cambridge University Press, Cambridge.
Gumperz, J.J. and Tannen, D. (1979) 'Individual and Social Differences in Language Use' in J.Fillmore, D.Kempler, and S.Y. Wang (eds.) Individual Differences in Language Ability and Language Behavior, Academic Press, New York, pp. 305-325.
Hoey, M. (1983) On the Surface of Discourse, George Allen & Unwin, London.
Hoenigswald, H.M. (1966) 'A Proposal for the Study of Folk-Linguistics' in W. Bright (ed.) Sociolinguistics, Mouton, The Hague, pp.16-26.
Hymes, D. (1972) 'Models of the Interaction of Language and Social Life' in J.J. Gumperz and D. Hymes (eds.) Directions in Sociolinguistics: The Ethnography of Communication, Holt, Rinehart & Winston, New York, pp.35-71.
Kreckel, M. (1981) Communicative Acts and Shared Knowledge in Natural Discourse, Academic Press, London.
Labov, W. and Fanshel, D. (1977) Therapeutic Discourse, Academic Press, New York.
Laver, J. (1972) 'Voice Quality and Indexical Information' in J. Laver and S. Hutchinson (eds.), Communication in Face to Face Interaction, Penguin, Harmondsworth, pp.189-203.
Leech, G.N. (1983) Principles of Pragmatics, Longman, London.
Levinson, S.C. (1979) 'Activity Types and Language', Linguistics, 17, 365-399.
Levinson, S.C. (1983) Pragmatics, Cambridge University Press, Cambridge.
Lyons, J. (1977) Semantics, Vol.1, Cambridge University Press, Cambridge.
McGregor, G. (1983) 'Listeners' Comments on Conversation', Language and Communication, 3, 271-304.
McGregor, G. (1984) 'Conversation and Communication', Language and Communication, 4, 71-83.
McGregor, G. (1985) 'Utterance Interpretation and the Role of the Analyst', Language and Speech, 28, 1-28.
Stubbs, M. (1983) Discourse Analysis, Blackwell, Oxford.
Wardhaugh, R. (1985) How Conversation Works. Blackwell, Oxford.
Widdowson, H. (1979) 'Rules and Procedures in Discourse Analysis' in T. Myers (ed.) The Development of Conversation and Discourse, Edinburgh University Press, Edinburgh, pp.61-71.

FIVE

HEARING YOU IN MY OWN VOICE: WOMAN AS LISTENER AND READER

Linda Anderson

To be seen and not heard. The nineteenth century injunction to women as well as children. '**Softly and kindly should the eyes be raised to those of the speaker, and only withdrawn when the speech, whatever it may be, is concluded**' (Ellis, 1981, p. 98). (Has this changed today? After the reading by a famous woman writer there is a space for questions. There are four questions by men which are neither urgent nor engaged before the first woman's voice from the floor is heard.)

> Every woman has known the torment of getting up to speak. Her heart racing, at times entirely lost for words, ground and language slipping away - that's how daring a feat, how great a transgression it is for a woman to speak - even just open her mouth in public (Cixous, 1980, p. 251).

I can remember starting to teach, hardly believing my own voice breaking the silence, rushing too quickly into questions, wanting a response, wanting other voices to be in dialogue with mine. Learning slowly that my speech as teacher has authority (male authority?) that is difficult to break, however hesitant I am.

> Look at a classroom: look at the many kinds of women's faces, postures, expressions. Listen to the women's voices. Listen to the silences, the unasked questions, the blanks. Listen to the small, soft voices, often courageously trying to speak up, voices of women taught early that tones of confidence, challenge, anger, or assertiveness, are strident and unfeminine. Listen to the voices of the women and the voices of the men; observe the space men allow themselves, physically and verbally, the male assumption that people will listen, even when the majority of the group is female (Rich, 1980, p. 243).

Women undergo a lifelong training - in repression/listening.

Listening becomes her special aptitude, her gift, 'a good listener'.

> Men expect to be listened to. It is in the very fabric of their experience that they can look to a woman to listen to them. Their mothers listened when they were boys; girlfriends listened when they were adolescents and women listen when they are men. Men look to women to validate themselves ... Very often men don't even want women to respond or give advice about something they are talking about - they just want to be listened to in the way their fathers were listened to. To be a man is to command attention and authority. Precisely because men have the continuity of being listened to, they believe that that is the way it should be (Eichenbaum and Orbach, 1984, p. 74).

Mother listens. '**The house seemed full of children sleeping and Mrs Ramsay listening**' (Woolf, 1977, p. 49). The silent presence, the presence in the silence, holding, containing, making safe.

To speak and not be heard. Cassandra-like. Who listens to women? If male/female interactions are asymmetrical (non-reciprocal?), if women are commonly given and take the role of listener in public gatherings (and private conversations) who is there (who is there?) to receive their speech?

> Women's speechlessness has its roots not only in the fact that they were so long subjected to silence, that what they *did* manage to say was not and still is not listened to (Breitling, 1985, p. 163).

'The deaf male ear' (Cixous, 1980, p. 251) which refuses hearing and the continual expectation of that deafness (experience or training? almost certainly both) inhibiting the possibility of speech, of self-expression. '**The silencing of her own voice, a silencing enforced by the wish not to hurt others but also by the fear that, in speaking, her own voice will not be heard**' (Gilligan, 1982, p. 51).

Women's voices heard as an assault, shrill, strident, monstrous. Does Mary Shelley's monster speak from the position of woman, begging an audience - '**Listen to me, Frankenstein**' - hiding his identity by covering Frankenstein's eyes, effacing himself.

> Averse to personal publicity, we veiled our own names under those of Currer, Ellis, and Acton Bell ... without at the time suspecting that our mode of writing and thinking was not what is called 'feminine' - we had a

> vaque impression that authoresses are liable to be looked on with prejudice (Charlotte Bronte, 1850).

(But the monster speaks, is, in fact, very eloquent.)

Women's writing as 'monstrous speech' to an audience that she is not sure will listen, to an absent/rejecting lover. **'Is it possible he cannot hear me when he lies so close, so lightly asleep?'** For the monster to be heard she must first obliterate herself. (**'My dear, my darling, do you hear me where you sleep?'** [Smart, 1966, pp. 126, 128].) In the house the children are sleeping and Mrs Ramsay is listening.

<u>Silent</u> <u>Listening/Listening</u> <u>Silence</u>. Recent criticism has undertaken the exploration of silence not as negation but as a field of multiple meaning, as spaciousness, potential. An Aesthetics of Silence (unheard of?) **'It has a presence / it has a history a form / Do not confuse it / with any kind of absence'** (Rich, 1978, p. 17).

> A genuine emptiness, a pure silence are not feasible - either conceptually or in fact. If only because the artwork exists in a world furnished with many other things, the artist who creates a silence or emptiness must produce something dialectical; a full void, an enriching emptiness, a resonating or eloquent silence (in many instances, of complaint or indictment) and an element in a dialogue (Sontag, 1982, p. 187).

Can we begin to think about speech and silence as in dialogue with each other (speaker and listener?), each deriving meaning from its dialectical relationship with the other? Silence can be the source of other hidden or potential meanings shadowing speech, unconscious meanings. (What do we mean by a meaningful silence?) How does this relate to the experience of silence in the psychoanalytical setting for both patient and analyst, each's experience of the other (the Other) as silent?

> Silence, as is more and more recognized, may have many meanings, each of them requiring different technical handling. Silence may be an arid and frightening emptiness, inimical to life and growth ... it may be a friendly exciting expanse, inviting the patient to undertake adventurous journeys into the uncharted lands of his fantasy life. (Balint, 1986, p. 276)

The patient's silence.

> Silence can be valid or invalid and it can be giving in important ways or it can be depriving (Langs, 1978, 71).

The analyst's silence.

Psychoanalysis as a mode of communication without redundancy, where everything is meaningful, where more must always be heard than is said. '**The art of listening is almost as important as that of saying the right thing**' (Lacan, 1979, p. 123). Almost?

> Listening to another, taking in, receiving, or accepting from another, are often seen as passive. However, they all generate a response, for one never merely passively receives, one also reacts. The reaction can take many forms. It is true men feel more pressured to cut short their receptiveness and to rush to put forward their own reactions. Often they clearly betray the fact that they have not received or heard much of what the other was communicating. Women, on the other hand, have often heard much more than was overtly stated and have gone through a more complex processing of information. Part of this processing, especially the part men are not permitted to observe, includes the knowledge that one had better not react directly and honestly to what has been said or done. This avoidance of direct expression has often been interpreted as evidence of inherent passivity (Miller, 1978, p. 58).

Do we break up (break into) the hierarchical structure of discourse (active speaker, passive recipient) by acknowledging a different, active space for the listener or reader? Imagine an analogy between the woman who has 'heard much more than was overtly stated' and the psychoanalyst. (But the woman is passive, patient). Imagine an analogy between the psychoanalyst and the reader.

> The reader is the space on which all the quotations that make up a writing are inscribed ... A text's unity lies not in its origin but in its destination (Barthes, 1977, p. 48).

If the idea of 'authoring' meaning is invalid the reader can only receive (but not interpret) the text or 'writing', hold it together in one place. (But is there still a danger that Barthes's reader has merely reversed the hierarchical model, pre-empted the author and kept the power? The problem is that the reader gains life only through the death of the author. And does it matter if the reader and/or author is a woman?)

For Helene Cixous, imagining the woman also means imagining a 'different' space within discourse, an almost unimaginable freeing of thought from a fixation on binary oppositions (male/female, speaker/listener, active/passive), where one term gains meaning only through the ´death´ of the other.

> To admit that writing is precisely working (in) the in-between, inspecting the process of the same and of the other without which nothing can live, undoing the work of death - to admit this is first to want the two, as well as both, the ensemble of one and the other, not fixed in sequence of struggle and expulsion or some other form of death but infinitely dynamized by an incessant process of exchange from one subject to another (Cixous, 1980, p. 254).

So finding the ´feminine´ within discourse (like finding the listener) also means exploring the space between and beyond the speaking subject, outside the oppositions which reduce woman (and listener?) to other.

Do ´woman´ and ´listener´ occupy the same position within a paradigm which always in the end turns out to be the same paradigm and do we liberate either (or both) by deconstructing the dominant system of thought? (But the listener is not simply the woman.) Can we talk about women and listening by talking about the organization of discourse? Can we talk about women and listening without talking about the organisationof discourse? How can I talk about both without meaning the same?

A similar emphasis on the ´process of exchange from one subject to another´ emerges if we think about the critical relationship to the text as being like a dialogue between people. (´Woman´ not as a function within discourse but rather discourse like a person.)

> Poetry is first of all a dialogue between human beings, and the poem is the person reaching out in relationship (Farwell, 1977, p. 203).

If the text is thought of as a person, listening to a text also introduces the idea of an emotional bond (a maternal bond?) which weakens the boundaries between subject and object. (What does it mean to be ´objective´?) The text could be part of a complex interplay between self and other and be responded to through identity and difference. (Or is it only women who retain the possibility of these different, oscillating forms of relationships, whose boundaries are fluid rather than fixed?)

> The psychology of women determines women´s relationships with their texts as well as the relationships among female authors and characters ... At times both writer

> and reader may relate to the text as though it were a person with whom one might be merged empathetically or from whom one might be separated and individuated (Gardiner, 1985, p. 138).

Does the idea of listening to a text (because it seems so inseparable from the person and specific emotional content) bring with it the idea of a 'subjective collaboration' (Rich, 1980, p. 108), a structure of mutuality, which has a special relevance to women?

Do I also listen in order to hear myself?

WOMEN'S WRITING AND LISTENING

Villette

The texts first of all take us back to the beginning: listening as a sign of oppression/repression. Charlotte Bronte's heroine Lucy Snowe accepts that she is peripheral to society (as a single woman without money) and positions herself at the edges, in the shadows ('a mere looker-on at life' [p. 206]), a place from which she can observe and listen but cannot easily speak and be heard. In rooms she sits away from the fire at the centre, out in the cold (her name from the beginning suggests her plight); from within the solitude of her own room she hears what is happening in the outside world, leans towards it, but cannot join in, cannot connect inside and outside ('thinking meantime my own thoughts, living my own life, in my own still, shadow-world' [p. 104]). Later, propelled by her own longing into the streets of Villette (who does she have to plead with to 'let me go - oh, let me go!'?) she still takes her place ('having neither wish nor power' [p. 411]) at the edge, alone, able to hear (and still be isolated in her internal world) and not see.

For her listening is self-effacement; it is also service and self-sacrifice. To Dr John she offers 'an ear and mind in perpetual readiness' [p. 169], however painful the communication he wants to make might be. When her role as confidante to Paul Emmanuel threatens to become a longed-for intimacy (give her pleasure, not pain) she runs away. ('He had something to tell; he was going to tell me something; my ear strained its nerve to hear it, and I had made the confidence impossible' [p. 350]). Her listening is a strategy of non-presence, comfortable to her only when it (and she) are taken for granted.

What choice does Lucy have but to keep quiet? Remember how she can speak and with effect both as a teacher (she quickly gains the respect of her pupils) and, because she can then hide behind the mask of a fictional character, as an actress. Fearful as it is for her to hear her own voice (this rather than the presence of other people) once she does start to speak within the play she breaks through all her physical repression, talks with passion, can actively woo (as man now, not woman), express her erotic energy. (Speech begins first of all in the body.) Constructed as male within the play, she displays the active 'male' abilities of expression which she cannot combine with her 'female' role as passive listener in the real world. Think too about the ways in which Madame Beck provides a grotesque parallel to Lucy (she is sneakingly admired but also rejected by Lucy), maintaining her 'male' authority through the female strategies of secrecy and indirection, 'her ear glued to the keyhole' [p. 111]. Lucy is even more attentive than Madame Beck, though in more orthodox ways, and like her gains knowledge through listening. Charlotte Bronte understands the ambiguity of silence and listening: Lucy's listening is not a mere absence of power but also <u>conceals</u> power (her own power to speak and the power she obtains through understanding) which it is too disturbing and risky for her to act on. In this way Lucy is positioned ambiguously in the novel, knowing more (as listener) than she tells (as speaker).

Lucy exists within a painful world of muffled desire and speech but this is not all. Lucy also tells <u>me</u> her story. I, the reader, listen. In this space between character and (female?) reader she identifies herself differently; there is room here for her vulnerability and for the acknowledgment of fear and pain. ('"Oh, hush! hush!" I said in my disturbed mind, dropping my work, and making a vain effort to stop my ears against that subtle, searching cry.'[p. 31]) The noise of the storm which threatens to overwhelm Lucy, metaphorically associated with her private grief and loss which remain substantially untold, returns at moments throughout the novel. It creates a powerful dynamic. As Lucy seeks to stifle the noise and her own emotions, so the reader listens all the more attentively, aware also of the undisclosed suffering and the struggle to contain pain. The silence creates an intense space for empathy. Lucy at times attempts to protect the reader and herself by her silence, providing hints of gloom but allowing space for happier conjectures; the result is inevitably a stronger sense of what is contained (in psychic and emotional terms) within the silence. I hear what I am not told. But Lucy's (silent) dialogue with the reader is not simply a plea for sympathy; in her struggle for autonomy and independence Lucy has to be able to contain the pain of her own life and not simply be destroyed by it. Moments of silence, indirection and even concealment from me, the reader (she hides the identity of Dr. John for instance) are complicated moments when I also recognize the strength of Lucy's pursuit of integrity, and her need to survive. Is this such a hard text because she shares with me so much of what she cannot communicate to others, the 'covert solidarity' (Showalter,

1978, p. 15) we create through the mutuality of our listening and the complexity and richness of that as both relationship and source of knowledge, but that I also experience myself as separate - motherless (like Lucy) and unable to mother? Lucy's strength also comes from a containment, an autonomy, however precarious, that excludes me.[1]

Bliss

Katherine Mansfield's story begins to explore the secret possibilities of women's silence and listening. It describes an awakening and a yearning towards an intensification of meaning. There is a passage in a letter she wrote to Murray, full of this longing:

> You know, darling, I have felt very often lately as though the silence has some meaning beyond these signs, these intimations. Isn't it possible that if one yielded there is a whole world into which one is received? It is so near and yet I am conscious that I hold back from giving myself up to it. What is this something mysterious that waits - that beckons? (Mansfield, 1977, p. 187).

To take the risk of exploring the secret (interior) world of one's own desires; is it possible that she will be received, heard, understood? For Bertha Young everything shimmers with potentiality; as repression weakens, as she discovers within herself 'that bright glowing place' so the external world is no longer resistant but 'melts', yields, becomes almost 'unbearably' meaningful.

> She hardly dared to look into the cold mirror - but she did look, and it gave her back a woman, radiant, with smiling, trembling lips, with big, dark eyes and an air of listening, waiting for something ... divine to happen ... that she knew must happen ... infallibly (p. 112).

Her listening is attention to a (strange) newly discovered self; it is also experienced as a turning towards other women. Her friend, Miss Fulton, provides another mirror, reflecting back, in her silence, a shared inwardness.

> Her heavy eyelids lay upon her eyes and the strange half-smile came and went upon her lips as though she lived by listening rather than seeing. But Bertha knew, suddenly, as if the longest, most intimate look had passed between them - as if they had said to each other: 'You too?' - that Pearl Fulton, stirring the beautiful red soup in the grey plate, was feeling just what she was feeling (118).

Together they look at the pear-tree 'quivering' in the moonlight, its perfect flowering and their shared (silently heard) understanding creating wholeness, the complete fusion of inner and outer meaning.

> How long did they stand there? Both, as it were, caught in that circle of unearthly light, understanding each other perfectly, creatures of another world, and wondering what they were to do with this one, with all this blissful treasure that burned in their bosoms and dropped, in silver flowers, from their hair and hands? (pp. 120-1).

But this is 'another world', a possibility which is brutally broken in on at the end of the story. What Bertha hears from her (female) position at the edge (this silent listening now in this [patriarchal] world taking on another meaning - powerlessness) is her betrayal by her husband and her friend, her exclusion, and the (necessary?) pain of unfulfilled longing. How can her listening (as potentiality) be brought together with what she actually hears (her negation)? This is the risk. (As a reader I have been a little more cautious; the author was always slightly [cynically?] undercutting her character's excitement - would not identify with her in that way.) '**I hold back from giving myself up to it.**' I (my reading positioned by the author's uncertainty) keep my distance, know/fear that surrender (emotional identification with the character/text) could lead to endless longing. (I, the reader, must give the story closure.)

<u>Memoirs of a Survivor</u>

> Instead of remembering here a scene and there a sound I shall fit a plug into the wall; and listen to the past ... I feel that strong emotion must leave its trace; and it is only a question of discovering how we can get ourselves again attached to it, so that we shall be able to live our lives through from the start (Woolf, 1981, p. 78).

The form of Doris Lessing's novel arises out of this desire that Virginia Woolf describes to explore the secret spaces of the self, to hear memory, to turn listening inwards. But the claims of the outer world (realism) are no longer in conflict (as they were for Charlotte Bronte and Katharine Mansfield). The structures of society in this (fantasy) novel are not solid but are exposed as frail and temporary. The turning inwards does not mean an exposure to a destructive contradiction between inner and outer but can embrace the outer too. The 'secret complicity' of reader, character and author is brought out into the open and made a condition of narrative; 'I' can merge with 'we', introspection is also a form of storytelling.

> We all remember that time. It was no different for me than for others. Yet we all do tell each other over and over again the particularities of the events we shared, and the repetition, the listening, as if we are saying: 'it was like that for you, too? Then that confirms it, yes, it was so, it must have been, I wasn't imagining things' (p. 7).

The discovery is that the inner story <u>is</u> the outer story, 'my own personal experience was common'.

For the narrator, 'realisation' or knowledge means beginning to listen, or learning to hear a possibility which has always been there.

> Looking back I can say definitely that the growth of that other life or form of being behind that wall had been at the back of my mind for a long time before I <u>realised</u> what it was I had been listening to, listening for (p. 10).

Listening <u>for</u> as opposed to listening <u>to</u> reality also means listening to the gaps, absences and silences, to what is unsaid. Again this listening means the exploration of potentiality, the exciting fantasy journey that can happen in silence, 'holding an egg to one's ear that is due to hatch' (p. 14). It also contrasts with the lack of listening which is experienced behind the wall (within the past). The mother talks endlessly because she must somehow make up for the lack of being heard: 'No one else was there for her, because she felt she was talking to herself: they could not hear, or would not' (p. 62). This voice (which is heard and absorbed by the child) truly becomes an internal voice for the adult: 'Often in my ordinary life I would hear the sound of a voice, a bitter and low complaint just the other side of sense' (p. 63). The cycle of unmet need is passed on from mother to daughter, the mother who has not been heard also does not hear her daughter.

> I heard the sobbing of a child, a child alone disliked, repudiated; and at the same time, beside it, I could hear the complaint of the mother, the woman's plaint, and the two sounds went on side by side, theme and descant (p. 125).

The narrator eventually finds the place which will allow her 'through' to quieten the uncomforted child, which is not Emily, the daughter, but her mother, as a child. The healing of the pattern must begin in the past; in order for the mother to comfort she must herself first be comforted.

This exploration of the psyche discovers the patterns which have already been lived in society in the past, the internalisation of relationships or deprivation. The narrator's listening unravels unacknowledged pain (unacknowledged by others first of all, then repressed and unacknowledged by the self). Self and other is not and never can be separate; relationships are embodied within the self, are the emotional experience of the self.

But it is also the experience of these shifting, fluid boundaries between inner and outer which allows the narrator's different emotional response which is also based upon a different mode of hearing. Going through the wall she is listening to herself as if she were other (as if this place, which has always been there, has also been discovered by her); she also 'mothers', emotionally identifies with, the child she finds there. The narrative mode is in many ways similar. I read the novel almost as if it were my own story, am both inside the story (incorporated into the narrative voice and expected to know the story as already having happened) and outside it as the receiver of the story. Does imagining this changed experience of listening and of the relationship between inner and outer, self and other, lead to the possibility of transformation? Is the she, mysteriously glimpsed at the end, also the (imaginary) whole, transfigured self?

The Storyhearer

The title is itself rich with meaning: teller is also hearer, listener is also speaker; interdependent, reciprocal.

Grace Paley situates her narrative voice among other voices, telling a story which can have no real beginning (what is the beginning of communication?). The story of her day is the story of many exchanges with people, where she has taken the role of both listener and talker. Going to the shops also means going out into the world and the seemingly trivial moments of conversation are full of wider emotional and political meaning - sexism, racism, history, the relationship of art and politics are some of the themes touched on - but ideas are first of all part of a dialogue. Conversations are also wry moments of acknowledging mutuality and its limits, a continuing experiencing of the self in relation to others. (The internal narrative cannot be separated from the external speaking voice, is always a voice in relationship) ('I said to myself, What a day! I think I'll run down to the store and pick up some comestibles.' [p. 135].) Thinking language (using the word comestibles) is also responding to something external ('But I do like this language - wheat and chaff - with its widening pool of foreign genes' [p. 135]), even though the word itself will only be thought and not uttered. Throughout the story language has to be both rejoiced in and fought with (again as if it were a person) in order for there to be a creative relationship with it. It must be made responsive to the emotional needs of the self.

The narrator tells her story to Jack, who both listens (with partial understanding) and interjects his own story too. Jack's mode of listening and talking are different. He likes beginnings (though he like middles too), and is contentious (prefers opposition to mutuality?). He is vulnerable but that is acknowledged by him only in his sleep when he has a bad dream ('That's O.K., kid, I said, You're not the only one. Everybody's mortal'). The narrator's desire for a child at the end of the story (though this, because of her age is impossible) is also a utopian image of language and creativity as a nurturing relationship between the child and the women who look after him. ('Oh, Jack, that Isaac, Sarah's boy - before he was old enough to be taken out by his father to get his throat cut, he must have just lain around smiling and making up diphthongs and listening, and the women sang songs to him and wrapped him up in such pretty rugs'). But this also exists in a world of violence (the father's violence) and dispute (Isaac and his brother, Jack and the narrator). The end of the story enacts the whole dilemma of women's listening: whilst she agrees with him (who has disagreed with her) she is still waiting for his acknowledgment, response, hearing at the end of the story. ('**Now all you have to do is to be with me**' [p. 144].) (Would this make the dream possible?)

> The notion that perfect mutual understanding - telepathy - is not the normal or the ideal outcome of speaking, frightens and confuses many people ... Until we do acknowledge that communication is to some extent an everyday triumph, until we get rid of our fantasies of what it never can be, we ... will be content to avoid the issue or to take it for granted (Cameron, 1985, pp. 142-3).

But we can also (must) imagine change, creating fictions which embody potentiality as well as repression, through which (given a hearing) we can be heard differently.

> To imagine an ideal speech situation is to envisage a way of life ... within an ideal speech situation, no compulsion is present other than the force of discourse itself; domination is absent; and reciprocity pertains between and among participants (Elshtain, 1982, p. 144).

Today I am thinking about this writing as if it were a letter. I am sitting at my desk, It is January, the afternoon, and in the winter sun the trees have distinct shadows. I listen to the silence, to the many voices that I have heard, that meet within me; I listen for my own voice, to the words that I want to say, that I need you to hear. I enter the silence. I write.

'Now all you have to do is be with me.'

NOTE

1. I am indebted to (though not totally in agreement with) the discussion of Villette by Brenda R. Silver (1983).

REFERENCES

TEXTS

Bronte, Charlotte, Villette, First published 1853; this edition Everyman, London, 1909.

Lessing, Doris (1974) Memoirs of a Survivor, The Octagon Press, London.

Mansfield, Katherine (1969) Selected Short Stories, Oxford University Press, Oxford.

Paley, Grace (1985) Later the Same Day, Virago, London.

SECONDARY

Balint, Michael (1986) 'The Unobtrusive Analyst' in The British School of Psychoanalysis: The Independent Tradition, ed. Gregorio Kohon, Free Association Books, London.

Barthes, Roland (1977) 'The Death of the Author' in Image - Music - Text, Fontana, London.

Breitling, Gisela (1985) 'Speech, Silence and the Discourse of Art' in Feminist Aesthetics, ed. Gisela Ecker, Women's Press, London.

Bronte, Charlotte (1850) in The Brontes: Life and Letters, vol. i, ed. C.Shorter, London, 1908.

Cameron, Deborah (1985) Feminism and Linguistic Theory , Macmillan, London.

Cixous, Hélène (1980) 'The Laugh of the Medusa' in New French Feminism, ed. Elaine Marks and Isabelle de Courtivron Harvester, Sussex.

Eichenbaum, Luise and Orbach, Susie (1984) What Do Women Want Faber, London.

Ellis, Sarah (1981) The Habits of Good Society in Victorian Women, ed. Erna Olafson Hellerstein, Leslie Parker Hume and Karen Offen, Stanford University Press, California.

Elshtain, Jean Bethke (1982) 'Feminist Discourse and Its Discontents: Language, Power and Meaning' in _Feminist Theory: A Critique of Ideology_, ed. Nannerl O. Keohane, Michelle Z. Rosaldo and Barbara C. Gelpi, Harvester, Sussex.

Farwell, Marilyn (1977) 'Adrienne Rich and an Organic Feminist Criticism', _College English_, 39, p. 203.

Gardiner, Judith Kegan (1985) 'Mind mother: Psychoanalysis and Feminism' in _Making a Difference_ , ed. Gayle Greene and Coppelia Kahn, Methuen, London.

Gilligan, Carol (1982) _In a Different Voice_, Harvard University Press, Cambridge, Mass.

Lacan, Jacques (1979) _The Four Fundamental Concepts of Psychoanalysis_ Penguin, Harmondsworth.

Langs, Robert (1978) _The Listening Process_, Jason Aronson, New York.

Mansfield, Katherine (1977) _Letters and Journals_, ed. C.K. Stead, Penguin, Harmondsworth.

Miller, Jean Baker (1978) _Toward a New Psychology of Women_ Penguin, Harmondsworth.

Rich, Adrienne (1978) 'Cartographies of Silence' in _The Dream of a Common Language_, Norton, New York.

Rich, Adrienne (1980) _On Lies, Secrets and Silence_, Virago, London.

Showalter, Elaine (1978) _A Literature of Their Own_, Virago, London.

Silver, Brenda R. (1983) 'The Reflecting Reader in _Villette_', in _The Voyage In: Fictions of Female Development_, ed. Elizabeth Langland, University Press of New England, Hanover and London.

Smart, Elizabeth (1966) _By Grand Central Station I Sat Down and Wept_, Granada, London and New York.

Sontag, Susan (1982) 'The Aesthetics of Silence' in _A Susan Sontag Reader_, Penguin, Harmondsworth.

Woolf, Virginia (1977) _To the Lighthouse_, Granada, London.

Woolf, Virginia (1981) 'A Sketch of the Past' in _Moments of Being_, Granada, London.

SIX

ANALYSING THE READER: A CRITICAL SURVEY OF RECENT PSYCHO-ANALYTICAL THEORIES OF READING

Norbert H. Platz

I

It is stating the obvious if I say that the mainstream of psychoanalytical criticism has been concerned with the decoding of a symbolic matrix in a literary work. What formerly quite often came to the fore, was a parade of phalluses, vaginas, anuses, oedipuses, when Freud was followed, or myths, when Jung was the chosen guide. In my present contribution I should like to draw your attention to psychoanalytical theories dealing with the reader and his response to literary texts. As can be seen from the bibliography, a great deal has been written in the US since 1957 about both the reading process and the reader from a psychoanalytical point of view. This was the year when Simon O. Lesser published his pioneering book *Fiction and the Unconscious*. Lesser's study exercised a marked influence on Norman N. Holland and David Bleich who have emerged as the major representatives of a theory of reading inspired by psychoanalysis. Those who are familiar with Bleich's work will perhaps wonder why I bracket him with Holland. Briefly, one reason is that his research practices bear the mark of a number of psychoanalytical assumptions about human nature. It has to be admitted, however, that his predominant concern with 'subjectivity' tends towards a philosophical rather than a psychoanalytical theory of the human mind. However, it is very interesting to see how both Holland and Bleich, each in his own way, arrive at concepts of the reader which are similar and comparable, at least if one views them from outside the discipline.

May I just add that quite a few of the other authors mentioned in the bibliography either retail or criticise Holland's and Bleich's ideas. So it is not only for reasons of space that I should like to give these two critical soloists cardinal attention, leaving out their accompanists. To be more specific, what I should like to do in this paper, is to offer a brief survey of Holland's and Bleich's theories of reading, postponing a critical evaluation till the final part of my paper. As Simon O. Lesser, to my knowledge, was the first to establish a link between the unconscious and the reader, a very few words about him are in place initially.

II

Simon O. Lesser

As one can imagine, New Criticism was still going very strong when Lesser ventured his foray into the unconscious in 1957. His book reflects that he was aware of the intense disapproval he was likely to earn after publication (cf. 297). For him, the reader of fiction is not the urbane synthesizer of the structural arrangements in the texts whom the New Critics identified themselves with. On the contrary, Lesser's reader is a pleasure-hunting creature, attempting to gratify repressed or displaced urges. Subscribing to Freud's theory that a perfectly satisfied person would not day-dream, he maintains conversely: 'We read because we are beset by anxieties, guilt feelings, and ungratified needs' (39). Reading in his view serves a two-fold purpose. On the one hand, it helps us to discover what our hidden needs and desires are, and, on the other, it assuages our pain or even grants us 'fulfillment of desires' (46) by means of 'substitute gratification' (47). Basically, the reader enjoys the privilege of playing with the fantasy material which the text offers to him in a disguised form.

Apart from the reader seeking gratification, a second concept has had a lasting impact on the psychoanalytical theory of reading. It is the kind of response which he calls 'analogizing'. By this term he designates our 'creation of stories parallel to the ones we read in which we play a part' (200). This concept of the reader creating for himself 'analogous' stories in which he imagines himself playing an active part has proved to be a fertile idea on which both Holland and Bleich have elaborated.

III

Norman N. Holland

Although my bibliography is not exhaustive, one can see from it that Holland is quite a prolific writer. For a long time he worked at The Center for the Psychological Study of the Arts at the State University of New York at Buffalo, and is the spearhead of what in America now is called 'Buffalo Criticism' (Leitch 146). His work as a whole represents a fairly consistent development of the insights gained in his first major publication _The Dynamics of Literary Response_ (1968). Because of the seminal character of this book, I should like to mention some of its key theses.

In its whole outlook Dynamics is based on a redefinition of Freud's concept of defence (Abwehr). With Freud, the term 'Abwehr' means both 'abwehren' and 'sich verteidigen'. 'Abwehr'/'Defence' aims at preserving the integrity and continuity of the ego by rejecting fantasies connected with forbidden wishes. Holland's own emphasis is that defence mechanisms (such as repression, symbolization, sublimation, rationalization) are not 'blocks to normal pleasure'; they are not 'in and of themselves pathological, undesirable, and to be removed in therapy' (5 Readers 116). On the contrary, defence is the very thing that enables us to indulge in both gratification and pleasure when reading.

In Dynamics, he is still in accordance with Lesser insofar as he maintains that literary texts store fantasy material which they 'transform' and 'defend': 'That . . . is the special and wonderful thing about literature: it does for us in an intense, encapsulated form what we must do for ourselves as we mature in life - it transforms primitive, childish fantasies into adult, civilized meanings' (32). The formal arrangement of the text is considered as the main index of the defence mechanism the text applies in order to control its underlying fantasy material.

The interaction between text and reader comes about because within the reader there resides his own store of 'defended' (abgewehrt) fantasy material. Both he and the text are said to share 'a central fantasy' (why, however, only one?) which reaches back into early childhood experiences. What actually motivates the reader to 'introject' (push inside) or, as Holland was to put it later, to 'ingest' the literary work is the 'promise of gratification'. In a kind of hallucinatory state, the reader slips through both the formal defence mechanisms of the text and his own habitual defences, plummeting back to the primal scenes of his life. So while reading, there happens within us a regression 'to our earliest oral experience of pre-self in which we are merged with the source of gratification' (89). Topologically, this merger is performed in what Holland in Dynamics calls 'a sub-system' of our ego and what later he will designate as 'potential space'. 'Potential space' is the psychoanalytical locality where the early interactions between mother and baby and the child's early responses to his social and cultural environment take place (5 Readers 127).

How do we know that the pleasure we enjoy while we are reading has its source in regressing to primal scenes which are stored in our unconscious? The only answer Holland can give to this question is to refer us to both Freud's theories and to clinical knowledge. There is no explanation, however, to which we may assent by relying on our own experience.

Parallel to the unconscious process of 'introjecting' a text, in Holland's model there runs a conscious process of

´intellecting´ it (180). This conscious process manifests itself predominantly in the reader´s attempt to arrive at a meaning of the text. Here Holland is not concerned with what Hirsch would call an ´intended meaning´, but with the reader´s need and desire to find a meaning which satisfies him, his very ego. This act of finding a personally satisfactory meaning is again explained in terms of the psychoanalytical concept of defence. To give an example: Supposing you read a text that harbours a sexual fantasy. As far as the text is concerned indulging in the sexual fantasy is often defended by the formal device of omission; this is to say, information about the lovers´ sexual activities is withheld. According to Holland´s model, you introject the sexual fantasy content unconsciously, but to enjoy it as a civilized adult person you have to make it acceptable to your conscious ego. The ego´s approval, however, can only be gained by finding a moral or a social meaning which, for its part, justifies your indulgence in the sexual fantasy. In other words, you are ´defending´ the crude fantasy material by finding a meaning for it. The particular kind of defence used in this instance is sublimation. The positive side of this defence process is that your pleasure is enhanced. Thus, in Holland´s overall hedonistic pattern, the quest for meaning becomes a second pleasure-maximizing principle, adding to the pleasure already achieved through unconscious gratification.

In Poems in Persons, Holland recasts and condenses some of the major ideas submitted in Dynamics. In this connexion, three new emphases deserve attention.

i. The theoretical introduction of the concept of an ´identity theme´. This is a category which becomes predominant in all publications following Poems in Persons. The ´identity theme´ is a conceptual device which is intended to explain how the human person remains the same although changing all the time (5 Readers 61). Leaning on the clinical knowledge evaluated by Heinz Lichtenstein (´Identity´), Holland argues that a person´s particular ego and the manifestations of all its reactions to the inner and outer world can be grasped in a single unifying theme, which conveniently may be called ´identity theme´. Through the ´identity theme´ the perception of a ´deep´ invariant core in personality structure or character becomes accessible to the inspection of the psychoanalytical observer.

ii. The application of this concept to the reading process is the second major emphasis of Poems in Persons. Here Holland rejects his former hypothesis that what comes about in reading is the coalescence of the fantasy material residing in text and reader alike. His new conception is that the reader is not at all challenged by the fantasy material which the text contains and offers to him. Rather the reverse is the case. The reader, in this revised view, only scans the text to actively find details that are compatible with his identity theme. The main discovery with which Holland surprises us here is that a particular reader's reading style is nothing else but a manifestation of his very private and deeply hidden 'identity theme' or - that's another term he is using - his 'life style'.

Correspondingly, we are given puzzling statements like this: 'A reader recreates a literary work so as to re-enact his own character' (100). Or: 'Each reader poems his own poem' (ibid.).

iii. A third point worth noting about Poems in Persons is procedural novelty. As in his following book 5 Readers Reading, Holland introduces tests and attempts to arrive at what seems an empirical verification of his radical hypothesis. The procedure is as follows. First Holland submits his test subjects to two psychological tests which are expected to reveal their respective 'identity themes'. The second part of the procedure is that Holland interviews his test readers about the text they have read. Finally he shows that each of his two readers has read an identical text quite differently. To be sure, there is nothing to wonder about that. But the really provocative thing, which, of course, exposed Holland to severe criticism, was his claim to have proved that the responses of his two readers had been governed exclusively by their 'identity themes' or 'life styles'. More precisely, on the little evidence he has got he tries to demonstrate, and does not hesitate to generalize about this, that every reader does not project any kind of fantasy into the text, but only that kind of fantasy 'that yields the pleasure he characteristically seeks' (77), all the time following his individual pattern of defence.

If this were true, it would mean that the text has lost its own dynamics to engage and to compel the reader. As there is no co-operation between text and reader, the only pole worth focusing on is the reader. Also, it's not the act of reading that deserves attention but the deep structure of the reader's personality. For if one knows about the reader's personality one can explain how he reads. So the new theory requires: Analyse the reader instead of the text. (It's this tendency which I have tried to indicate in the title of my paper!)

Furthermore, as each reader recreates his own personal text, the same item of literature generates as many texts as there are readers. Here Holland's argument verges towards the epistemological stance of utter subjectivity which, in spite of finicky terminological squabbles between Holland and Bleich, is the trademark of their criticism.

In 5 Readers Reading, Holland has arrayed five students, instead of two, in the same kind of reading experiment as he had arranged in Poems in Persons. In 5 Readers Reading he does not bring forward any new arguments worth special attention, but his repertoire of arguments is presented with a more coercive rhetoric. Thus, for example, the way in which a reader reads is comprised in four formulas:

i. 'Style Seeks Itself' (113). This means that the reader responds only insofar as a literary text acts out what is within him.

ii. 'Defenses Must Be Matched' (115). This is to say, the reader activates his own defence mechanisms.

iii. 'Fantasy Projects Fantasy' (117). This formula indicates that all fantasies are provided by the reader. The text itself is devoid of them.

iv. 'Character Transforms Characteristically' (121); in other words, the meaning of a text is engendered by the reader's own 'identity theme'. Here, however, one has to ask whether it is still adequate to speak of 'the meaning of a text'.

To remain with the notion of the 'literary text' for a moment, according to Holland it can only be defined in negative terms. The literary text is nothing special but just an external object like so many other things to which we respond. It contains neither fantasy material nor meaning unless they are given it by the reader.

All you can deal with as a critic is readers' responses which, for their part, deserve correlation with personal 'identity themes'.

Apart from the books mentioned so far, Holland has also written a considerable number of essays (see bibliography). In them he repeats his arguments in a condensed form over and over again, without making any really new points. However, the essays are interesting to read because they are well-written and cover, e.g., the classroom situation as well as 'gender-linked' responses to Gothic novels (see Holland/Sherman). In his attempt to drive home his views to as many people as possible, Holland has also coined an acronym - 'DEFT'. So if you feel inclined, you may read 'DEFTly', meaning that you rely on 'Defense', 'Expectation', 'Fantasy' and 'Transformation' ('New Paradigm' 338). Holland also offers a new tradename for his kind of criticism. Reacting to a controversy with David Bleich, Holland calls his criticism 'transactive', thus basing his criticism on the far-reaching epistemological assumption 'that humans cannot separate subject and object', but we can know 'the transaction between self and other . . . very subtly and intricately indeed' ('New Paradigm' 343). The statement sounds good. Yet I am not so sure whether <u>we</u> <u>really</u> <u>know</u> much for certain about the transaction between self and other. With his 'transactive paradigm' he challenges, and competes with, what David Bleich calls 'the subjective paradigm'. This leads me on to David Bleich, the third major figure I want to deal with.

IV

David Bleich

Like Holland, Bleich is also preoccupied with analysing what happens within a reader. In fact, there are a lot of conceptual and procedural similarities stimulated by Holland, which Bleich acknowledges (<u>Readings</u> 113). Bleich, too, wants to demonstrate 'how, why and what happens when people write and read' (3). Inspired by Holland, Bleich is also aware of the importance of the reader's personality in the reading process. Reading, for Bleich just as much as for Holland, above all means an encounter with oneself.

Yet there are differences which cannot be denied and are thus worth pointing out. As has been shown, Holland analyses the reader as a person. Bleich also analyses the reader; but instead of the reader's personality structure whose basic individuality he takes for granted, Bleich focuses on the reader's <u>act</u> <u>of</u> <u>response</u>, which, admittedly, emanates from his personality. Holland's reader is one who seeks gratification by managing his defence mechanisms; Bleich's reader, on the other hand, is the a priori hermeneut: He wants to make sense out of what he reads; he is genuinely pre-occupied with value judgements, with what Bleich calls 'literary importance', and last but not least with 'interpretation'. The psychoanalytical assumption that human reactions are manifestations of evaluative 'emotions', which reveal themselves in 'affects' and 'free associations', leads Bleich to a thorough and radical examination of how people read and arrive at meaning.

Pitting himself against all literary theories which justify objective meaning, Bleich argues as follows: When I as a reader say 'this means that', I actually camouflage my subjective response to the text. I had better say: 'feel this'. For my decision on what is 'of literary importance' in a text is derived from my own 'perceptual initiatives' (<u>Subjective</u> <u>Criticism</u> 96). But it is an essential part of my normal behaviour that I depersonalize my most personal response. So in all we say about literature we had better acknowledge the subjective origin of our objectifying statements.

In Readings and Feelings and Subjective Criticism, the two books I mainly refer to in this paper, Bleich deals with the subjective origin of our objectifying statements about literature in two different ways.

To begin with Readings and Feelings, this is a practical 'let's-do-it' book devised for the classroom. Bleich thinks it is the emotions that set his reader's mind in motion. Accordingly, he elicits - and gives advice on how to elicit - direct responses from the students by encouraging them to indulge in free-association and not to suppress their emotions. He also shows how the individual responses can be 'negotiated', or converted, into shareable experiences in the classroom. Each response statement that is communicated, in spite of its high personal content, enshrines a 'truth-value' vis-a-vis the text, and this 'truth-value' can be shared by others participating in the group process of interpretation. So what emerges are interpretations bearing the mark of a 'collective subjectivity' (93).

The metacritical principles underlying Readings and Feelings are projected on a larger canvas in Subjective Criticism. Here Bleich aligns himmself with leading representatives of 20th century thought (one of whom is S. Freud) to demonstrate that reality can only be understood in terms of what he calls 'the subjective paradigm'. Using T. S. Kuhn's notion of 'paradigm' as a characteristic way of perceiving the world, Bleich attempts to establish a 'subjective paradigm' which questions the validity of the traditional 'objective paradigm' as derived from Descartes and Newton. The main characteristic of the 'subjective paradigm', if set against the objective paradigm, is the involvement of the perceiver. Placing himself under this all-embracing epistemological umbrella, Bleich goes into linguistics to emerge with the theory that language is a system of symbols. Once this is admitted, he is able to entertain with favour the thesis that literature is a symbolic object which consequently needs resymbolization or interpretation. It is in this very concept of resymbolization or interpretation that the subjective factor gains momentum: For it is not the text that puts forward the claim to be resymbolized or interpreted; on the contrary, the motive of resymbolization resides within the interpreter. He wants to know what literature as a symbolic object means to him on a given occasion. Now, between the concepts of symbolic object and resymbolization Bleich cunningly wedges the notion of 'response' as an added dimension. 'Response' is in Bleich's definition 'a peremptory perceptual act that translates a sensory experience into consciousness' (97). This also implies that 'response' is a primary act of evaluation manifesting the person's highly individualized mental and psychic structure. 'So far, so good´, one may say. But what is the relationship between response and interpretation? Here Bleich stipulates that it is not the text, but our response that needs resymbolization: ´. . . the response, not the text, is the symbol that the interpretation resymbolizes´ (147). In other words, the "response" is ´our text´ which we have created out of the literary text. If this is the case, interpreting ´our text´ is the method through which we adapt it to our own desire because the meaning we find for it redeems us from uneasy feelings. Ideally, the purpose of constructing a meaning for a text can be pursued in a classroom situation. There, I can compare ´my text´ with the texts the students have developed in their response statements. Moreover, we can try to compare all our private texts with the words on the printed page, thus responding anew to the chain of correlated texts we subsequently have become aware of. Predictably, in Bleich´s view, all meaning we construct and formulate in what seems objective statements bears the marks of the process we have shared with other subjects. For only whatever we have approved of in our own and other people´s responses can be negotiated into specific knowledge about the text. This specific knowledge is, of course, of limited validity. The other, more positive, side of the coin is that any response statement, however inadequate it may appear to me basically implies a processual ´truth-value´. For, if I feel displeased with my neighbour´s response, I am motivated to arrive at a more satisfactory interpretation that pleases me (Readings 63). The message Bleich wants to drive home, however, is ´that any meaning is a construction whose topical fluency and objectivity need no longer deny its subjective origins´ (Subjective Criticism 237).

V

Critical Summary

Critically reviewing the psychoanalytical theory of reading surveyed here, let me now first point out what this theory does not account for.

The most obvious feature, of course, is: We do not find in it any readiness to acknowledge that a historical awareness of the text might be important. This means, the historic distance between the production and reception of a literary text is hardly taken into consideration as a fundamental problem. This disregard of the historical factor clearly stems from the overriding interest in pleasure and from the emphasis on intuitive perception.

Another striking point is the radical denial of a meaning residing in a written text. Whereas other theories ascribe to the text the capacity to harbour potential meanings, a fixed set of intentional meanings (Hirsch, Validity) or contrariwise, 'an indeterminate hierarchy of meanings' (Sparshott 10), and, as Paul de Man would have it, an inexhaustible infinitude of meaning (Ray 148), the psychoanalytical theory deals with this problem in a legerdemain way by just giving the reader a monopoly of meaning. Furthermore, there is a complete negation of the efficacy of conventions and ideologies. Cannot conventions easily interfere with a reader's individual style of responding? To ask the question is to answer it. Significantly, the notion of stock responses to typical situations has not at all been made the topic of critical reflection. Even more alarming is the total neglect of the reader's ideological preoccupations. Are they not also part of his mental structure? If they are internalised, the reader is not conscious of them. Thus, it seems that a huge body of motives of which the reader is not immediately aware but which, all the same, govern his personal way of reading has been condemned to deliberate neglect. This is all the more deplorable since both Holland and Bleich, with compelling rhetoric, pretend to offer a satisfactory explanation not only of the reading process but, reaching out towards universal conclusions, of the way in which human beings understand reality.

Unlike other directions of reader-oriented criticism, the psychoanalytical theory of reading takes away from the text the capacity to stimulate, leave alone control, what the reader does to it. Whereas structuralists accommodate an 'inscribed or encoded reader' (Suleiman/Crosman 14) within the text, without, however, considering what happens to the actual reader outside, both Stanley Fish and Wolfgang Iser deal with the lively interaction between reader and text; in their view, it is this interaction which leads to the engendering of meaning. With Holland, Bleich and their followers, however, we encounter a reversal of the primacy granted to the text by the structuralists; at the same time we find an upsetting of the balance on which both Fish and Iser rely. Instead, undue pre-eminence over the text is given to the external reader-person.

By tradition, the historical and formalist varieties of criticism (structuralism being an exception) adhere to the belief that literature notches up a high degree in the hierarchy of values and, consequently, deserves special attention. The psychoanalytical theory of reading takes a less exalted view of literature. To Holland, a literary text is an 'external object' just like any other external object; and to Bleich it is a 'symbolic object' just like any other symbolic object (a map e.g.). The literary text is thus thoroughly reduced to the status of an 'occasion' or 'promptuary' (Holland, 5 Readers 285). The reader avails himself of this occasion in order to 'poem his own poem' or to 'story his own story'. It is the private text that matters, nothing else.

In view of the many different avenues critics have taken at the crossroads of fundamental dissent during the last two decades, the very concept of literature has become questionable. Intrigued by this development, some critics, such as Hernadi and Eagleton e.g., have felt challenged to ask anew: 'What is Literature?' Indeed, such a perplexing question does not really worry the psychoanalytical critic. According to Bleich literature simply is what the individual reader considers as such. This simplistic view requires no further reflections as to the essence and the ontological status of literature.

On the other hand, in spite of the radical opposition to a consensus of values agreed on by rival schools of criticism, the psychoanalytical theory of reading has one important principle in common with the reader-oriented theories of all shades. Like them, it capitalizes on the importance of reading and interpreting although what is read and interpreted is the reader's own text instead of the printed one. Interpreting, however, - and this is a principle ratified by all schools except perhaps the deconstructionists - aims at establishing a unity of a 'higher or deeper' order among separate, and frequently discordant, elements (Culler 61, 64).

Historically, the psychoanalytical reader concept was developed as a grumbling reaction to what Crews called 'anaesthetic criticism', meaning New Criticism and the systematic rigidity of teaching practices based on the theoretical insights offered by Northrop Frye's *Anatomy of Criticism*. What American psychoanalytical criticism since Lesser targeted at was the former emphasis on scientific procedure and the insistence on detachment from personal concern, features which were predominant in the American university teaching of literature. Both Holland's and Bleich's crusades have mightily boosted and popularized the reader's justifiable claim 'to come to grips with [his] deepest responses' (Crews 73). According to the evidence recorded in *College English*, the application of reader-centred pedagogics has had a vitalizing effect on teaching at some American universities. I personally believe that it might well be worthwhile to experiment with some of Bleich's study assignments at German universities as well, if only to initiate the students' interest in literary texts and to make them think about what we are doing when we are reading.

There is another positive facet which I should like to acknowledge. It is the fact that Bleich considers feelings and emotions as important factors which permeate our reading experience. As academic criticism almost universally avoids dealing with emotions and has, to date, not been capable of offering operational conceptualizations, Bleich seems to point in a direction where more research would be necessary and perhaps even yield promising results.

Having become sensitized to the question of how personal all value-statements are, may I conclude my paper by saying quite simply what I like and dislike about the psychoanalytical concept of reading. I do like the challenge it offers to a purely formal and structuralist consideration of literature which simply turns a blind eye to the personal element always manifesting itself in our understanding of literature. What I dislike is the inflated epistemology and the far-reaching claims associated with it. What I also dislike is the over-emphasis on the reader's ego-concerns.

To me this preoccupation with the reader's ego seems to be just another expression of a narcissistic attitude which has become recognizable in many other sectors of American life and culture since the 1970s (see Lasch). The greatest complaint I have to make, however, is that I, as a reader, am to be forbidden from letting myself be challenged by a repository of meaning which is located outside my own person. Am I a coward if I prefer to deal with 'Shakespeare's Macbeth' rather than with 'my Macbeth'? To be frank, I have not yet discovered the 'Macbeth within me', and I can live quite happily with the idea that Shakespeare, and not myself, is Macbeth's progenitor. Let me mention a final aspect that makes me feel uneasy. Both Holland and Bleich pay lip-service to the conscious mind. In their practical procedures, however, they seem to forget that reading also means a constant involvement of the conscious mind. Basically acknowledging the general pull of the unconscious, I, all the same, feel more at ease if I may engage in what according to Fish might be called 'the spectacular mental athletics of the conscious mind reading' (Erlich 767).

REFERENCES

Alcorn, M. W., Jr., and Bracher, M. (1985) 'Literature, Psychoanalysis, and the Re-Formation of the Self. A New Direction for Reader-Response Theory'. Publications of the Modern Language Association of America 100, pp. 342-354.

Black,S.A.(1977) 'On Reading Psychoanalytically', College English, 39/3, pp. 267-274.

Bleich, D. (1967) 'The Determination of Literary Value', Literature and Psychology 17, pp. 19-29.

Bleich, D. (1969) 'Emotional Origins of Literary Meaning', College English 31, pp. 30-40.

Bleich, D. (1971) 'Psychological Bases of Learning from Literature', College English 33, pp. 32-45.

Bleich D. (1975) Readings and Feelings: An Introduction to Subjective Criticism, Urbana, Ill: National Council of Teachers of English.

Bleich, D. (1975) 'The Subjective Character of Critical Interpretation', College English 36/7, pp. 739-755.

Bleich, D. (1978) Subjective Criticism, Baltimore/London: The Johns Hopkins University Press.

Bleich, D. et al. (1978) 'The Psychological Study of Language and Literature: A Selected Annotated Bibliography', Style 12/1, pp. 113-210.

Crews, F. (1975) Out Of My System: Psychoanalysis, Ideology, and Critical Method, Oxford University Press, New York.

Culler, J. 'Prolegomena to a Theory of Reading', in S.R. Suleiman and I. Crosman (eds.), pp. 46-66.

Eagleton, T. (1983) Literary Theory: An Introduction, Blackwell, Oxford.

Elliott, S. M. (1975) 'A New Critical Epistemology', Hartford Studies in Literature, 7/2, pp. 170-189.

Erlich, V. (1975) 'Reading Conscious and Unconscious', College English 36/6, pp. 766-775.

Fish, S. (1980) Is There a Text in This Class? The Authority of Interpretive Communities, Harvard University Press, Cambridge, Mass.

Fish, S.E. (1967) Surprised by Sin: The Reader in Paradise Lost, Macmillan, St. Martin's Press, London.

Franzosa, J. C., Jr. (1973) 'Criticism and the Uses of Psychoanalysis', College English, 34/7, pp. 927-933.

Hernadi, P. (1978) (ed.) What Is Literature? Indiana University Press, Bloomington/London.

Hirsch, E. D., Jr. (1967) Validity in Interpretation, Yale University Press, New Haven/London.

Holland, N. N. (1968) The Dynamics of Literary Response, Oxford University Press, New York.

Holland, N. N. (1975) 5 Readers Reading, Yale University Press, New Haven/London.

Holland, N. N. (1982) Laughing: A Psychology of Humour, Cornell University Press, Ithaca/London.

Holland, N. N. (1975) 'Hamlet - My Greatest Creation', The Journal of the American Academy of Psychoanalysis, 3, pp. 419-427.

Holland, N. N. (1978) 'Literature as Transaction'in P. Hernadi (ed.), pp. 206-218.

Holland, N. N. (1976/77) 'Literary Interpretation and Three Phases of Psychoanalysis', Critical Inquiry, 3, pp. 221-233

Holland, N. N. (1975) 'The New Paradigm: Subjective or Transactive?', New Literary History, 7, pp. 335-346.

Holland, N. N. (1973) Poems in Persons: An Introduction to the Psychoanalysis of Literature, Norton, New York.

Holland, N. N. (1978) 'A Transactive Account of Transactive Criticism', Poetics, 7, pp. 177-189.

Holland, Norman N. (1977) 'Transactive Teaching: Cordelia's Death', College English, 39/3, pp. 276-285.

Holland, N. N. (1970) 'The 'Unconscious' of Literature: The Psychoanalytic Approach', Stratford-upon-Avon Studies, 12, Contemporary Criticism, Arnold, London. pp. 130-153.

Holland, N. N. (1975) 'Unity, Identity, Text, Self', Publications of the Modern Language Association of America, 90, pp. 813-822.

Holland, N.N. and Schwartz, M. (1975) 'The Delphi Seminar', College English, 36/6, pp. 789-800.

Holland, N.N. and Sherman, L. (1976) 'Gothic Possibilitities', New Literary History, 8, pp. 279-284.

Iser, W. (1978) The Act of Reading: A Theory of Aesthetic Response, Johns Hopkins University Press, Baltimore.

Kuhn, T. S. (1962) The Structure of Scientific Revolutions, The University of Chicago Press, Chigaco/London.

Lasch, C. (1978) The Culture of Narcissism: American Life in an Age of Diminishing Expectations, Norton, New York.

Leitch, V. B. (1977) 'A Primer of Recent Critical Theories', College English, 39/2, pp. 138-152.

Lesser, S. O. (1957) Fiction and the Unconscious, University of Chicago Press, Chicago/London.

Lichtenstein, H. (1963) 'The Dilemma of Human Identity', Journal of the American Psychoanalytic Association 11, pp. 173-223.

Lichtenstein, H. (1961) 'Identity and Sexuality: A Study of their Interrelationship in Man', Journal of the American Psychoanalytic Association, 9, pp. 179-260.

Lichtenstein, H. (1965) 'Towards A Metapsychological Definition of the Concept of Self', International Journal of Psychoanalysis, 46, pp. 117-128.

Ray, W. (1984) Literary Meaning: From Phenomenology to Deconstruction, Blackwell, Oxford.

Roland, A. (1978) (ed.) Psychoanalysis, Creativity and Literature, New York.

Schwartz, M. (1975) ´Where Is Literature?´ College English, 36, pp. 756-765.

Shrodes, C. (1960) ´Bibliotherapy: An Application of Psychoanalytic Theory´, American Imago, 17 pp. 311-319.

Slatoff, W. J. (1970) With Respect to Readers: Dimensions of Literary Response, Cornell University Press, Ithaca/London.

Sparshott, F. E. (1978) ´On the Possibility of Saying What Literature Is´ in P. Hernadi (ed.) pp. 3-15.

Suleiman, S. R., and Crosman, I. (1980) (eds.) The Reader in the Text: Essays on Audience and Interpretation, Princeton University Press, Princeton, N.J.

Tennenhouse, L. (1976) (ed.) The Practice of Psychoanalytic Criticism, Detroit.

Tompkins, J. (1977) ´Criticism and Feelings´, College English, 39/2, pp. 169-178.

Steig, M. (1975) ´The Challenge of Subjectivism: A Personal Response´, West Coast Review, 10, pp. 15-23.

SEVEN

THE NATURE OF LISTENING IN READING POETRY: A CONVERSATION

R. A. Lumsden and John Pellowe

> It takes two to speak the truth - one to speak, and another to hear.
>
> Henry David Thoreau
> A Week on the Concord and Merrimack Rivers

[Editors´ Note: A book on listening as an active function hardly seems complete without a conversation. The following is a partial transcription of a conversation between two lecturers in the National University of Singapore, one primarily a teacher of literature, the other primarily of linguistics. The editors have, without any particularly consistent rationale, omitted some sections (signalled by ...) and we apologise to the interlocutors for any cuts which they may think are insensitive. We have not edited out apparent digressions, misdirections, misunderstandings, misquotations since the theme of this book is that these phenomena are more correctly analysed as new directions and separate understandings. The conversation, we believe, not only comments significantly upon these matters, but also exemplifies them. Each reader, like each of the editors, may find areas of interest and non-interest which will differ in the individual case. An initial handwritten transcription was made by one of the interlocutors, typed by a third person and proofread by both speakers. Further typing and proofreading were the responsibility of the editors, who no doubt have introduced new variants, silent witnesses to the creative nature of the communicative process.]

-- ... This seems true; perhaps you´ll agree with this. The type of listening determines the type of poetry, that is, the way in which the poetry´s perceived. The first question, to me

anyway, is whether the type of poetry also compels or invites a certain kind of attention, that is, a certain kind of listening. In short do we have a circularity here; a reciprocal relationship, or an exchange in which either the listener or the poet has the determining part? It is the old reader/writer debate again, in different form, or at least it could be.
-- [Puffing pipe] Mm; mm?
-- Now if we have a circularity, are the difficulties of apportioning dominance to one side or the other in particular cases insuperable? What kind of methodology can we arrive at? It's the solipsism question again. And there's a further complication. We're listening to our selves anyway now, in a ghostly way, listening to our other selves back there as we imagine ourselves reading poetry, so we're already at one remove in discussing it, we're already at one remove from when we actually do it.

It seems to me that if we take an extreme example (and I'll get on to Eliot in a moment), that of symbolist poetry, it shows that different types of listening are <u>required</u> because it's different from ordinary poetry; I take symbolist poetry as an extreme example of poetry.
-- Who's that, Verlaine?
-- Let's say Verlaine, Rimbaud, the classic case of Coleridge's 'Kubla Khan', Mallarme; it's more difficult to find cases in English, but if we match the English examples against those great French prototypes then we come close to it; Eliot to a degree, when he's not being discursive. The point is that most English people (and even those people who have the English tradition inculcated, such as Singapore students) take as the norm something which is non-symbolist, something which is much more discursive, narrative, epic, explanatory, indicative. They have such great difficulty in changing their way of listening, their way of reading, and I think this has to do with themselves listening to themselves reading.
-- Right.
-- They commonly misunderstand, misconstrue, wrench out of true, have difficulty with symbolist poetry; they can't <u>adjust</u> their listening.

So I take from this the lesson that different types of listening are required and that what goes wrong with most beginning students, at least, when they're listening to symbolist poetry, is that they try to hear it as though it were instructing them, as though it were discursive.
-- Mm, polemic.
-- Polemic, right. To apply an ancient grammatical term - a rough attempt to categorise - it's as though symbolist poetry were indicative, but it's not, it's probably closer to optative, expressing a wish (Kubla Khan) or counter-optative - expressing the disappointment of a wish or noting the details

of a world in which wishes do not come to pass (Plath's 'The Moon and the Yew').

These are talking points. I'm not promoting these categories as total or explanatory, or adopting some kind of crude Freudianism: I'm trying to mark a distinction between the type of listening that beginning students incorrectly do when they're trying to read symbolist poetry and the type of mood this poetry would demand of them, which is closer to the truth.

-- Can I stop you there? When you were talking about symbolists something struck me. We might need to make a distinction between the mere process of reading, which is some kind of silence, and reading with your ears open.

We're talking about reading poetry. There's a text. There's black stuff on white stuff in front of you and it's going into your eyes. You're talking about modes of listening as metaphors superimposed on the fact of this black stuff going into your eyes, right?

-- Yes.

-- You're pointing to how the dominant listening mode is often inappropriate, especially in beginning students. That seems to me to be right, but maybe there's a prior question which is that the reading mode shouldn't ever be silent. I mean that all the listening modes should be actively potential (I know that's paradoxical): if one is reading properly, it seems to me that all the listening modes are active, but they're only potential, and that somehow there's a very dense but cyclic interaction between the merely silent business of getting the print from the paper, to eyeballs to brain (or wherever it goes) and which of those listening modes finally becomes post-selected as the most appropriate. I take it that that is one of the sources of differential readings.

You've got some students who expect everything to be polemical discourse. But imagine someone who was thoroughly overtrained as a symbolist/imagist reader. That person would be listening with their three-dimensional eye, with their visual eyes, not with their print-receiving eyes. Listening for pictures of some sort.

Somehow we have to sort out priorities. The eyes aren't being eyes when they're reading print. Reading is a perversion.

-- We're agreeing here on that.

-- I think we are. How do you expect - going back to my reason for interrupting - to select the right listening mode?

-- OK. This is the question.

Our starting point seems to be the same. I'm treating reading - and I think you're right to distinguish seeing a tree, or a picture, or a human face, from seeing print; it's not the same sort of activity -

I'm treating reading as a kind of silent listening to oneself reading over [Ryle: The Concept of Mind]. Some kind of internalised subvocalisation is going on. It's different from seeing. Once we've established (and this is the point of the symbolist example) from empirical evidence that it is different from seeing a picture (because of the difficulty students have with such poetry), then we've cleared the ground for the central question of how we can distinguish between appropriate modes. This is the big problem and may be one we can address. We have to decide which way to turn. Are we going to again turn to look for scraps of data which will help us? Are we going to introspect first?

My own feeling is that we should listen - a way of introspecting by way of other people - listen to practitioners; Barthes, Eliot.

-- This is a footnote. When you said 'how can we encourage people to adopt the appropriate mode?' -

--I think I know what you're going to say. Maybe we can't. Maybe we shouldn't.

-- Is there an appropriate mode? If a student reads Verlaine (who's the first one, Verlaine or Rimbaud?) -

-- Please don't ask me historical questions.

-- (Oh sorry.) - as if he was reading Pope or Dryden can we say that that's inappropriate? It's a footnote.

-- It's marginally central in the way of Derrida, because we're challenged to disclose our criteria at the very time when we're trying patiently to investigate these criteria - pretending that we can discover what is likely to be embedded already within us. All I can say is what my own feeling about it is.

From the symbolist example, it seems that there's a circular relationship here. We can't have the readers listening in a vacuum and making something totally out of nothing. We have a text which is predisposing them in some way. Why do I say so?

I fall back in this way on something like a Johnsonian consensus - it happens so often. In this way I'm laying aside theoretical problems of solipsism, and so on, that we know so well. I have X number of students and I find that all but two or three of them have the same difficulties of adjusting their frame of reading to symbolist poetry. I assume from this, in people who are otherwise so various, that they are responding to stimuli which are bringing their differences back to some mean which suggests that the promptings from the text are in some way single, coherent. Their responses are much less variable than the variance amongst their personalities. Some kind of circularity is thus in evidence.

-- There might be another explanation.

-- Just one more thing. The problem you mentioned before also arises here: How do we find the techniques that they can usefully adopt?

-- The narrowness of the range of 'erroneous' modes that people adopt might not have anything to do with the primacy of novels. They assume that _poetry_ is discursive. Why? Because the only thing that people really understand when they read these days is novels. They understand something fictive, linear, non-optative. They don't have any idea of indexical understanding, they don't _feel_ for metaphor. (Language works in such and such a way, there are rules, the dictionary entry is right. They don't understand that metaphor is the middle of everything. Indexicalness is your only hope. We all duck that all the time. Daily living would be thought impossible if we acknowledged how non-contiguous the metaphorical and the literal were. And how rare the latter, as we feel things, is.)

The problem with poetry might come from the dominance of novels.

--If I can retranslate you in my own terms - I think you are saying and I think you are in your own - forgive me for putting words into your mouth -

-- I'd rather someone else did it -

-- - if you're saying that the reason people have such a similar range of responses, is because there are certain conventions that have been imposed upon them' markedly similar difficulties. That they've been led to expect (by teaching, by background, by environment, by educational context) something of poetry which brings their personalities down to a mean which is artificial, then I agree with you. It's a very strong possibility. It's one that has to be confronted. It's one that Marxist and neo-Marxist writers from Benjamin on have been very interested in. It's virtually irrefutable. (Foucault, Barthes, all of them, have been interested in this.)

This brings me to Barthes. Barthes (in a marriage to Eliot which Eliot would have regarded as grounds for instant divorce) from _Mythologies_ on, when he's easing himself out of structuralism to something more free-wheeling, makes a distinction between readerly and writerly texts.

-- Can you explain that?

-- OK. He thinks a readerly text is one (paraphrasing and debasing him, simplifying - _Writing Degree Zero_ is the central book here) which leans very heavily on its ability to provide a whole ambience of classicalness, of normativeness. He also calls them classical texts. Such a text leans _authoritatively_ on the reader to accept that the text is given as it is. It should be received respectfully, unquestioningly; it should be honoured; it should be handled with reverence and awe and it has a certain style which is a non-style because it isn't _noticed_, it's taken as so normal that one doesn't have to _do_ anything with it as a reader, one simply ingests it.

-- Jane Austen? _Volpone_?

-- Right. Balzac. He distinguishes between that and another kind of text which he regards as writerly, that is where the reader is thrown, thrown back on his own experience more, on his own ability to make sense of what he's given. In other

words the reader is aware that he has to reconstruct, he has to 'write' as he goes along through the text, in order to make sense of it. For Barthes this is the dividing line between the classical and modernist. (I'm really simplifying these.)
-- So Sterne and Trollope and Shakespeare(?) and Beckett would be writerly.
-- Shakespeare probably classical. Sterne the great precursor of the writerly because he built so many anti-determining devices into his text. There's no way you can get around him and put him in tidy order.
-- So Thomas Mann has got to be writerly as well.
-- I don't know. He's an interesting case. Some of the Marxist writers, Lukacs for example, regard him as classical.
-- Really?
-- Yes, an exemplary social realist.
-- But Dr. Faustus is constantly making the reader, making me, aware of the fact that he, Mann, through the narrator, is constantly saying 'Look, you as a reader should be far more critical, I've just spent a whole chapter digressing, and you haven't complained, but I'm complaining about it on your behalf, and I'm not going to do anything about it.' So he hauls you out of the classical into the writerly, and as soon as you've got there he promptly dumps you.
-- Yes. This was Gabriel Josipovici's line in his modernist seminars at Sussex. You can see how Faustus can be used as a classical text by people who are pushing the social-realist line; and you can also see how certain of his books (Joseph and his Brothers is another) do throw the reader onto his own resources and don't give him something that he can fit comfortably into the received form.
-- But I have a terminological problem.
-- What's that?
-- It's that Barthes' terminology is the wrong way round. What he calls a writerly text is actually a readerly text in my terms, because it requires the reader to be fully intelligent, to have no masking cards, to be aware of everything, to be prepared to make his (the reader's) own text out of the writing.
-- To live with his own uncertainty.
-- Yes. So what Barthes calls writerly texts require very patient, hard-working readers and I would call those readerly.
-- I see why too.
-- In what he calls readerly texts, you don't need to know anything: that's how it works, that's how it always ever did work. That's the writer having an ego trip and the reader doesn't have to do anything. Stick your hand out, the bus stops, and on you get, you're carried along. You know how it's going to work, you know where the catharses are going to come.
-- I see your point. I'm trying to dredge my memory. I'm not sure whether Barthes hasn't used the terms with some sense of irony. He's perfectly capable of it. We'd have to check that.

-- I keep disrupting you.
-- Anyway why not. It's useful. The point about readerly texts is that they are strongly socio-politically tied. This comes back to your earlier point about my students who are trying to understand symbolist poetry - their apparent commonest difficulties being culturally determined - Barthes is making the same point but about readerly texts. That such texts turn people into readerly listeners, and they need to be taught how to handle their own uncertainty.
-- There are two poles, two sources for that problem. One is the writers themselves. A writer who, in Barthes' terms is readerly, is emasculating the reader; and the education system that we all play a game in (though we try to play a part in it) encourages _us_ to turn _them_ into merely readerly readers. So that when they're faced with Beckett they're either blown to bits or they can't take it.

We haven't got that far away from listening, but we have to clear all this stuff (what stuff?) away. In Bunting's sense of listening we're not talking about listening at all yet; we're talking about why people read; when Barthes says people are readerly and when you say students don't understand symbolist poetry, we're saying the same things - that people are just ruined by education modalities, and writers are riding on the same bus. Writers themselves are being readerly (Harold Robbins, in part Eliot).
-- You've brought me to Eliot. Eliot after Barthes. To recapitulate about Barthes: readerly and writerly texts, the former those which are thrust upon us socio-politically, the latter those which we have to reconstruct, where we are more free agents in our ability to find meanings.

I'm thinking in connection with this of T. S. Eliot's conception of what happens when a poet or a critic writes (that is when _Eliot_ writes, since all of his criticism is about himself). He envisages the writer at the moment of writing as not being able to write anything of value unless he imagines an audience and I think he conceives of four different kinds of audiences. One is an audience of one, a close friend who thinks similarly. Another is some kind of projection of the writer's ideal self. The third is a broader audience of one's peers, the people one might have been educated with, the people who agree with one, whatever. I've forgotten the fourth. But the principle holds, that he thinks that in order to write at all the writer has to project into the role of a reader. He has to listen to himself through the ears of those he imagines before he even writes.

My point about this, aligning it with Barthes, is that though Eliot doesn't realise it himself what he's giving us is a picture, an exemplification of the readerly text, not the writerly at all. Because all these images are projections of the way in which he, Eliot, bourgeois, is tied by his socio-political context. It _seems_ to be more free-play-like than it

is because he's throwing it out a-historically. But it's actually Eliot defining himself as a socio-political animal and he's exemplifying in this way Barthes' readerly writer.
-- If your connections between Eliot and Barthes are right, then the reason why texts which are produced under those conditions are readerly is because his imaging of the reader-in-himself is part of a tradition, an educational, political tradition.
-- Yes. There are two directions which I take after this. One is a little to one side of the title of this paper, because it doesn't bear on poetry. However, it's an important point because it shows the way in which a study of poetry can apply in the real world. There are fairly obvious parallels between what Eliot, unbeknownst to himself, was doing there, and what politicians do more or less consciously. Politicians and 'political' speech writers, the government, employ media men in order to align what they have to say to an audience which is envisaged or imaged in a very similar way to the way Eliot was envisaging his audience.

There's a difference in that Eliot is not trying to tailor what he has to say, to qualify it, at the outset. This is presumably why poetry is felt to be more honest, even poetry of Eliot's sort, than political speeches. What the politicians try to do is to please their audience in a certain way; they project themselves towards an image of the audience that they have; they take it as a sign of failure if they're not throwing themselves towards a sense of audience that they themselves helped to create. Alignment of what is to be said to an image of audience.
-- Can I butt in again? It's a bit worrying this, because it means that poetry could be as perverting and trivialising as politics. (Eliot's imagined readers constitute a specification of expectation - where do writers get expectations from? - if you're producing a text which matches what you believe to be the expectations of the reader.) The only question of distinction here is that of the degree of honesty of the imaged expectation. The poet could get it wrong. The poet's imaged expectation might be just as much of an imposition upon the creation of readerliness as the politician's. The <u>degree</u> of imposition is the only thing which varies. Another source of potential collapse comes from your use of the phrase 'at the the outset' ('Eliot is not trying to qualify what he has to say at the outset') but I don't know what 'the outset' is.
-- The phrase is mine, not his.
-- But the notion of a writer having an outset preceding the establishment of an expectation is peculiar. Furthermore, what about the writerly writer? According to Eliot's distinction it ought to be impossible to write because you can't imagine the audience. What has the writerly writer to do or what is he doing over and above what the readerly writer is doing. A logical problem.

-- I take your point about the parallel between poets and politicians. I'm allowing Eliot the great credit of being more honest than politicians. It's a thorny, prickly problem because we only have the word of the person for it that he _is_ being more honest. I suspect Eliot himself precisely on this point. One way of getting around it is to make a distinction between Eliot the critic and Eliot the poet. There are various ways in which Eliot the poet offers more of an invitation to writerliness than Eliot the critic. _The Four Quartets_ contain long sections, but those where he's seeming to be discursive, pretending to be explaining himself - where he's really throwing the reader back on his own resources, to make sense of something which, he, Eliot, _seems_ to have made perfectly good sense of to that point. At those points I think you _can_ say that he's offering the invitation to writerliness to the reader, and is therefore being more honest. In other words, he's being more self-doubting, whereas in his criticism he seems to be full of himself to the point of being officious if not authoritarian. You know the sections (of _Four Quartets_) I mean, where he finishes 'that was a way of putting it', etc.

So I concede your point, that there _is_ a difficulty in making the kind of distinction I've made between politicians as such and poets per se, as though poets were not susceptible to the same kinds of dishonesty as politicians evidently are. And I say 'evidently are' because it's common knowledge, isn't it, that nobody much believes in politicians. People don't read political speeches in the way they read poetry, they don't read them with anything like the same suspension of disbelief. They're much closer to asking of political speeches, as one journalist did, 'why is this bastard lying to me?' Well it's not likely that many people would adopt that attitude in respect of a poet. Poets have the reputation of being truer to themselves. But I do concede. Eliot might be a good example, a case in point, that it doesn't always make sense to give them this degree of credit.

-- Do people ever really suspend their disbelief? Maybe this is irrelevant. But do they? You say - 'when you read a political speech, don't suspend your disbelief'?

-- Not if you're wise.

-- In such cases the listening mode you adopt is one of doubtfulness. One is always on the doubt. I can see that the notion of 'suspension of disbelief' is OK for drama, but I don't know if it is for poetry.

If I'm reading a newspaper, or instructions, I read in different ways, with different masking cards. If I'm reading for a well-defined purpose, that has the effect of masking out all kinds of critical faculties I have. If I'm reading poetry, I _can_ do it in the same _way_ as I have read political speeches, I apply all my critical faculties, I remove all the masking cards for different well-defined purposes. I read in all ways

at once. ('Why does the person say this and then this and then that?' 'This has to do with putting off these types of readers, this has to do with mollifying these people', etc.) There are all sorts of hooks in this piece of political writing which hedge off types of criticism. Well, don't I read a poem the same way? The poet is here trying to make me see or hear or feel or know this, here something else.
-- I do think there's a difference.
-- The only difference is that for a poet I don't have the overriding notion of doubt. I assume that somebody who is willing to live in a garret to tell me the truth about the world is not the same as the man who is taking the money out of my pocket after a hard day's work.
-- Now, that's a crucial difference, the element of doubt. I don't think you can read them in the same way. If you doubt a poet in the same way that you're wise to doubt a politician I don't think the poetry will work for you. I don't think it can work.
-- And isn't that why so few people find it easy to read poetry?
-- Yes because ...
-- Because doubt is a critical faculty which is active all the time.
-- That's right. Because in order to survive in this naughty, not to say many times nasty, world, we have to doubt. It's a skill we've developed. If we're smart we'd better. So it's very difficult in the reading of poetry because one has to make oneself vulnerable.

You mentioned earlier that it was beyond the readerly/writerly distinction. I wonder if it is? It seems to me that it applies, roughly, in that, when you're reading the poetry you are in a sense, from the other end, listening to a part of yourself. Eliot may have been right in part. You're hoping to hear some part of yourself which is enlivened; something close to yourself which you're reminded of through another person. If you approach, for example, political speeches in that way you're giving yourself over into the hands of an enemy. (We recognise this, don't we, since the Third Reich?) Poets don't have this sort of image. To that extent the term 'honesty', although it's a misnomer, does mark the difference.
-- OK. Honesty and something to do with ends.
-- I'm saying that poets encourage you to listen to part of yourself from which you might have been estranged, which the poet is re-aligning you with.
-- OK. Estranged precisely because of all your experience of politicising.
-- Yes.
-- The poet is encouraging you to be vulnerable in a way which is going to turn out to be suicidal, given what you said before about the need to doubt for survival. The poet is

trying to make that little part of us bigger which will make us more vulnerable in the world. He is trying to do that for so many people that the sum total of personal revolutions and revelations makes the maintenance of doubt unnecessary, and brackets off politicians.

-- This is something I hadn't thought about at all. It's an uncomfortable conclusion. (One little point of resistance - writer intention: not so much trying to do, but doing in a certain way.)

It may well be the logical conclusion of what I've been suggesting, and I don't know what to do with that, I don't know where we can go from there.

If this is true, if we go through some examples and we find that this is the trend for poetry, and we can recognise it, is poetry then a good thing or a bad thing given the state of the world at the moment? It might be a tremendous risk. It may be one of the reasons why it's not very popular.

-- Yes. Young people, I suspect, find it pretty difficult to read because it's asking them to do things which daily life tells them are dangerous ... and reading poetry in the way we're suggesting is a dangerous remedy for a disastrous end. An act of faith by the poet for the whole world. If enough people took the risk to read poetry in the way in which it has to be read then you might have a Krishnamurti revolution.

-- This ties in with the ancient, much re-iterated, idea that poets are a little crazy (unrealistic) and that poetry is basically anarchic.

--It's the only reason I read the stuff.

There's something else I want to ask you about 'the outset'. I understand how Austen etc. operate, those writers getting people on the readerly bus. First of all you've got to read all the previous readerly stuff. OK there's the mainstream tradition, here's a sidestream tradition, just do it again Sam, play it again. And that's what you're doing, by imagining your peer group or whatever it is. What I still don't understand is what does a writer who is writerly draw upon in addition? Because it has to be something 'in addition' or something 'in spite of'. What sort of a thing is it? It's not the tradition, it can't be everything that's gone before. What is it that gives the writer the ability to be revolutionary/writerly? Where does it come from? How can you produce something which you don't understand?

-- We could go two different ways here.

(But first, another point about poetry's place in an increasingly dangerous world. We can draw support for the idea from the perceived shift in the attitude to poetry and the attitudes to one's world as between the '60s and '80s. The '60s was an age of optimism when poetry was very popular, a very free kind of poetry (poetry readings, e.g.). It's only because the world has been perceived to be the enduringly nasty place it is internationally in the '70s and '80s, that poetry has fallen into some kind of desuetude from that earlier time. Remind me of your question again.

-- What is it that the writerly writer has?

-- Oh OK. I think we've got to say about Barthes - since we've been building on his theory - that it's very vulnerable here, it assumes a great deal. The Barthes of Mythologies assumes something not a long way away from what Freud assumes. He assumes that if you show or tell people what informs the bourgeois mythologies by which and under which they live, then they'll be able, in some sense, to free themselves. Just as Freud believes that if you bring unconscious contents into the conscious mind, the rational mind will deal with them and will give you power over your malaise.

We can go one of two ways, neither of them particularly attractive. The romantic way, the one which I think you've suggested, is that we can say there's something extracontextual, extrasocietal, something independent, free, which we can have access to by way of freeing ourselves from the social constraints which shape us. It's not attractive because the romantic revolution seems to have led nowhere, except into some kind of narcissism.

The other way is to say that Barthes is wrong; that there's no such thing as independent action. That even those actions he regards as independent, as recognition of the writerly, have to do with something in his background. I mean there's plenty of room in the bourgeois tradition for Barthes, for people who seem to think independently; there's room made for the maverick in the bourgeois tradition, and it may be no more than an expression of that Hyde Park Corner loophole that bourgeois structures allow.

If there is a third alternative - and here we come back to the solipsism question again - I don't see what it can be, I don't see the fulcrum on which a third choice could turn. I don't see what the God's-eye view is which we can adopt to arbitrate between these two. All we can do at this point is to go to something like introspection,or an empirical sifting through of data, or seizing upon data which we think is significant.

-- Yes. That's what I was going to suggest. Both 'writerly' and 'readerly' are text-interpreting notions, but you could try to step behind that to text-making notions, and you could simply say that the readerly writer lives with the tradition and the writerly writer attacks the tradition formally (in terms of form). That's totally non-Barthesian isn't it?

...

What was my point about 'incorrect'? Oh, that it was simply too judgmental of us. That if a student reads something symbolic - Verlaine, Empson, Auden - direct or higher-order symbolism as discursive, we can't call that 'incorrect'. But what we have to do is to consider the whole framework within which the student has that inappropriate response. It's a whole new subject area and I don't think we've discussed it. The range of modalities of types of listening is actually much narrower in the world at large than it is for us. So we can see when, according to our lights, they are reading something inappropriately, but *they* have no way of seeing it. They can't bootstrap out of that because there isn't anything else for them. If all they can listen to is the discursive, it may be an unteachable situation.

-- I see what you're saying and it's interesting. It in a way reverses what many have said, and what we ourselves have said at other times, about the relative *narrowness* of academic ways of doing things compared with ways of experiencing that go on outside. Here you're suggesting that it's the other way round: that in this particular there are frames available to academic ways of doing things that are *not* available outside. I'm inclined to agree with that. So that the question *here* would be - let me say something else before I go on to the methodological problems. There are theoretical problems involved. There's a case at this point for some kind of typology of reading. There's some very close work to be done on what particular frames we're using; that the problem with literary discussion is at this point that it's too impressionistic still, that it needs a data base of some sort. Not that these frames would be taken as objective or exhaustive but that at least both tutors and students should have a shared knowledge of what kinds of expectations are being promulgated. That's a practical move one could make.

-- The *type* of approach you're planning to use in your introduction to poetry thing would be the basis for a typology, because you're providing people with techniques precisely to help them bootstrap. Even if they only believe they've got one reading-listening mode; once you start giving them things like logical tools to work on their own reading methods with, and tools which practitioners themselves use (Pound's 'efficiency') then they might be able to create another form of reading. Once they've got two forms of reading then they can have ten, or twenty. The problem for most of them is they've only got one, and they can't see it's a problem because they think that reading is just one thing.

...

-- One example occurred to me. The situation was that I was in a first year tutorial and I'd given them two poems to read. One was Donne's 'Death be not proud' and the other was Milton's 'On Time'. Actually I'd given them the poems in the other order (I'd mentioned Milton first and they'd taken them down in that way). We were talking about the poems for about twenty minutes I think and by and large agreeing. It was a class where there was a lot of agreement going on. We'd struck up some kind of rapport.

-- Agreement is a good thing?

-- Perhaps not? I was referring to the Milton text. We were talking about it in a general way. They were chipping in. The conversation was going on. There were a couple of flat spots where we didn't quite seem to be engaging - a couple of veiled interpretations of lines which I interpreted in a way which would enable me to keep talking about the Milton poem and for them to keep engaging with me. It was really quite a lively discussion and, one felt, quite productive.

-- Convergent?

-- Yes. At about the twenty minute mark it became clear that I'd been talking about and referring to Milton's 'On Time' while they'd been talking about and referring to Donne's 'Death be not proud'! To place this in our discussion: up to the twenty minute mark we'd been having what might be pretty close to an immediate (relatively unmediated) experience of the text and of each other. We hadn't noticed that we were talking about different texts. At the twenty minute mark it became clear that we were. I made a joke of it. Everybody recognised something that they hadn't recognised before. What did we do with this? We did two things. The first thing that happened was that there was a strong tendency on the part of the group not to deny their earlier readings, not to deny our earlier agreement, even though these had been generated by reference to two different texts. In other words what was predominant was our agreement - the meanings that we were making, and they tried very hard, and I think on the whole they succeeded, in shoring up the agreement that we'd had, radically reinterpreting the poetry so that it would fit the frame that we'd decided to put around it. We were, of course, projected out of the luxuriance of the enjoyment of agreement and we saw where we really stood. Where we stood was that we were making our own meanings and agreeing upon them, and the text was simply prompting us. We were much more contingently involved with the text than many of these first year students might have expected. What happened then was that they saw the point in a way that they would not have been able to see it before about, for example, the writer's intention being a very tenuous way to try to focus meaning - a very dubious way. One could have spoken to them at length and not got through in anything like this way at all, but because they were distancing themselves from the original experience, because they'd been able to work out from their practical experience to the theoretical component, they really did get the point about intention, were not disturbed by it at all. They were taking it back into the heart of that experience which we'd just had; accepted it; got to grips with it. So here again, working out from a practical base, it's much easier to see the importance of the theoretical level and from then on the class has been much more critically aware, and adept and not frightened, much better able to follow their own instincts.

This kind of distancing is actually a way of clarifying in such cases the types of reading that people are able to perform. It's not necessarily, as it's often represented, a way of confusing them.

-- This seems crucial to me from a mere, if it's mere, pedagogical point of view, that if people suffer from having only one mode of reading available, then one way of inducing other types would be to develop theoretical distance in practical situations.

-- Yes, I agree.

-- So how could this be done in a day by day way? It could be done by adopting some semi-outrageous critical positions in respect of a text and, assuming that the students are going to take a lowest-common-denominator reading, then make them see how the two can converge.

-- Yes.

-- It's a paradox isn't it?

-- Yes.

-- We're talking about close listening to reading and we're saying it's only possible by going away from the text.

-- That's right.

-- Only by being aware of the fact that you're making the text can you be aware of everything there that could be seen to be in the text.

-- Yes.

-- Yes. That's old hat, is it?

-- I don't think it is, because current practice in English Departments, I gather, still is to try to involve students directly with an appreciation of the poetry.

-- I like that 'I gather'. That's a nice distancing factor.

-- And that appreciation is basically uncritical, basically dissolves any distance between the reader and the poetry. It refuses to acknowledge or recognise the distance. This distancing is my basic understanding of what listening is. Even when one is talking about a provisional reader one is listening to a reading that's being made. Listening, I take it, is something which is closer to the present, closer to vocalisation even if you're not doing that to it. When we're adopting the methods you suggest (deliberately adopting the heresy of paraphrase, or the intentionalist fallacy or whatever it might be) we're offering them a way of listening to what they would have been doing, and hearing themselves quite clearly, where previously that might have been obscured from them altogether. In fact it might be the only way as far as I can see. Simply saying 'listen to yourself read' would be totally counterproductive presumably.

-- Yes.

-- I don't know if there's a cultural difference of any

importance. It seems to me quite likely that a lot of people do read with zero listening; that is, it's just ocular, marks on the page to marks on the brain, and there's no audition at all. I take it that that's one of the reasons why the notion of 'tone' in listening studies is very difficult for students (and a lot of critics) to get hold of. And tone must be to do with listening.
-- I think that that one is an immense problem which is simply swept under the carpet. It's simply ignored. Surely one of the basic hints to interpretation is the tone of voice. And you can't translate tone of voice accurately to (or from) written script. If we're taking the intention of the speaker, or merely a piece of tape, putting the speaker's intention to one side, any attempt to translate that to a page of script is going to show what is a substantial part of its meaning.
-- Even if you put a tone of voice analysis on top of it you don't recreate it.

The notion of tone is at the centre of our trying to say that theory can never be ignored. Because tone, by definition, must be created by the listening process.

The tone of a poem can only be provided by the reader who is listening in some mode or modes. That's an axiomatic indication that the reader must make the meanings.

...

-- As the transcriber I suppose I've seen more of what we've said and I suddenly realise I haven't really been thinking properly about the phrase 'the art of listening while reading poetry'. In this context 'listening' is both a metaphor and is very literal. You are listening to the euphoniousness of things - metre and assonance and many other things which are thrust upon us at too young an age. But taking up the notion of distancing again, when you are reading you're listening to a completely abstract connection betweeen what the text suggests and who you are. (It's no longer anything to do with the text.) And those two are in some kind of resonance.
-- Who's listening?
-- I'm listening. I'm reading a text. I am listening but not to metre. I'm listening to the resonances between what I currently construe as my self and selves - the internal, inchoate, unspeakable me and something prompted by the text. Hence abstract - quite a high level of abstraction.
-- So what poetry is doing for you is setting aside a part of your mentality as specialised, projecting you into a frame of mind where you can judge amongst selves. Is that it?
-- That's part of it, yes, but that is resultative. What I'm trying to focus on is a completely abstract component or process.
-- It's almost a definition of poetry you're arriving at.
-- There's text on my hands: part of listening is metre,

collocation, syntax, lexis, metaphor and the melding of all those merely linguistic. That's a fairly concrete notion of listening. What I'm trying to say is that there's a higher order of that concrete listening which is more abstract, which grows out of that concrete listening, but is of a different type in Russell's terms. In that higher-order listening what I'm doing is deriving something from the first order of listening and I'm deriving it cyclically, interactively also from what I need. But I don't even know what I need.
-- At the first level there are two totally disparate 'things': the text and my selves as currently construed. Then I read. And the listening I do takes me away from the text and it takes me away from my pre-reading pre-listening construal of who I am. So the one lifts the other. But then there is a kind of fusion of those two: a redefinition of 'me' (my selves) by the higher order listening, and a redefinition of what the higher order listening is by my selves. And this is where I wanted to bring context in.
-- If you're lucky, if you're having a good day as a reader, your whole life can be changed by a poem. It's a kind of listening (I can't get hold of it properly) which depends on - you used a lovely metaphor earlier on that by distancing you somehow swoop closer to the poem - what I'm trying to say here is that by letting that higher order listening and that newly dislocated sense of self interact you can swoop into the subconscious. You can see the manifest/immanent range of selves that you could be. (That's too much?)
-- No. It makes a lot of sense to me. You're really explaining a comment of yours from last time which was something like this: you listen to the internal conversation, but at some point it becomes non-linguistic.

What you've offered is a definition of poetry according to the effect it has on your ability, the way it prompts or primes your ability (perhaps always implicit) to distinguish between selves which are otherwise irresolute. You're taking my remarks about distancing from the poem in order to get back to the poem and transferring them to the realm where they really belong which is what happens in the psychology of the person when this sort of movement is going on. It complements that image I was dealing with earlier.
-- What interests me about this is that the primary evidence - OK we've just grazed against the necessity or the irrefutability of solipsism a few times -
-- I want to come back to that by the way, centrally.
-- OK. What I'm suggesting here is that. (What you've just said indicates this.) We can't get through this problem because we're lumbered with this metaphor of listening. Listening implies a source and a goal. Picking up what you were saying about Eliot, what I'm trying to suggest is that you can't write unless you listen to your self. Take that in Lacanian terms. You can't write until, at least to some

extent, you can tap the subconscious. (I'm assuming that's a possible interpretation of Eliot.)

When the writer is listening to the subconscious that's one side of the pattern. But the reader also listens to his self. So all the text is a completely transparent current which, if it's successful, is not between a source and a listener, but between two listeners; those listeners turn out to be the same because they're both listening to something non-linguistic viz. their subconscious.

-- I'm persuaded by this against every theoretical tide that I can discern because if you're right you're positing a confluence of subconscious minds which totally knocks on the head any notion of solipsism altogether.

-- But this is what I want to say - it doesn't - though it appears to do so.

-- Why not then?

-- It knocks solipsism on the head if what we're talking about is rational, conceptual, linguistic communicability. But if we're talking about communicability sub-lingua, under the tongue, then solipsism is still intact. We're communicating not because of, but in spite of, language. The poet's joy when he succeeds is that the transparent cement between two subconsciouses works <u>in spite of</u> the vehicle being linguistic. It seems to me that that is beautifully balanced between the irrefutable necessity of solipsism and the fact that no one can actually live with it. If we didn't have poets solipsism would be a great deal starker. It's precisely because the poet uses that vehicle (language) to deny itself that solipsism is both there but mollified.

-- I take as a small indication that you may be right, that in going through social preferences and social movements of our time you find that poetry has become less popular, less influential, do we agree?

-- Yes.

-- At a time when the privatisation of consciousness in a very unhelpful way (anomie, plain loneliness) is becoming more and more recognised. The second thing, and maybe more important, is that we have to be quite sure that we're clear that we're making a distinction between your use of solipsism with which I'm inclined to agree (that is that the poetic refutes/ confutes it), and solipsism as it's usually, generally understood. Solipsism in this sense is the absence of assurance that there's communication of <u>any</u> sort, of <u>any</u> sort. I don't think it means absence of communication through language merely. Here, we're positing not only a form of communication which is extra-linguistic but one which is prompted by the linguistic.

-- But if I do that [**the speaker slaps and holds the hearer's arm**] is not that communication? You can feel the heat my hand and your pain cells are ready to get it again right? Is that communication?

A Conversation

-- You´ve got a problem because it only becomes communication when we talk about it. How can I specify the immediate without language? If we use the term ´solipsism´ we´re already using language, using something which is philosophically, lexically, linguistically, comprehended and we´ve got a problem, a circle which is so tight that it´s at the very inception of usage itself.
-- OK. So let´s relax the definition of solipsism a bit and say whether it´s metaphysical or epistemic, not that it is impossible to have knowledge blah blah blah but that there is no guarantee that the knowledge will be reliable. On this definition, what I´ve said about the transparent permeable window between subconsciousnesses that´s made possible by the pain of the poet is not a refutation of that type of solipsism.
-- I need more.
-- A poet, with great pain, consults his subconscious and expresses it in a vehicle of signifiers. A reader, possibly with equal pain, works at that string of signifiers to enable him to consult his subconscious. That´s all. I´m saying that in the ideal case the types of pain and the types of consultation between subconsciouses might be measurable, they might have some qualitative characteristic in common. God knows how you could specify it, but I´m not concerned about that.
-- I don´t think you can break the circle by appealing to feelings. It seems to me that you can only go one of two ways. We can weld the terminology and try to talk about the impossibility as I take it (as you know I´m not convinced by any of the philosophical arguments against solipsism) of refuting solipsism. If we´re talking about it in terms of theory, then we´re using language, and we can´t break out of it that way. Unfortunately we can´t break out of it by appealing to our feelings either. Not only because we make the case of our feelings linguistically (as you did when slapping my arm), but also because feelings as such, when appealed to, are not in themselves proof that the solipsistic circle is broken. One imagines or feels that bridges are thrown across by means of poetry, which are not thrown across by other methods of discourse between person and person. That feeling is demonstrably no proof against solipsism. We shouldn´t deride the empirical world: people have felt all kinds of things with great intensity and passion, including the fact that the world is flat, which most people would no longer subscribe to.

...

-- I wanted to say something about context. People talk about context as if it was easily publicly agreeable; I just want to say that context is infinitely subtle and unspecifiable

because it is, for each individual, on each occasion, some refraction of his or her inexpressible conscious and unconscious experience of living. (Context is not, contra Parker-Rhodes, a set of unspoken, but speakable, sentences; but rather, who you are, who you believe you are, who you have been, who you could be.)
-- This is good because it leads me into deja-vu. But let me support what you're saying. The points you've made are the points that are relevant. In addition there is an interesting distinction between people who think of themselves as literary and those who think of themselves as scientific. There's been a vogue since the '50s or '60s of people recognising fiction as being fictional and leaking this into ordinary life. There are articles from social psychologists about the way people daydream, the way people fictionalise their own lives. So the join between real life and fiction is totally indiscernible. It's recognised that people make up stories about themselves all the time. The stories are ongoing. Now what are these stories if not ever-shifting, ever changing contexts. The contexts you make for the utterances which are made about you and by you aren't suitable to you, therefore you change those contexts, you change the story about yourself. You sit at a factory bench and you make up a story about yourself winning the lottery... What I had to say about deja-vu bears on this all important question of context. Context is continually, amazingly fertile, it's ongoing, and privately projected, private. And if one's context for oneself overlaps with the context of another, then my suspicion is that we do that to our context (by fictionalising if necessary) in order to gain support. (This fits with your question of why readers read, and why writers write.) Because we need to survive and to do that we need other people to agree with us and shore up our notion of what is excellent, what we think is excellent, and thus the excellence which we ourselves publicly manifest.
-- Even that may be a terminology problem: 'one's context may overlap with another'. It's impossible that that be the case. We may be prepared to impute to the context of the other some overlap with our own (though because of its immanence, latency, inexpressibility, we can never know) but even to so impute is a voluntary giving up of the true nature of our experience. Experience is private, inexpressible, incommunicable...
-- Your point about context is that it's much more definitive than usually recognised. I think that deja-vu is a good example of that. It seems to be something which people chat about and decide about without really examining the context which they're creating for the decision they make. There's some kind of undeclared conversation with oneself that goes on. What interests me are the premises beneath it. I'm also interested here - picking up from before - in the way in which private context comes to be projected into the socio-

political arena, and comes to seem normative. A lot of our squabbles as human beings, very serious squabbles involving the deaths of many many people, have to do with the lack of recognition of what is essentially private (or what cannot be demonstrated to be not private) being projected onto the public sphere as a norm. And then the projectors fight tooth and nail and commit genocide in order to have their theoretically very shaky idea of normativeness accepted by other people. Let's take deja-vu as an example: a small, modest, non-genocidal model.

We can go one of two ways with a case of deja-vu. We can say that it's an instance of what we might call the numinal: that the experience is an indication of actual connection with cosmos as it's not usually experienced. Or: we can take the physicalist line and say that the experience can be explained by reference to the unusual behaviour of the cells of the brain (some kind of electrical discharge). My interest here is not in the details, which I don't know anything about, but in the reasons for adopting these attitudes.

When the physicalist view is preferred, it's preferred because intellection (explanation) is thought to be superior to a consultation of the way one feels about these things. When the numinal view is adopted it's because feelings are consulted before an explanation is sought. It's not important, in a sense, which way one goes, but mark that a preference has to be evidenced, and that one's sense of the world will be dependent on this undeclared premise. This is the kind of decision that goes on undiscovered, unrevealed, sub rosa.

-- For a long time.

-- Just to finish off this stuff about deja-vu. What I'm saying is that it's an instance of the way in which we must be careful to try to work, so far as possible, down to the premise beneath the premise of an apparently self-sufficient experience.

This is a VERY IMPORTANT POLITICAL POINT that we're making out of our talk about listening to poetry and the way we decide about poetry. (I'm taking deja-vu as 'poetic', that is immanent, experience.) Unless we're clear, unless we hook onto these experiences critically, it's not too much to say this: we're going to go around killing each other, because we don't believe the same way, because we don't interpret in the same way. We're going to be prisoners of our ideology. And we're going to be prisoners of our ideology because we don't understand that these ideas of normativeness are STUPID. These ideas of normativeness are the result of not working down quietly and with average intelligence (I emphasise average) to the premises beneath decisions about experiences which are apparently self-sufficient.

This is why Pol Pot killed 1,500,000 of his own people; that is why Hitler made war on the world, because these people thought the rest of the world was stupid because it did not see things in their normative way. And we go on and on and on in the same way.

The study of poetry and the critical appreciation of poetry is very important because it's a useful laboratory way of sorting out the ways in which one reasons about one's world. It's important to the extent that, carried on into the political sphere, that line of reasoning, that way of thinking can save people's lives. And if anyone says that the critical sense that comes from poetry is not important, then that person is saying that the cost in human lives is also not important.

-- Right. On.

...

[The speakers did indeed go on. No doubt in some way or another, in solitude or in other company, they are continuing the conversation. For the sake of the proportions of this book, however, we make this arbitrary ending. EDITORS]

EIGHT

SHAKESPEARE AND THE LISTENER

R.S.White

Conversations are events which we would all, presumably, say we have been involved in from time to time. Therefore, they have the rare merits of not only being suitable subjects for close, even analytical inspection, but also democratically open in the sense that anybody can offer an opinion which will be as valid as the next person's. It can also be presumed that those who choose to read this essay will have had at some time the experience of watching or reading the dialogues in Shakespeare's plays, as a set of created or artificial (in the most precise sense) conversations intended to be enacted by living people on the stage, who will seek to convince us that their roles and discussions are as 'real', if only observed and overheard, as those we become engaged in outside the theatre in our own unscripted language. The consequence of these two presumptions is a third. A close inspection of what goes on in Shakespeare's dialogues, informed by a commonsense reference to our own individual understandings of conversation can reflect analytically upon what we do in our own social interactions, while at the same time lighting up some of the recognisably 'human' qualities of Shakespeare's texts.

In order to create a context for discussion, I ask for a 'greeting of the spirit' (Keats's phrase) in asking a naive question of myself and offering as honest an answer as I can manage. When I say 'I had a good conversation with X today', what do I mean? Obviously not a single thing, nor even necessarily a similar thing whenever I say it, but some essentials can probably be abstracted. I would almost certainly mean that I became aware of X's presence through his/her responses, and felt reasonably confident that X was aware of my presence through my responses. This would account for the words 'conversation with' as distinct from 'diatribe to' or 'sermon from'. There was mutual awareness and a belief that we were listening to each other, although the only source for such a belief is an observed responsiveness to each other. What about a <u>good</u> conversation? Here I could mean a range of things. We seemed to be understanding each other throughout, we seemed to reach agreement after some false starts or misunderstandings, individually we seemed to become spurred by what the other was saying into an excited responsiveness, we seemed to be discovering something together in a train of logic or association which was helped along by the questions/statements/answers offered by the other. I may have seen or understood something I had never before realized, or reached an idea or feeling which I would probably not have formulated in such a way without somebody helping me. Or X expressed a change of opinion precipitated or influenced by what I had said in answer to his/her ideas ... and so on. What gathers all these feelings together (whether X shared them or not) is a personal experience of the unexpected outcome from what might have started as a bored, apparently predictable, even ritualistic exchange. If we did not so readily ignore or take for granted the mystery of the commonplace (what Dickens calls 'the romance of the familiar'), we should describe this whole process as a miracle. But the main point I wish to make is that the process itself, at every step as we are forced to explain it, depends on notions of responsiveness, listening, interacting and interpreting - and not primarily on speaking, saying, uttering. What we <u>hear</u> is what enables us to <u>speak</u>, and what we say is what enables the other to hear and speak, and so on. It is the listening function which is, far from being passive, of prime creative importance in determining the direction and future course of a conversational interaction. If either party neglects the speaking function (by a nod or a wink) he is still involved in a conversation; but if either party abdicates listening and responding, the conversation is over. A conversation is defined by responsive hearers, not by eloquent speakers, and it is the function of 'active listening' which dictates the direction in which speakers proceed.

You, the reader, may have found already so much to disagree with, qualify, or reflect upon in what I have already 'uttered' that you may wish to stop reading, discuss the issues with somebody else ('talk about it'), debate them inwardly, think about the substance, ask for clarification, or move onto the next section of the essay, or simply put it aside in boredom. In every case, your reaction is confirming my analysis, for it is your response that determines our next step. It is your choice of a level of interest and hearing which leads into the future, and what I have written for you is merely an occasion or a <u>con</u>text for your ideas, a basis for your creation of 'a text' from 'the writing'. On the other hand, since I am engaged in writing rather than speaking, my listener (reader) is either imputed or nobody but myself. Therefore, I can impose choices about the direction of the argument. For example, what I do not choose to develop in this essay (although the subject is important and implicit) is the nature of the response of a reader or an audience to Shakespeare's plays, the sort of problems raised in so-called Reception Theory or Reader-Response Criticism. Instead, I shall be examining the ways in which Shakespeare constructs and conducts conversations between his fictional characters, and later the ways in which listening can be seen as a central concern at the 'thematic' level of his plays. Furthermore, in the discussion that follows I do not expect to <u>prove</u> the proposition that listeners determine the direction of conversations in Shakespeare, but instead to show that it is a proposition which is not contradicted by the evidence, can be amply illustrated, and, satisfying Popper's criterion, that it is useful in providing analytical insights into the phenomenon of Shakespearean conversation.

SHAKESPEARE'S CONVERSATIONS

Literary critics, while tacitly acknowledging what every audience knows, that characters in Shakespeare's plays hold responsive 'conversations' with each other, have never investigated the matter with anything like the rigour they apply to other subjects (character, imagery, ideas, etc.). And yet surely if we want criticism to follow questions genuinely raised in the theatrical experience, or in the experience of reading, the topic should be somewhere at the top of our agenda.

Some critics do at least recognise the centrality of conversation and interaction between characters:

> ...the manner of [*As You Like It*], when once it settles down in the forest, is to let two people drift together, talk a little, and part, to be followed by two more. Sometimes a pair will be watched by others, who will sometimes comment on what they see. Sometimes of course there is a larger group, once or twice even a crowded stage; but most often two at a time. When they part they may arrange to meet again, or they may not ... it is rare that anything happens in any particular encounter between these people of the sort that changes the course of their lives , anything, that is to say, that goes to make what is usually called a plot. Yet the meetings may properly be called 'encounters', because of the impact the contrasting characters make on one another and the sparkle of the wit they kindle in one another. (Jenkins, 1955, p. 50).

The play, then, is centrally one of 'conversation' and we should expect that the task of criticism is not to presuppose this but to analyse it. On *As You Like It* in particular, a start has been made by Joan Rees in her book *Shakespeare and the Story: Aspects of Creation* (Rees, 1978) in an elegant and sensitive chapter called 'Doing without Events; or the Art of Conversation' which extends commentary to Twelfth Night:

> In a 'conversation scene', a scene in which Shakespeare 'does without events', the talk at once conceals and reveals a network of responses and reactions whose vibrations decisively affect the development of the play (Rees, 1978, p. 90).

The writer effectively draws attention to the 'artistry' of such scenes, but she by no means exhausts the rich vein she has opened in drawing attention away from large, abstract concerns and towards the minutiae of the dialogue. Another critic, equally helpful but equally limited in scope, in writing on Measure for Measure takes as his belief that 'it is precisely confrontation of characters, in specific predicaments, that I am trying to reinstate at the expense of thematic concerns' (Maxwell, 1974, p. 14). Even his tone indicates that our subject, 'the Art of Conversation', supremely important in the theatre and surely also to the reader, has been overthrown or neglected in the critical study of Shakespeare.

Why? The general answer seems to be that the tools for analysing verbal interaction are not so well developed as those used in discussing either the content of dialogue (at the expense of form) or, when matters of form are addressed, they are discussed only from the point of view of one function in conversing - speaking. We talk happily of puns and quibbles, wit, stichomythia and soliloquy, of rhyming and blank verse, of poetry and prose and of the tone in which something is said. But what have these matters, undoubtedly of academic interest, to tell us about 'the impact the contrasting characters make on each other...'? They give information about how something is said but not how it is received and therefore not how the conversation develops. They leave out the magical process whereby reception and response determine the next stage of the dialogue, the meaning which has been discovered or created by a listener from the words of a speaker.

For example, Love's Labour's Lost is always seen as a play in which people have an effect on each other through discourse, and yet how many of the following randomly collected comments tell us much about the interaction between people?

> The dominant theme of this play ... is the overwhelming event of the English language and all that had been happening to it in the last twenty years or so (Willcock, 1934, pp. 8-9).

Judging from such a statement the characters are defined solely by their individual accent, idiom and vocabulary, in short by how they say things.

> Navarre has the tendency to want words to match his wishes. Words are his servants. There is a slight but unmistakeable, touch of oafishness about him; a favourite word of his is 'chat' ... 'chat' is the utterance of a man who does not understand words, and does not respect them (Berry, 1969, p. 70).

More interesting this, because the critic hovers on the edge of saying that Navarre is a bad listener, but instead switches to concentrate upon 'utterance'. He ignores the context in which the King's statements are exposed as vacuous 'chat' even though it should be clear that the context must be central in forming this judgment. The context, as commonsense tells us, crucially involves hearers who respond to the King's statements, and our feeling about him come largely from how he reacts or fails to react - the quality of his responsiveness. In one particular moment at the end of Love's Labour's Lost, for example, we are shown the insensitivity of a man who, after hearing news of the death of his beloved's father, having witnessed her grief-stricken state, merely returns to a proposal of marriage as if nothing has happened. We know of his tactlessness not primarily through the content of his statement (in another situation, indeed, it might have been sensitive), but through our awareness of the context as monitored by the Princess's reaction which starkly pinpoints the King's callous listening: 'I understand you not; my griefs are double' (V.ii.740). Are these things so obvious that they do not need stating, let alone analysing? Or has the critical procedure, by and large, given us conclusions as if they are premises, without revealing, investigating or even acknowledging the existence of the process which throws up the conclusion? I believe there is more evidence to support the latter than the former possibility, even though it leads us close to the position of virtually having to begin all over again in our analysis of Shakespearean conversation.

In order to explain more satisfactorily, and analyse more acutely, the ways in which Shakespearean dialogue appears to imitate the strategies of plausible conversations which in turn depend upon active listening, we must look at the context in which a statement is made rather than dwelling solely on the content of a series of utterances as if they are more or less isolated from what they grow out of and what follows them. When dealing with words on a page (or on the stage) put into the mouths of 'characters' apparently speaking to each other, the context that really matters is how the statement is received. This means looking closely at the response of the listener. To actors rehearsing their parts this will be self-evident, if not fully conscious, because they must accept that in choosing a 'tone' in which to deliver a line they automatically look at what it is supposed to answer, and what the next speaker reveals about how his line has been understood.

Without arguing that only Shakespeare among his contemporary dramatists reproduces recognisable conversations, nor that he is invariably successful in doing so, an initial contrast might clarify what underlies much of his reproduced conversation. Here is a dramatic dialogue from Marlowe's _Tamburlaine the Great_:

Re-enter Techelles

Techelles. I have fulfill'd your highness' will, my lord:
Thousands of men, drown'd in Asphaltis' lake,
Have made the water swell above the banks,
And fishes, fed by human carcasses,
Amaz'd, swim up and down the waves,
As when they swallow assafoetida,
Which makes them fleet aloft and gasp for air.
Tamburlaine. Well, then, my friendly lords, what now remains
But that we leave sufficient garrison,
And presently depart to Persia,
To triumph after all our victories?
Theridamus. Ay, good my lord, let us in haste to Persia;
And let this captain be remov'd the walls
To some high hill about the city here.
Tamburlaine. Let it be so; - about it, soldiers; -
But stay: I feel myself distemper'd suddenly.
Techelles. What is it dares distemper Tamburlaine?
Tamburlaine. Something, Techelles; but I know not what. -
But forth, ye vassals! whatsoe'er it be,
Sickness or death can never conquer me.
(_Exeunt_)

The primary effect of this dialogue is to give us information about what is happening at the level of story. Each statement adds to our knowledge of the sequence of events. Only Techelles' 'What is it _dares_...' gives us a hint of information about the 'character' of Tamburlaine and the way the world views him, and it is the exception that proves the rule that narrative dominates the dialogue. Although each statement has signals of responsiveness ('Well, then ...') the effect is not one of naturalistic conversation. This is not to say it is 'inferior' dialogue, but that it has a different function which is largely to do with advancing the narrative rather than revealing what is happening between the people. The way we know this lies in the analytical perception that each personage is _speaking_ rather than responding. Although fairly insignificant in itself, the passage is not untypical of Marlowe's drama in general and _Tamburlaine_ in particular.

It is essentially a speaker's play and the absence (or the only very occasional existence of) conversational responses is an indication of its extroverted, rhetorical, basically narrative manner.

As a contrast, take this snatch of dialogue from Shakespeare's Julius Caesar, a play which is just as much concerned with power, politics and 'historical' narrative as Tamburlaine:

> Brutus. What means this shouting? I do fear the people
> Choose Caesar for their king.
> Cassius. Ay, do you fear it?
> Then must I think you would not have it so.
> Brutus. I would not Cassius; yet I love him well.
> But wherefore do you hold me here so long?
> What is it that you would impart to me?
> (Julius Caesar, I.ii.79-84)

This extract, although brief, is typical of a section lasting some 170 lines. The obvious point is that the lines could not be put into the mouth of a single speaker. It is an encounter between two independent speakers not only imparting information to each other but measuring and adapting their counter-statements in the light of what they have heard. They are holding a conversation in a way that Marlowe's characters did not, even though both passages are integral parts of the respective 'plots' in each play. Each man in the passage from Shakespeare shows himself to be consciously aware of what the other is saying, the respondent in each case linking his statement to the one he follows. The specific linking is subtly different on each occasion, and the difference depends upon what the hearer chooses to hear and respond to. Cassius catches the word 'fear' rather than lazily interpreting it as 'think' as a less motivated listener might do. Brutus then responds to what he regards as a conversational strategy adopted by Cassius, whom he sees as 'holding' him, for a reason which has not yet been explained. Readers of the whole passage will realize that Cassius is involved in testing Brutus's attitudes to Caesar, and is waiting until he is sure of his ground before he makes any explicit statement about the conspiracy to murder Caesar. By pouncing on insignificant words rather than merely following the drift, Cassius is revealing himself as a selective listener on the lookout for certain hints. It is not clear whether Brutus knows this or not, but at least we can say that from Cassius's point of view there is a 'subtext' underneath the interaction and he is involved in 'decoding' it. When Brutus asks for explanation he is at least recognising that Cassius has not been ingenuous and that he is 'up to something'. By simply paying attention to the ways in which the men are listening to each other, we become more acutely aware of the 'network of responses and reactions whose vibrations decisively affect the development of the play' (Rees, 1978, p. 90). Although again it is a small example, it is not unrepresentative and some conclusions can be drawn which will have broader significance in the analysis of Shakespearean dialogue: (1) Shakespeare represents in his dramatic dialogue more of the complexities of spoken, unspoken and selective interaction than does Marlowe: that is, he has given a representation of a _conversation_ rather than a set of statements designed to give information to the audience about the action alone. (2) We can draw this conclusion from our perception that each person is _listening_ to the other, and responding, each with subtly different things in mind, depending on indvidual preconceptions. (3) The contrasted passages, one of which we see as a conversation and the other not, illustrate the fact that what we call a conversation is identified not by the content of one statement as it is spoken, but by the way it is heard and answered - in short, by the listening function.

The kind of analysis conducted above would, I believe, if systematically carried through, enable us to define with a new precision the radical differences between the kinds of drama written by the two greatest dramatists of the 1590s. Shakespeare's rival in the years after 1600 was Ben Jonson whose _forte_ was wit, a mode used also by Shakespeare but with some differences. Here is the climax of _Volpone_ as the scavengers gather to hear Volpone's 'will', as the parasite Mosca takes an inventory of the possessions:

(_Mosca gives them the will and continues writing_)
Corbaccio. Is that the will?
Mosca. Down-beds, and bolsters -
Volpone. (_aside_) Rare!
Be busy still. Now they begin to flutter;
They never think of me. Look, see, see, see!
How their swift eyes run over the long deed
Unto the name, and to the legacies,
What is bequeathed them there.
Mosca. Ten suits of hangings -
Volpone. (_aside_) Ay, i'their garters, Mosca. Now their hopes
Are at the gasp.
Voltore. Mosca the heir?
(_Volpone_, V.i.15-22)

The dominant mode here is satirical wit, but it depends on our relish of a situation rather than the way the people converse. Volpone interprets on behalf of the audience, enjoying the ironies of a situation where everybody thinks him dead and reveal the greed of potential legatees. Meanwhile, Mosca stage-manages the scene by ignoring the others and casually allowing them to make the fatal discovery that it is he himself who is named in the will as heir. The whole strategy of the scene exemplifies the classical and Renaissance concept of satire and wit, the Schadenfreud of characters with superior knowledge, closely collaborating with the audience, taking amusement from the discomfort and distress of caricatures who have diminished knowledge and exaggerated traits of folly and vice. It is humour of manipulation and power (even Volpone and then Mosca are exploited later) where character is essentially subservient, not to narrative as in Marlowe, but to 'plot' in the more conspiratorial sense. The information released to the audience by Jonson tends to diminish 'character' in the Shakespearean sense at least, for the people surprise us in their ingenuity (or lack of it) rather than in their capacity for change or for complex verbal and emotional interaction. Through his dramatic strategy the playwright enhances the sense of a witty social and economic pattern playing itself out, since the events and 'discoveries' and modes of manipulation do surprise us. As with Marlowe but for different reasons, to speak of 'conversation' is largely irrelevant to the enjoyment of this kind of theatre. On the other hand, we can identify people reacting and responding, not to each other but to events. The predators are not listening to each other but rather they are listening for information about their gulls which will allow them to exercise power. There is more acute listening in Jonson's witty plays than in Marlowe's pageants, but it is still not the conversational listening (sometimes as an end in itself) which we find in Shakespeare. It is, rather, listening which gives power or dominance.

Shakespeare does sometimes use the Jonsonian form of domineering, situational wit, especially in The Comedy of Errors and the 'eavesdropping' scene in Love's Labour's Lost and so we must be careful not to generalise too far. But the kind of wit which is more normally associated with his drama is rather different:

Don Pedro. In faith, lady, you have a merry heart.
Beatrice. Yea, my lord; I thank it, poor fool, it keeps on the windy side of care. My cousin tells him in his ear that he is in her heart.
Claudio. And so she doth, cousin.
Beatrice. Good lord, for alliance! thus goes every one to the world but I, and I am sunburnt; I may sit in a corner and cry 'heigh-ho for a husband'!
Don Pedro. Lady Beatrice, I will get you one.
Beatrice. I would rather have one of your father's getting. Hath your Grace ne'er a brother like you? Your father got excellent husbands, if a maid could come by them.
Don Pedro. Will you have me, lady?
Beatrice. No, my lord, unless I might have another for

> working-days; your Grace is too costly to wear every day. But, I beseech your Grace, pardon me; I was born to speak all mirth and no matter.
>
> Don Pedro. Your silence most offends me, and to be merry best becomes you; for, out o'question, you were born in a merry hour.
>
> (Much Ado About Nothing, II.i.281-300)

Such a 'civil war of wits' takes its energy from a centre which is rather different from Jonson's. The characters are hardly furthering the action through the dialogue. They are only obliquely commenting on the events of the narrative, and there is no relevant manipulation occurring. The real point lies in what is revealed about how the characters think and feel about each other, and the means of revelation can be seen as multi-layered. Beatrice establishes the tone by answering Pedro's observation in a lighthearted way, keeping herself and him on 'the windy side of care'; but her mode of merriment then allows her to say something rather serious about herself (her desire for a husband) by first mentioning her cousin and without actually risking a serious response. If Pedro's reply is a veiled proposal, she deflects this by a verbal pun on 'get' to maintain the lightness, and he, protected by the general atmosphere of wit, apparently risks an overt intimacy in asking 'will you have me, lady?'. In theory such a statement could provoke a very serious or a very evasive answer. In fact, Beatrice parries it again with a more or less verbal play on work and pleasure, subtly reminding Pedro of the social difference between them by addressing him as 'your Grace' several times. But when she instantly realises that her words may seem like a blunt refusal to the 'costly' duke she politely excuses herself in a manner which enables Pedro honourably to retreat to his initial stance ('you were born in a merry hour'). The exchange is remarkable for how much could be found in its nuances. Has the Duke seriously proposed to Beatrice and been politely rebuffed? How deeply are her feelings engaged? Does he notice the skill with which she saves him embarrassment? All these emotional potentials have been kept under the surface of prevailing wit in the Shakespearean sense of the word. It would seem clear first that it is Beatrice who is establishing the tone in which intimacy can be proffered but withheld, and secondly that both characters are carefully collaborating to limit the extent of self-revelation. Fundamentally, each is responding to the other, intellectually and probably emotionally, and it is precisely this which is the 'point' of the dialogue. In plays like Much Ado, As You Like It and Twelfth Night this special, Shakespearean version of 'witty conversation' is the dominant and unique mode within which we instantly discriminate between those who listen carefully (Beatrice, Rosalind, Viola) from those who do not.

I have used the word 'tone' as if it can be taken for granted as a term of art. Literary critics as a group use it in a similarly loose sense and certainly not so strictly as linguists. Generally speaking, it means the same as when we describe conversationally the imputed attitude behind the manner of a statement: 'He spoke in an angry/resentful/ cheerful tone'. The stress is on imputed. I may say, attempting to be frank or straightforward, 'Did you know you made a mistake as chairman of the meeting yesterday?' hoping for a similarly frank, non-personalised discussion of the matter. If, however, the listener says 'I don't like your patronising tone' then I realise that what I had hoped for cannot now happen, since the listener has found in my statement a different level from the one intended. The listener's response governs the future of the conversation, since it may prove impossible for me to specify what I intended in such a way that the listener will proceed on that basis rather than his own chosen assumption. I may feel upset, frustrated, eventually angry that the situation seems to be irretrievable, but I cannot honestly believe that my statement was anything but a 'starter' to an interchange, holding in it a range of options which can (unexpectedly to me) be chosen by the listener, depending on his or her mood or personality. The classic, common experience is when a person, after offending somebody without having considered this result, expostulates 'I was only joking!' Tone, then, as understood in ordinary conversation, exists relevantly in how a statement is received rather than how it is uttered, since the former is the issue which will effect the future of the conversation. The same generalisation is helpful in dealing with tone in the literary or dramatic work.

Another example from Shakespeare may illustrate this important point.

> Rosalind. ... they are in the very wrath of love, and they will together. Clubs cannot part them.
>
> Orlando. They shall be married to-morrow; and I will bid the Duke to the nuptial. But, O, how bitter a thing it is to look into happiness through another man's eyes! By so much the more shall I to-morrow be at the height of heart-heaviness, by how much I shall think my brother happy in what he wishes for.
>
> Rosalind. Why, then, to-morrow I cannot serve your turn for Rosalind?
>
> Orlando. I can live no longer by thinking.
>
> Rosalind. I will weary you, then, no longer with idle talking ... If you do love Rosalind so near the heart as your gesture cries it out, when your brother marries Aliena shall you marry her.
>
> (*As You Like It*, V.ii.36-63 *passim*)

Taken out of context, it is impossible to impute a tone to Rosalind's first statement with any certainty that Orlando would agree, although actors and critics would wish to make some choice. On its own, it seems simply to be a statement that two people are about to copulate. But as soon as Orlando speaks, we can begin to define the significance of Rosalind's words from his point of view. He chooses to interpret the events she is describing as leading to a marriage, 'cleaning up' her message by ignoring the image she uses and instead using the formal word 'nuptial'. He then speaks of his own feelings, emphasising words which, if we take the option, could describe his tone of voice (the attitude imputed) - 'bitter' and filled with 'heart-heaviness' because he cannot marry and is envying his brother's happiness. Rosalind (who is in disguise although it would not much matter if Orlando knows this) asks a question which is designed, it seems, to elicit some clarifying response from Orlando. He has a range of responses available and he chooses one which glosses 'serve your turn' as a frustrating, mental game: 'I can live no longer by thinking'. We cannot yet say what attitude lies behind this (anger? yearning? reproof? poignancy? whimsicality?), and all we can be interested in is how Rosalind will respond, and which option she will choose to impute into his words. She chooses: 'I will weary you, then, no longer with idle talking', and she decides to alight upon his own stated topic, marriage, after at first avoiding it. The whole passage, small as it is, can be interpreted as marking a turning-point in the play, showing that apparently idle chatter is capable of carrying serious messages and effecting changes to the narrative and to the emotions, when the speakers are acting as independent respondents.

One conclusion to be drawn from this brief analysis is that we cannot rightly speak about the 'tone' in which a statement is spoken. We may impute a tone but there is no way of knowing if it was intended. What we can properly talk about is the way in which the statement is received by the listener who indicates what he has found in it. Each statement merely sets up a range of options (most of which the speaker will be ignorant of) and the response may be something which surprises the initial speaker. The exchange is a brilliant, miniature example of conversation as negotiation of the emotions and the mind alike. Here we are close to the mysterious heart of Shakespearean conversation. It is not centrally the spoken wit, or even the diversity of 'spoken' tones which dazzles us, but more the unpredictable range of responses which statements elicit from his fictional characters, that make us feel we are in a conversational world akin to our own. Shakespeare's people are 'characterised' for us not primarily by what they say or even how they say things, but by the extraordinarily diverse and surprising manners in which they listen and respond to each other.

In the examples we have looked at so far, the characters involved are, at least semi-consciously, testing each other, and they are more or less aware of what is going on in the conversation. The process becomes more complicated and exciting when the audience becomes involved with superior knowledge in an interchange where the characters are for some reason at cross-purposes.

> Desdemona. I say it is not lost.
> Othello. Fetch't, let me see't.
> Desdemona. Why, so I can, sir, but I will not now.
> This is a trick to put me from my suit:
> Pray you let Cassio be receiv'd again.
> Othello. Fetch me the handkerchief: my mind misgives.
> Desdemona. Come, come;
> You'll never meet a more sufficient man.
> Othello. The handkerchief!
> Desdemona. A man that all his time
> Hath founded his good fortunes on your love,
> Shar'd dangers with you -
> Othello The handkerchief!
> Desdemona. I'faith, you are to blame.
> Othello. Zounds!
> (EXIT OTHELLO)
> (*Othello*, III.iv.85-99)

The audience has prior knowledge of what is going on. Othello, assured by Iago that he will find 'proof' of Desdemona's adultery with Cassio by interrogating her as to the whereabouts of 'the handkerchief', thinks he is being met by evasion which, even more incriminating, involves Cassio's name. Desdemona, knowing none of this, is innocently trying to restore Cassio in Othello's estimation and service. At a superficial level, the audience is witnessing a 'misunderstanding', but it is clear that the two characters feel quite certain that they are understanding each other. We know that quite inadvertently Desdemona is inflaming Othello simply by mentioning Cassio's name, and we also know that Othello is forming a 'perfect understanding' from her words. Similarly, Desdemona in trying to make sense of her husband's somewhat odd obsession with her handkerchief, instead of realising there is a misconception, hits upon a formula which fits her sense of his character and of the moment: it is a practical joke to put her from her suit, a kind of domestic tease. She also believes she is in command of complete understanding, even as the evidence mounts that she is not. It is legitimate to say the audience does not necessarily have 'better' knowledge but instead it has access to a third 'perfect understanding' (that is, potentially just as imperfect as Othello's and Desdemona's). It is quite possible to say that there is not a misunderstanding but three, equally coherent systems of understanding, all held with equal conviction of the truth. Unless the parties realise something has gone wrong, they will continue to struggle to make sense of what is given to them in the context and the words they hear, constructing a point of view which excludes or accommodates contradictions. It is only when one or all systems break down that a misunderstanding can be acknowledged and rectified, and in the meantime misunderstandings are new understandings. Some such analysis as this lies at the centre of Iago's whole strategy of dividing people and undermining trust and relationship, so the discovery is of considerable significance for our understanding of the play as a whole. It is also a favourite ploy of Shakespeare's, perhaps reflecting the frequency with which such situations occur casually in our 'ordinary' social life, though rarely with such tragic consequences.

One of Shakespeare's most subtle and masterly deployments of the 'misunderstanding strategy' (more properly 'separate understandings') comes in Angelo's testing of Isabella in Measure for Measure. Spread over two long and intense scenes, spellbinding in the theatre, the process is too long to illustrate by quotation, but even a paraphrase gives an idea of the murky complexity of interaction. At first Angelo dismisses Isabella's plea that he, the law-enforcer, should pardon her brother for the sexual offence he has committed. He simply reiterates statements like 'I will not do't' (II.ii.51), resisting even appeals to mercy and pity on the legal maxim that hard cases make bad law. The young novice persists, vehemently and passionately attacking authority in a way which makes him say 'Why do you put these sayings upon me?' (II.ii.133). She replies that he, as an authority figure, may have some experience like Claudio's in his own memory, and should recall his humanity and soften his harsh judgment. At this stage Angelo speaks aside:

> She speaks, and 'tis
> Such sense that my sense breeds with it.
> (II.ii.141-2)

To the audience as eavesdroppers, the aside can hold different meanings, each of which may be equally valid. For those who know the play it can refer to Angelo's own skeleton in his cupboard, the relationship with Mariana which will disgrace him. Those who do not know this may think either that Angelo is taking Isabella's statement as she intended it and realising that even judges may err in their imaginations, or that irrespective of Isabella's message he is beginning to respond to her as a woman despite her own determination to exclude this dimension. Such is the force and ambiguity of 'breeds'. Inadvertently, Isabella sets up the conditions for a 'misunderstanding' if the third interpretation is the true one:

> *Isabella*. Hark how I'll bribe you; good, my lord, turn back.
> *Angelo*. How, bribe me?
> *Isabella*. Ay, with such gifts that heaven shall share with you.
> (II.ii.145-7)

As she leaves we learn again in private from Angelo that he, who has been immune to the strumpet's temptations, is sexually aroused by 'this virtuous maid'. It does not come as a great surprise, since we cannot help noticing the gradual change in his responses from curt abruptness to invitations to Isabella to prolong the interview. Shakespeare at this point breaks the scene, presumably because he wishes to give us the opportunity of hearing from Angelo the full power of his lust as it struggles with his religiosity, and because the dramatist is reserving his most potent effects for a later scene, II.iv. Given the information now available to the audience, we follow a whole gamut of inter-responsiveness between Angelo and Isabella, from his tentative advances, oblique insinuations which are met with Isabella's completely accidental appearance at one stage of acquiescence in worldly sin, to his dawning realisation that she either does not understand him or is deceiving him:

> Your sense pursues not mine; either you are ignorant
> Or seem so craftily; and that's not good.
> (II.iv.74-5)

It is precisely her 'ignorance' which pushes him gradually towards reluctantly having to verbalise his intentions of sleeping with her in return for her brother's life, and the audience should be under no illusions about who is trying to 'bribe' whom. It happens very slowly, for whatever tack his suggestions take, she interprets him (*Gestalt*-like) as having as innocent a mind as she, while at the same time, as the audience appreciates, she is saying things which he interprets (equally *Gestalt*-like) from his own point of view as being 'craftily' intended. (It is perhaps ironically significant that many critics have, with their own interpretative powers of imputation, convinced themselves that Isabella is indeed sublimating her own sexuality in this scene.) When Angelo is forced to be explicit it is as if a guilty secret has been wrung from him under duress and interrogation, whereas in truth he has been the one with the presumed responsibility of power. His manipulations have failed simply because they are not seen as such. When Isabella is finally made to 'understand', she recoils in horror. Unlike some critics I do not believe the two scenes are arranged to make us think about some 'idea' such as justice or mercy. The real point is the rivetingly theatrical and humanly dismaying spectacle of two people locked in separate understandings while in fact responding to each other with a mutual certainty of individual understanding. As Angelo is crafty and domineering, so he sees Isabella. As Isabella is innocent and passionate for justice, so she sees the ruler. The listeners reveal themselves through their responses,and the scenes are amongst the most powerful of Shakespeare's exploitations of 'listener-orientated' conversations.

For little reason but to lighten the tone, I quote an example showing how there can be a creative conversation even as one party is trying to avoid verbal contact, completely understanding while he pretends otherwise:

> Chief Justice. ... Call him back again!
> Servant. Sir John Falstaff!
> Falstaff. Boy, tell him I am deaf.
> Page. You must speak louder, my master is deaf.
> Chief Justice. I am sure he is, to the hearing of anything good. Go pluck him by the elbow, I must speak with him.
> Servant. Sir John.
> Falstaff. What! A young knave and begging? Is there not wars? Is there not employment? ...
> Servant. You mistake me, sir.
> Falstaff. Why, sir, did I say you were an honest man? ... I had lied in my throat if I had said so. ...
> (2 Henry IV, I.ii.61-77)

And so the master of evasion goes on, his brilliance lying in turning everything back on the speaker with a perverse creativity in his unpredictable and clever responses. For a critic solemnly searching for themes, image-patterns, 'essential identity' and 'universality' such an exchange can be a conspicuous irrelevance. For an audience in the theatre, on the contrary, it engages interest at the most powerful level as the kind of conversation which gathers to itself the sense of mysterious surprise and self-generating creativity which recalls the underlying process of many of our own conversations. That the audience has the last say in this matter is evidenced by the fact that there are far more tears shed over the rejection and death of the master-in-response, the multitudinous Falstaff, than ever can be found for the fate of the master of ceremonies, the giver of orders and eloquent speaker, Henry the Fifth.

LISTENING AS A SHAKESPEAREAN THEME

Having formulated the general ideas above, I coincidentally attended a performance of Love's Labour's Lost given by the Royal Shakespeare Company. It was not so surprising that I realised that I was more sharply aware of the ways in which the actors must have studiously analysed and rehearsed their dramatic responses to each others´ lines in an attempt to allow the audience to feel it was ´eavesdropping´ conversations. What was perhaps odder was that, although I had read, seen and even written about the play many times over fifteen years, I gradually realised that I was hearing and thinking about, perhaps for the first time, lines which formerly I had merely noticed. These lines were specifically and insistently about the act of listening itself, and they became more and more noticeable (to me at least) as the play neared its end:

> Holofernes. Via, goodman Dull! thou has spoken no word all this while.
> Dull. Nor understood none neither, sir.
> (V.i.133-5)

> Rosaline. What´s your dark meaning, mouse, of this light word?
> Katharine. A light condition in a beauty dark.
> Rosaline. We need more light to find your meaning out.
> (V.ii.19-21)

> Princess. Well bandied both; a set of wit well play´d.
> (V.ii.29)

> Princess. No, to the death, we will not move a foot,
> Nor to their penn´d speech render we not grace;
> But while ´tis spoke each turn away her face.
> Boyet. Why, that contempt will kill the speaker´s part
> And quite divorce his memory from his part.
> Princess. Therefore I do it.
> (V.ii.146-51)

> Moth. They do not mark me, and that brings me out.
> (V.ii.172)

> Berowne. Tell her we measure them by weary steps.
> Boyet. She hears herself.
> (V.ii.193-4)

> Rosaline. It were a fault to snatch words from my tongue.
> (V.ii.382)

> Armado. Sweet royalty, bestow on me the sense of hearing.
> (V.ii.655)

> Princess. I understand you not; my griefs are double.
> Berowne. Honest plain words best pierce the ear of grief.
> (V.ii.740-1)

> Dumain. Our letters, madam, show´d much more than jest.

<u>Longaville</u>. So did our looks.
<u>Rosaline</u>. We did not quote them so.
(V.ii.772-4)

<u>Katharine</u>. I'll mark no words that smooth-fac'd wooers say.
(V.ii.816)

And finally, most resoundingly:

<u>Rosaline</u>. ...
You shall this twelvemonth term from day to day
Visit the speechless sick, and still converse
With groaning wretches; and your task shall be,
With all the fierce endeavour of your wit,
To enforce the pained impotent to smile.
<u>Berowne</u>. To move wild laughter in the throat of death?
It cannot be; it is impossible;
Mirth cannot move a soul in agony.
<u>Rosaline</u>. Why, that's the way to choke a gibing spirit,
Whose influence is begot of that loose grace
Which shallow laughing hearers give to fools.
<u>A jest's prosperity lies in the ear</u>
<u>Of him that hears it, never in the tongue</u>
<u>Of him that makes it</u>; then, if sickly ears,
Deaf'd with the clamours of their own dear groans,
Will hear your idle scorns, continue then,
And I will have you and that fault withal.
But if they will not, throw away that spirit,
And I shall find you empty of that fault,
Right joyful of your reformation.
(V.ii.838-57, my underlining)

Keeping at the front of our minds these speeches about listening (or more properly, not listening), we may state the 'plot' of this play in which nothing really happens: the courtiers swear an oath (give their <u>words</u>) not to speak to a woman, and decree that no woman shall speak to them on pain of losing her tongue. When the Princess and her three women arrive, the men refuse to 'entertain' them in the court itself and leave them in the fields. The men then individually fall in love and write sonnets (a way of speaking without speaking), eventually abandon their oaths (as 'but words') and decide to woo the women. At this stage the women begin to exact revenge by wilfully not responding to the advances of the men, disguising so as to be wooed by the 'wrong' man, withdrawing the 'grace' of conversation and substituting mockery and refusal to engage with their words. When some stern concessions are made by the women, the courtiers agree to allow the entertainment of the 'low' characters presenting a little play, but they then refuse to enter the spirit of the masque and instead (to try to regain their own pride) jibe the players into silence, ridiculing them by picking up their words in perverse senses. 'The scene begins to cloud' when the Princess responds sombrely to Marcade's announcement of the death of her father and from the gravity of her feelings he refuses to carry on the courtship. At last, reluctantly, she agrees to resume relations in a year's time, meanwhile imposing upon the men various tasks which all turn on taking responsibility for their words, learning to listen and learning to speak with the listener in mind. Simply by stating the action in this way it is possible for the literary interpreter to claim as a central concern - a 'theme' - of the play the importance of learning and teaching the 'grace' or generosity involved in compatible social interaction (and, of course, most pertinently in love relationships) of speaking with the listener in mind, of listening with a 'greeting of the spirit'. It is probably true (as Rees and Maxwell were quoted as saying) that critics too readily speak of themes and ideas at the expense of the momentary effects and textures of a play, but in this case there is an intimate relationship between the two levels as there is, I hope to show, in other plays.

On another occasion of watching or reading the play, with different preoccupations in mind (Elizabethan love conventions, the formal concerns of comedy), I should almost certainly 'find' a different theme, or rather a different way of stating my overall understanding of the play. This does not mean the words have changed, nor even that certain stock responses of mine have changed. What has changed on each occasion is my own awareness of a new prominence of certain statements in the text and an experience of recreating with a new set of priorities my own overall responses. The lesson I take is that a body of writing such as a play is a neutral artefact holding no more than a body of potential meanings which can be activated and understood subtly differently by each actor who plays a part, each director, each member of the audience, each reader in his study, and each critic who attempts to present a case about the play. Most important, for each of these co-participants the understanding will also be different, to a greater or lesser degree, on each occasion. Such a position does not abandon us to a hopeless subjectivity in which each lonely recipient 'hears' something unshareable and forever cloistered in the individual mind. In fact, in the act of communication (writing, speaking after the play) there will be the give and take, the mutual sharing of ideas allowing a different kind of 'objectivity' which others can agree upon, a rigorous but tactful inter-subjectivity. The whole process is an extension of the kind of mental and conversational 'grace' which is implicitly advocated by the action of *Love's Labour's Lost*. In a play which explicitly deals with the rules of conversation, we find a pattern which can help us understand the nature and methodology of interpretation itself.

Much Ado About Nothing

Shakespeare, in this other play of 'witty conversation', discriminates between characters and groups by giving them all distinctive modes of speaking and listening which have a crucial bearing on the plot and the play's significance. The aristocratic characters are, if nothing else, wonderful speakers. Their exchanges are full of elegant, poised ripostes. The basic strategy of wit, however, as we saw in the brief exchange between Beatrice and Don Pedro, is to respond vivaciously at the level of words while deflecting attention away from the feelings which are hidden behind a smokescreen of impressive verbiage. The barbed conversations between Beatrice and Benedick are central in establishing that, while each is evading the other at the level of emotions they are, as it were, locking minds and tongues through the process of listening keenly to the semantics of the other and turning words back in puns and verbal aggression. We gain the impression that they know each other extremely well, but refrain from revealing important information about themselves. We even wonder if they know themselves very well, for there is a note of personal repression of feelings as well as evasiveness. Claudio takes to an extreme the tendency of responding only to a surface meaning and judging purely on appearances, since he falls in and out of love with Hero on simply seeing her and then hearing a rumour about her (based, moreover, on no more than her reported silhouette in a window at night). All the qualifications and doubts we hold about these eloquent speakers who are deficient listeners make them ripe for deception, and the whole plot hinges on this. Claudio is deceived into thinking Hero is unchaste merely by an unsubstantiated report. Beatrice and Benedick are drawn to admit their love for each other (perhaps even create their love), only after a trick has been played on them, as each overhears prearranged statements by others. At the head of this gossiping, 'noting', prying area of society stands Don Pedro, a gracious speaker and an effective, if benevolent manipulator of events as of words. All the complications of the two love plots turn on words which are heard only superficially, the characters being too concerned about an impression created by speaking and not with careful listening. The spectacular proof of this lies in the fact that Hero's father, Leonato, before the crucial 'broken wedding' scene is about to be given information of the plot on his daughter's reputation, but he is too much in haste to listen:

Dogberry. One word, sir: our watch, sir, have indeed comprehended two aspicious persons, and we would have

> them this morning examined before your worship.
>
> Leonato. Take their examination yourself, and bring it me; I am now in great haste, as it may appear unto you.
>
> (III.iv.42-6)

While the scene acts as a reassurance to the audience that comic revelation will eventually come, it is also a reproof to Leonato who could have avoided the terrible scene to follow, simply by listening now. In the 'wedding' scene itself we find also that it is not only words which can be expressive to the acute listener for the truth, when the Friar interprets the blush of Hero as denoting her innocence while others are jumping to conclusions based on rumours. Another, more unobtrusive hint that problems could be avoided by listening, lies in the fact that Beatrice is continually giving hints to Benedick about her desire to marry him (reluctant to turn the hints into forthright statements apparently out of fear of being hurt), but Benedick, unlike the audience, is such a defensive and generally poor listener that he does not hear them.

On the other side of the social divide stands the official 'watch'. Dogberry is made memorable purely by his inspired inability to speak 'correctly', and his malapropisms are, of course, famous. The irony is that he, admittedly in a rather accidental fashion, is the one able to hear, for he and his men stumble on the plot, interpret it as mischief, and eventually bring the 'benefactors' to justice. He can also hear an insult when he is called 'ass', even though, with magnificent dignity, he does not take the accusation of being 'tedious' as anything but a compliment. His 'headborough', the old man Verges, is equally incompetent at speaking to the point, for he is inclined to wander, but he too is instrumental in apprehending the criminals. Although they are ostentatiously not good speakers, these characters are able to find the truth more effectively than their eloquent social betters. The most delicious irony is that while the aristocrats are constantly watching each other, leaping to conclusions from overhearing snippets of conversation out of context, they rarely see facts which are staring them in the face. Meanwhile, the official 'watchers' discover truths even as they determine not to look:

> Dogberry. ... You are thought here to be the most senseless and fit man for the constable of the watch; therefore bear you the lantern. This is your charge: you shall comprehend all vagrom men; you are to bid any man stand, in the Prince's name.
>
> 2 Watch. How if 'a will not stand?
>
> Dogberry. Why, then, take no note of him, but let him go; and presently call the rest of the watch together, and thank god you are rid of a knave.

...

> You shall also make no noise in the streets; for, for the watch to babble and to talk is most tolerable and not to be endured.
>
> 2 Watch. We will rather sleep than talk; we know what belongs to a watch.
>
> (III.iii.20-35 passim)

Standing at the opposite moral end from Don Pedro is his own bastard brother. Don John is a man who speaks little ('I am not of many words' I.i.135), watches much, and uses his perceptions to create mischief. It is not wholly insignificant, although he is no speaker, that he is related to Pedro, for he uses for destructive ends the same tactics of rumour-spreading as Pedro uses for creative purposes. Unlike Dogberry and the watch, he too is involved in appearances rather than the substance of truth. The whole play is dominated, complicated and eventually resolved by a range of competences in speaking and listening. The eventual happy ending is determined by the decision of Benedick (for once) to listen to and trust the spirit behind the serious words of Beatrice when she asks him to 'Kill Claudio' (IV.i.287), a line which devastatingly strips away the pretences, falsities, misdirections and illusions of a society of dazzling speakers who congenitally choose not to listen.

Hamlet

It is a curious fact that Shakespeare sometimes uses the same dramatic strategies for opposite ends in a comedy and a tragedy respectively. In its social ethos, Hamlet's Elsinore has some radical similarities to the Messina of Much Ado. The play begins with a watch on the battlements, who report to Prince Hamlet the sighting of an apparition. We discover the existence of a large plot to cover up the truth, initiated by the head of state who is, in this case, guilty of murder. Thereafter, we realise that there are many spies around - Polonius sets a spy on his son Laertes, as Claudius sets Rosencrantz and Guildenstern on Hamlet. Hamlet, meanwhile, spies on his stepfather in order to confirm the murder of his own father. Privacy is almost impossible to attain and there are many eavesdropping scenes. Polonius and others watch Hamlet and Ophelia, Hamlet watches Claudius praying, Polonius dies while watching Hamlet and Gertrude, Hamlet and Horatio watch the funeral of Ophelia. We even get the feeling that when Hamlet is alone he is watching his own thoughts as closely as he observes the king in the 'mousetrap' scene, so introspective, reflective and self-critical are his soliloquies. And yet, with all this watching, very little 'truth' is realised. Polonius thinks Hamlet's 'madness' is for love while Claudius thinks it a trap; Hamlet thinks Claudius is praying but the audience discovers he is not able to pray; Hamlet thinks it is Claudius behind the arass whereas it is Polonius. Behind all these misapprehensions the real point being made is not that the characters are in ignorance but that they hear what they are predisposed to hear. Claudius, indeed, is one who understands and skilfully exploits this phenomenon of selective listening, for example in his brilliant manipulation of Laertes into vowing revenge against Hamlet (IV.vii), a scene in which the adroit politician draws from the hotheaded young man precisely the responses he wishes, with only a minimum of statement and inference. Significantly, it is a mere bystander, an unnamed Gentleman, who utters the line most central to this aspect of the play, in a scene which, structurally and spiritually is at the centre of the play's vision whilst being at the periphery of the narrative. In IV.iv, a strange and long scene, the distracted Ophelia is witnessed by other characters at the court, and her mad statements, appearing to hold some deep consistency, are interpreted or decoded by each character differently. The Gentleman describes the process:

> Her speech is nothing,
> Yet the unshaped use of it doth move
> The hearers to collection; they yawn at it,
> <u>And botch the words up fit to their own thoughts</u>:
> (IV.iv.7-10, my underlining)

The world of Elsinore under Claudius is one of obsession with secrecy, of limited knowledge eked out with inference and suspicious presumptions. Even the spellbinding presence of the innocent, pathetically deranged young woman, mercifully taken out of the context which has driven her insane, oddly liberated through madness from the politics of the court, is not sufficient to shame the others into realising their ignorance and arrogant duplicity. The fragmented honesty of her subconscious mind exposes by contrast the even more fragmented dishonesty of conscious plotting. In broad terms this is a world of politics, expediency, self-centredness and calculated deviousness. It is not really surprising that Hamlet's need for 'proof' or even meaning is thwarted, for such a state denies the existence of meaning itself. Ophelia's mind is ruined by the absence in her social world of reliable, consistent touchstones of meaning. Hamlet is driven to reckless murder as the only appropriate response to the same conditions. It is a society where people listen only for what they want to hear, and as a consequence divisive individualism is supreme. The lack of shared assumptions about meaning which may be mutually held in common between people is present only between 'minor' characters on the watch who all see the ghost, the players from the 'outside world', and to a lesser extent between Hamlet and Horatio. Beyond such tolerant camaraderie there is only the loneliness of a prince who cannot share his secret, nor even prove its existence. It is a world where communication cannot operate, shared meanings be discovered, because instead of listening to others, people botch words up to fit their own, preconceived notions. It is the tragic interface of the benevolent world of Much Ado where at least we are given a sense of providence working through and rectifying the mistakes.

King Lear

The tragic sequence of events in King Lear is precipitated when one man does not hear what he wants to hear:

> Lear. ... Now, our joy,
> Although our last and least, to whose young love
> The vines of France and milk of Burgundy
> Strive to be interess'd; what can you say to draw
> A third more opulent than your sisters? Speak.
> Cordelia. Nothing, my lord.
> Lear. Nothing!
> Cordelia. Nothing.
> Lear. Nothing will come of nothing.
> Speak again.
> Cordelia. Unhappy that I am, I cannot heave
> My heart into my mouth.
> (I.i.81-90)

Since this exchange, above all else, has the most cataclysmic consequences for the state and for the individuals in the play's version of 'history', we need not feel reticent about examining it closely, as many commentators have done. Here we can emphasise the strategies of interaction, and how they shape the future development. Reading 'forwards' there seems little to trouble us in Lear's first speech, especially since the responses of Goneril and Regan have been pitched at exactly the level which Lear expects and appreciates. But with Cordelia's 'Nothing', some facade is shattered and we are forced to reassess what has happened. When she says 'I cannot heave My heart into my mouth' we realise that she has taken Lear's question ('How much do you love me?') totally literally and at face value. Everything in his responses tells us that this is not what he foresaw or intended. Her 'Nothing' is in direct answer to his question 'What can you say...?' when in fact his manifest satisfaction at the replies of the other two sisters shows, in conjunction with his wording, that he was really asking a different question: 'How can you say you love me with more rhetorical flourishes than your sisters?' In fact, presuming upon the very thing he is about to relinquish, authority, he is not asking a question but making a command: 'Flatter me in the way which will please me most'. In short, when we read 'backwards', we discover that Lear has not placed himself in the context of a conversation or discussion at all, but has attempted to exercise power by severely limiting the options open to his interlocutor, while politically pretending that all options are open. Cordelia asserts the only power available to her, the option of honesty in treating the utterance of her father as a genuine question intended to evoke a true response (or, paradoxically, it might be argued that she is disingenuously calling her father's bluff in calculated fashion - though her conversational tactics are the same on either glossing). The result is a deadlock marking the end of real communication and tearing the stage audience (and perhaps the audience in the theatre) in two. There are those (like Burgundy, Goneril and Regan) who know that if Cordelia will 'Mend [her] speech a little' (I.i.93) she will redefine her 'Nothing' as an aberration or a joke and all will be well. There are others (Kent and the King of France) who see the fault as lying in Lear for demanding what should be given freely and without solicitation or bullying, and they feel it is he who should mend his speech: 'See better, Lear!' (I.i.157). Even if there is more moral support for the second argument, none the less Lear, manifesting a trait which is curiously symptomatic of people in Shakespeare's plays who wield power, refuses to admit a mistake. Fortunately for the cause of truth (as both Kent and France point out), but unfortunately for her own wellbeing, Cordelia is unable to retract a response which is measured and honest. Having been asked to state her 'bond' to her father she has done so. She is disowned, and Kent is banished, simply because she chose to respond directly to a question which is put to her. The pathetic core of the matter is that Lear never intended his words to be taken as a genuinely open question. Her misfortune was to act as a truthful listener instead of as a projection of the speaker's intentions.

The consequences of this exchange (not a misunderstanding but an obstinate definition of opposing positions) are so drastic - civil war, madness, torture, murder - that we can only wonder at the profound seriousness with which Shakespeare viewed the simple act of human interaction. If such a short dialogue, and such a tiny word as 'Nothing', can be so far-reaching in their effects when traced figuratively and with remorseless logic, then by implication every time we converse with another person we may hold an awesome responsibility for our responses. In Othello Shakespeare takes such logic to similarly disastrous limits in the domestic sphere. Obviously, and luckily, there are more checks and balances, more negotiation towards shared understanding rather than independent understandings, in 'ordinary' conversation, but this may simply be due to the happy cause that we do not all have to face an obdurate figure alienated from his humanity to his position of authority which he briefly wields, one who hiding behind his power will not obey the simple decencies of listening to the other person.

Lear makes more mistakes. When Kent tells him he has been placed in the stocks by Regan and Cornwall, Lear refuses to believe him, again because he just does not want to hear the truth. He is shattered by both Regan and Goneril because he did not countenance the possibility that once he has given up his authority as king he is also relinquishing his expectations as a father because these daughters are ones who bow only to instituted power and not to moral obligations or 'bonds' of kindness or conscience. He foresees a dream-existence with his reinstated daughter, living 'like birds in a cage' only to be brutally disappointed by the murder of Cordelia. But on the other hand there are rare moments when Lear gives signs of having listened and - too late - of being prepared to respond in vulnerable and generous spirit. His 'noble philosopher' (III.iv.168) is Poor Tom the beggar and his mentor Caius the stouthearted servant, both _personae_ of noble characters liberated to listen and teach others to do the same:

> Poor naked wretches, wheresoe'er you are,
> That bide the pelting of this pitiless storm,
> How shall your houseless heads and unfed sides,
> Your loop'd and window'd raggedness, defend you
> From seasons such as these? O, I have ta'en
> Too little care of this! Take physic, pomp;
> Expose thyself to feel what wretches feel,
> That thou mayst shake the superflux to them,
> And show the heavens more just.
>
> (III.iii.28-36)

The bleak logic of this play is that, no matter how many characters call on 'the heavens' to hear their pleas for justice, there are no gods available and that the human beings who are 'Dress'd in a little brief authority' (_Measure for Measure_, II.ii.118) seem occupationally disabled from listening except for things which will incriminate their subjects or pose a threat to themselves. When they are made accessible to truths from outside themselves, it is only because they have lost their power. At the beginning of his play, King Lear is a peremptory and overbearing speaker because he does not listen. At the stage when he blesses the beggars (as 'Mr. Lear, private citizen') and when he is reconciled to Cordelia, he is a morally convincing speaker because he has chosen to listen and to respond vulnerably. The end of the play can only mean that holding power and being able to listen in generously responsive fashion are incompatible. The tragedy of this, however, is not to the King or the powerful, but to the innocent who in order to survive require of others only that they should listen.

In other plays (such as (Timon of Athens, Othello), Shakespeare deals with the tragedy that comes from 'bad listening', while in the romantic comedies he portrays the delightful entertainment that springs from the greeting of the spirit exercised in 'good listening', and sometimes the comedy arising from 'errors' in listening. The four plays briefly examined here are not the only ones in which Shakespeare raises the issue to the status of a thematic centre. Judged from virtually any standpoint (time, language or cultural context) Shakespeare emerges as one of the greatest communicators of all time. A part of his secret must lie in the simple fact that he was inveterately curious and enquiring about the very act and modes of communication between human beings, a subject which finally centres on the capacity to listen and to respond.

REFERENCES

Berry, Ralph (1969) 'The Words of Mercury', Shakespeare Survey, xxii, pp. 69-77.

Bradbrook, M.C. (1951) Shakespeare and Elizabethan Poetry, Chatto and Windus, London.

Jenkins, Harold (1955) As You Like It, Shakespeare Survey, viii, pp. 40-51.

Maxwell, J.C. (1974) Measure for Measure: The Play and the Themes, British Academy Shakespeare Lecture.

Rees, Joan (1978) Shakespeare and the Story, Athlone, London.

Shakespeare, W. (1951) The Complete Works , Collins, London and Glasgow.

Willcock, G.D. (1934) Shakespeare as Critic of Language, Shakespeare Association Pamphlet, London.

NINE

LISTENING TO HER SELF: WOMEN'S DIARIES

Rebecca Hiscock

> 'Time does nothing to my companions in school. For me each day is a novelty, and it seems to me that my character changes every day. If I do rise at the same time, I have different impressions each day. Even if I wear the same dress, it seems to me that I am not the same girl. Even if I repeat the same prayers during one year, each time they appear differently to my interpretation, and I understand them differently' (Nin, 1973, p. 256).

> 'Sometimes I feel that if I did not write in here I would cease to exist' (Unpublished Diary).

This essay hinges on a paradox. It examines secret writing, and as such demolishes that which it seeks to examine. Of course, even in scientific thought - the last bastion of objectivity - it is now recognised that 'observed phenomena can be understood only as correlations between various processes of observation and measurement' (Capra, 1982, p. 77). In this way it is inevitable that the nature of the examined should be acted upon and changed by the examiner. The writing, produced in secret and not destined to be read, becomes the diary, now read and rewoven into an analysis of itself as not read. I do not address diaries written to be published, of which there are many, but diaries, few though they are, that have become available despite their initial privacy. I also emphasise women diarists, although I do not assume all my observations to exclude men, nor to include all women. As an ex-diarist myself, I have not attended to one of the most obvious assessments of diary writing - narcissism. It undoubtedly plays its part, but it also figures in many other forms of writing and modes of behaviour. The peculiarities of both the diary and the impulse behind this form of writing are rarely addressed.

Diaries are usually lumped together with autobiographies, letters and memoirs. In its project autobiography obviously comes closest to the diary in that both involve reflection upon one's own subjectivity moving through time. In diaries, however, this reflection takes place on a more or less day to day basis, whereas in autobiographies a preselected section of one's past life is scrutinized. This distinguishes the diary both in its form and in the relationship the writer has with her text. In a diary the material constraints of time and space are perpetually apparent in the course of the text's production. This factor which speaks of the mechanics and materiality of literary production is effaced from most other texts. In diaries pens run out, the writer falls asleep, thoughts are interrupted and never returned to. More significantly, the allocation of meaning to experience is revealed as often arbitrary or deluded, perpetually open to reassessment and reinterpretation. Events which may be seen at one moment to have great significance can be exposed as irrelevant and trivial through the progress of pages and time, and subsequent changes in the writer's experience, self-awareness or ideological position. In autobiography such unevenness is ironed out by hindsight. Thus one may perceive significance where it had never been experienced, but where it emerges in terms of subsequent events. The meaning of an event is fixed through its relationship to a passage of time rendered textually as a unified past. In this way autobiographies can have an ordering effect on experience which was random, endowing it with sequential logic. This is an obvious advantage, but one that can give rise to problems and limitations. Anna Wulf in Doris Lessing's <u>The Golden Notebook</u> articulates one of them: 'The trouble with this story is that it is written in terms of analysis of the laws of dissolution of the relationship between Paul and Ella. I don't see any other way to write it. As soon as one has lived through something, it falls into a pattern. And the pattern of an affair ... is seen in terms of what ends it. That is why all this is untrue. Because while living through something one doesn't think like that at all' (Lessing, 1973, p. 231).

This realisation is from Anna's Yellow Notebook where she recreates her experience into stories, and is part of the problem of narrative form eloquently addressed by much twentieth century fiction. Objective realism is no longer deemed an adequate tool for the representation of experience, and the writer's emphasis is placed upon an inner subjective truth. This 'truth' seems constantly to defy conclusive formal arrangement. The text of a diary with its disregard for pattern and its ongoing relationship to the self in time, would seem to come close to it, conveying what Virginia Woolf described in <u>Modern Fiction</u> as 'this varying, this unknown and uncircumscribed spirit, whatever aberration or complexity it may display ...' (Woolf, 1966, p. 106). The diarist is able to capture the immediate sense she has of her own experience, however it may subsequently be contradicted, avoiding the kind of 'untruth' that Anna Wulf describes. As Anais Nin puts it in her diary:

> What is remembered later does not seem as true to me. I have such a need of truth! It must be that need of immediate recording which incites me to write almost while I am living, before it is altered, changed by distance of time (Nin, 1973, p. 72).

Autobiographies demand that the writer fix herself in the text at a static point in order to view herself in process. Robert Sayre sees this as 'a denial of a continuing historical nature in order to repeat the past' (Sayre, 1964, 182). While autobiographies cannot merely 'repeat' the past as if it were a film waiting to be rerun, the 'gesture of denial' would seem to be an inevitable consequence of taking up a position from which one might describe one's history. The writer is positioned as other to the written self - the self in process. And the self in process is revealed as becoming the self who writes. A similar enactment takes place for the diarist, except that the writing self is not fixed in time. The relationship to the written self is much more intimate; they both move through time together, with no apparent intention of ending. Autobiographies written in retrospect and generally adhering to a linear movement of time, have a determining narrative which must reach the point at which the writer fixed herself in order to view her past - ultimately the present moment of writing. There is an inevitable closure of the form, and it is at this point of closure that the diary opens.

...

> So that my dreams may be my own, so that they may never become real, so that I may always call them back to keep me company, to help me live, I keep them in the deepest part of my being or in the most secret pages of my diary. (Nin, 1973, p. 258)

...

But of course the diary does not actually open. It remains silent and hidden, secreted in private places. While in the fixity of the authorial position and the subsequent ending, the autobiography would appear to be a 'closed' form and the diary a text in process, the privacy of the diary renders this rather irrelevant. In its ending the autobiography can be seen as just beginning. The apparent closure of the form, rather like the cutting of the umbilical cord, the tying of the knot, is vital to the release of the writing, like the subject, into the world. There it is constituted and named, produced and reproduced within a network of relationships. It is made available as a literary product, capable of a multiplicity of readings. As Umberto Eco observes, 'the author should die once he has finished writing. So as not to trouble the path of the text' and 'When a work is finished a dialogue is established between the text and its readers (the author is excluded)' (Eco, 1985, p. 47). The diarist will not risk the 'death' or exclusion indicated here and described more forcefully by Roland Barthes in his essay 'The Death of the Author'. For Barthes the concept of the author as an ultimate source of meaning must be destroyed in order to liberate the text, which can then be 'disentangled' rather than 'deciphered'. 'To give a text an Author is to impose a limit on that text, to furnish it with a final signified, to close the writing ...' (Barthes, 1977, p. 147). The possibility of opening the text resides with the reader. Only when a text is separated from its author and read can its multiplicity be released. The diarist writes against such separation. She seeks to remain the 'Author' of her text, defining its limits, determining its meaning, keeping the diary closed. Paradoxically this means that she must never become the author - in the sense of being named as such by a reader - but must be ever the writer, her text eternally unfinished.

To this end she may take all practical measures to ensure that nobody has access to her text. The diary is hidden in secret places, kept under lock and key. Orders may be left for it to be burned on the writer's death, or it may be written in cipher. The Reverend T. Dugard's whole diary consists of an abbreviated form of Latin, and this initial deterrent is strengthened by his microscopic handwriting (Ponsonby, 1923, p. 154). But while such ingenuity is directed at an actual reader, it is also an attempt to diminish the effect of an imagined reader. The diarist who is intent on secrecy is plagued by the paradoxical nature of her act. For such a rendering of inner life into an exterior form necessitates the use of a material structure of communication, easily possessible and constantly begging an addressee or recipient. One way of dealing with this is to construct an addressee, specifically defined by the writer. This is the opening of the diary Fanny Burney began at the age of fifteen:

> To have some account of my thoughts, manners, acquaintances, and actions, when the hour arrives in which time is more nimble than memory is the reason which induces me to keep a Journal. A Journal in which I must confess my every thought must open my whole heart! But a thing of this kind must be addressed to somebody - I must imagine myself to be talking - talking to the most intimate friends - to one whom I should take delight in confiding and remorse in concealment: but who must this

friend be? (Ponsonby, 1923, p. 171).

Burney comes to the conclusion that it must be 'nobody', and addresses her diary accordingly to 'a certain Miss Nobody', mastering the paradox of an addressee who is both present and absent. Miss Nobody is a listener and Burney sees herself talking within a secure relationship. The fact that a text is created in the process is not at this stage seen as problematic. For other writers, more conscious of their text, the ghost of a recipient is less easily exorcised. This is Emily Shore writing in 1838 at the age of eighteen, after keeping her journal for seven years:

> I am sure it is a memoir of my character and the changes and progress of my mind - its views tastes and feelings. But I am conscious that, at the same time, it is far from being as complete as with this end it ought to be ... I have poured out my feelings into these later pages; I have written them on the impulse of the moment, as well as from the coolness of calm deliberation. I have written much that I would show only to a very few and much that I would on no account submit to any human eye. Still even now I cannot entirely divest myself of an uncomfortable notion that the whole may some future day when I am in my grave be read by some individual and this notion has without my being often aware of it, cramped me, I am sure. I have by no means confessed myself in my journal; I have not opened my whole heart; I do not write my feelings and thoughts for the inspection of another - Heaven forbid! - but I imagine the vague fear I have above mentioned has grown into a sort of unconscious habit, instinctively limiting the extent of my confidence in ink and paper so that the secret chamber of my heart of which Foster speaks so strikingly, does not find in my pen a key to unlock it (Ponsonby, 1927, p. 205).

The imagined reader Emily Shore sees here as present in and informing upon her text's production, separates the writer from her text rather like an actual reader, making it partial, and releasing or concealing meanings in a way that the writer has little control over. Just as the written self, separated from the writer, is acted upon and changed by a reader, so the writing self is acted upon and changed by a consciousness of a reader. The threat of a break in the ongoing, exclusive unity and correspondence between writer and written is seen to inhibit and distort, preventing access to the 'secret chamber of the heart'. This can be reached only in total solitude, when the diarist is confident of that exclusive relationship with her text. Emily Shore resolves to keep a second diary even more secret than the first:

> Let me do it feeling certain that it will never be seen

> by human eye and let me take effectual means that this shall be the case (Ponsonby, 1927, p. 206).

The secrecy of the diarist can be seen as the manifestation of a desire to capture the self alone, removed from the dynamics of relationship. Therein is seen to lie the 'truth' of one's self, and it is the transcription of this 'true' self that the ghost of a recipient - the sense of a reader - is seen to threaten. In this light the diarist appears to be retreating from a relativist world into a private realm of singular absolutes, seeking a Cartesian self: an innate core of human identity over which one might have total control. She appears rather like the Idealist critic searching for the nugget of truth, perceived as fixed within the literary text. Both would appear to see themselves as 'deciphering' a pre-given essence which in its meaning - its truth - refers only to itself and cannot be seen as constructed within a network of relationships. However, for the diarist it is the very recognition that the self is susceptible to construction in relationship that sets her on her obsessively private course. Her aspiration toward transcription of the self alone, as a 'true' self, is perhaps best understood by looking at how the self might be experienced in relationships; the context of women's social and psychological experience of selfhood.

...

> Probably a crab would be filled with a sense of personal outrage if it could hear us class it without ado or apology as crustacean, and thus dispose of it. 'I am no such thing,' it would say: 'I am myself, myself alone' (James, 1901-2).

...

There are varying psychoanalytical formulations of gender difference and female identity, but I would like to draw upon Nancy Chodorow's discussion of the relationship between difference and the process of differentiation/separation (Chodorow, 1979). Initially the child experiences itself, the world and in particular, its caretaker, as an undifferentiated symbiotic unity. The process of differentiation occurs as the child comes to perceive a division between itself and the object world, recognising the subject/self as distinct and separate from the object/other (initially the caretaker). Chodorow foregrounds the fact that in our highly gender organised, patriarchal society the primary caretaker is almost invariably female, and this is shown to have particular implications for the process of differentiation and the concomitant acquisition of gender identity. Because of the primacy of the mother in the early years compared to the more shadowy male presence, a boy's gender identity is learned as not female, not mother, building upon the process of differentiation. Gender identity develops away from the mother, involving a denial or repression of the primary identification with her. Consequently difference and separateness become a much more integral part of differentiation; the me/not me distinction is more fixed. For the girl gender identity involves a recognition of being like the mother and builds upon the primary identification with her. In the act of differentiation there is also continuity and similarity. Consequently the female self is less separate, involving a less fixed me/not me distinction. In Chodorow's analysis difference and separateness are not seen as vital components for a satisfactory sense of self, and the cultural assumptions that 'individualism, separateness, and distance from others are desirable and requisite to autonomy and human fulfilment' (Chodorow, 1979, p. 67) are questioned. But in the context of such assumptions and the identification of a negatively valued gender identity, women can experience 'problems of sense of separateness and autonomy'. Merger and fusion of the self in relationship can be problematic.

Within this formulation of female identity it is easy to see a role for the secret diary. The very boundedness of the book offers definition and containment, and its secrecy is a defence against invasion. Anais Nin relishes an absence of boundary, a sense of self as unlimited and undefined:

> Allendy may have said: 'This is the core.' But I never feel the four walls around the substance of the self, the core. I feel only space ... What interests me is not the core but the potentialities of this core to multiply and expand infinitely. The diffusion of the core, its suppleness and elasticity ... (Nin, 1973, p. 209).

And yet she keeps a diary, 'an inviolate island', a place where she can 'think of a self portrait today in order to disengage the self from dissolution'. Without the diary she sees herself as a snail without a shell, vulnerable and uncontained, lacking a protective division between herself and others. And a snail without a shell is no longer a snail; dependent upon the diary for a sense of separate self, the diary becomes an intrinsic part of one's identity. It is carried about, accompanying the diarist everywhere, becoming a material expression of selfhood. Diarists exhibit a great fear of losing their endless volumes, and a preoccupation with binding and storage. Anais Nin kept her journals in iron boxes and later an Arabian wedding-chest, 'violet velvet with gold nails. Lovely to see the coffer open, brimming full.'

Eventually they were transferred to a bank vault. Final physical separation from the diary is feared as much as the separation from the text effected by the reader.

> I need to return to the diary, it has been neglected ... people have been stealing it away from me, stealing away the time I used to spend here, tempting me to escape, and I so easily tempted, idle evenings away playing with words outside myself, never captured, always fragmentary, chipped from an amorphous whole by another person's blows. In here I can explore all the shapelessness without the hindering qualification of another presence - which while it stimulates can also - with a self that's vaporous, absorbent, undefined - restrict by imposing or implanting thought which I must have space to investigate, discard or make my own (Unpublished Diary, 1977).

'Words outside myself' are synonymous with words outside the diary, and created in interaction are seen to be partial, uncontrolled. Interaction is seen as a process of self formation, but formation through fragmentation - at the hands of another. The diary's private space is seen as one in which the fragments can be bound, in all their shapelessness, and the formation of the self in language is felt to be under one's own control. In this way the diary is less a search for definition than a resistance to definition in relationship, a fear of becoming fixed in any single fragment which, in interaction, will inevitably masquerade as a whole.

This has implications for the way women may experience their social construction as women. The development of large scale capitalism through to corporate consumer capitalism led to work in the form of wage labour being removed from the centre of family life to become the means by which the family was maintained. As Eli Zaretsky argues in his study *Capitalism, the Family, and Personal Life*, 'society divided and the family became the realm of the private' (Zaretsky, 1976, p. 57), a refuge from social relations experienced as fragmentary, anonymous or coerced; a place where a sense of one's own unique individuality could be validated in personal relationships removed from the mechanized forces of production. Women presided over this private space, becoming a symbol of the personal. But far from being a refuge, for women the family was a place of work, denying her any personal space. As Charlotte Gilman pointed out, only the man of the house was permitted a study (Zaretsky, 1976, p. 113). And though labour may be deemed 'alienated', social identity is still constructed around what one 'does'. Woman, cut off from the public world of production and isolated within the 'private' world of reproduction, cannot be recognised in terms of 'doing'. Her work, and the economic and power structures that determine her relationships in the family, are effaced by the ideological representations of romance, sexual love and motherhood. Rather than being resolved within the realm of personal relations, feelings of alienation and a lack of autonomous self are actually promoted in that realm. Problems of merger and fusion become problems of dependency and powerlessness. Under patriarchy, men have the power to define the limits of 'femininity'. As Chodorow argues gender difference and differentiation are much more closely linked for men. Masculinity is learned as not female, and women are the object/other against which they need to define themselves. Consequently they have a psychological as well as a political/economic investment in the representation of women. The inevitably negative ideological representations of 'femininity' under a male cultural hegemony will fit uneasily with any other sense a woman may have of her self - as a rational self-determining 'human' being, for instance. But the dominant ideology will be internalised as 'natural' or inevitable, and any contradictions or dislocation will be experienced within the woman as splits, divisions, fragmentation.

> This is why I think political and not just literary work is started as soon as writing gets done by women that goes beyond the bounds of censorship, reading, the gaze, the masculine command, in that cheeky risk taking women can get into when they set out into the unknown to look for themselves (Cixous, 1981 p. 53).

...

As an adolescent I maintained two diaries. In one I recounted my day to day experience in the framework and language of the collective identity of my adolescent peer group - one of romance, preoccupation with appearance, sexual bravado, fun and laughter. In the other were aspects of myself that disrupted or contradicted that representation. The two diaries grew into an inner/outer split; the exterior self being the self in relationship - the self as one is seen or wishes to be seen, and the inner as the internal sense of unspecified dislocation, or of that outer self as inadequate or 'false'. My second diary was maintained with much confusion, loathing and a paranoic secrecy. Its very existence was testimony to my failure to be whole in the first diary; a successful adolescent female. I wanted to eradicate the discordant 'inner' self, and maintaining the first diary was an attempt to do so, by creating a false harmony between how I was seen and named in relation to others and the world: the object self, and myself as subject. It was not surprising that the object self was recognised as more important, and the inner voice was kept so secret. Under patriarchy, women, like small children, should be seen and not heard.

> The only time that I think I might be real is myself screaming or having hysterics. But it is these times that I am most in danger ... of being told that I am wrong, or that I am not really like what I´m acting like, or that he hates me. If he stops loving me, I´m sunk; I won´t have any purpose in life, or be sure that I exist any more. I must efface myself in order to avoid this and not make any demands on him, or do anything that might offend him ... I have to be noticed to know that I exist. But if I efface myself, how can I be noticed? It is a basic contradiction (Tax, 1970, p. 7).

In a sense the secret diary exists within this contradiction, described here by Meredith Tax. The diarist can both notice and efface herself. In its secrecy the diary is rendered silent and invisible and its silence is a virtue - a very ´feminine´ virtue. This is not to imply that the act of writing is an easy or guilt-free course for women. It is impossible to assess how many women have been or are writing in this way, but of those whose texts are available, many regularly punctuate their writings with cringing gestures of apology for having put pen to paper in the name of their selves. But while in this, and its personal nature, it may appear to be no challenge to the public world of men, the act of ´noticing´ oneself obviously is. The vital dependency upon one´s self as object - upon external recognition for a sense of self - is weakened. It was my second diary that survived; the initially discordant subjectivity comes to be seen as a secret resistance to both the seductive and violating fixity of being named by another. Anais Nin writes here of an encounter with Antonin Artaud:

> He embroidered on the meaning of my name. Anais, Anahita, the persian Goddess of the moon. Anais, the Grecian external me, lovely, luminous, not the somber me. Where is the somber me who matches Artaud´s despairs? In the diary. Secret (Nin, 1973, p. 237).

And that secret resistance to being named is also resistance to the definitions of others who have the power to construct one within very specific terms - those that fulfil their own needs.

> Playing so many roles, dutiful daughter, devoted sister, mistress, protector, my Father´s new found illusion, Henry´s needed all purpose friend, I had to find one place of truth... (Nin, 1973, p. 296).

The diary can offer the possibility of a space where Meredith Tax need no longer `hear herself´ scream from a position of object identification. The scream need no longer be discordant, but can be self validated away from the powerful controlling presence of 'he' who will say 'you are wrong' or 'you are not really like that', imposing an objectification that conceals or questions the subjective. Of course 'he' is internalised in the form of specific representations of womanhood, as my two diaries demonstrate; and such internalisations, like Virginia Woolf's 'Angel in the House', can assist in producing the 'unconscious habit' of self censure that Emily Shore describes. In this context the attempt to shake off the 'unconscious habit' (for Emily, the sense of being read) is an extension of the attempt to overcome the sense of watching oneself, of oneself as object. The exclusive relationship the diarist aspires to between her writing and her written self can be seen as a bid to escape the internalised male surveyor and his limiting self constructions, constructions which inevitably fragment or negate one's subject self. Anais Nin's father's jealousy is quite well founded:

> Father too is jealous of the journal. 'My only rival' he says. (All of them would slay the journal if they could) (Nin, 1973, p. 224).

Her relationship with her text excludes him, and on the blank pages she is actively inscribing herself, challenging his desire for her just passively to appear.

It becomes clear then that the aspiration toward exclusive privacy takes place in a context where women can feel a lack of control over a sense of separate, self-affirming identity for very concrete historical and political reasons. It is also understandable, in the context of such fragmentation and alienation, why the privacy of the diary should be seen as a means of reaching 'the secret chamber of the heart', 'a place of truth'. But in regarding the diary as a repository for the self alone, the 'true' self, the diarist is in part responding to the cultural assumptions that 'individualism, separateness and distance from others are requisite to autonomy', and seeking to resolve contradictions by positioning herself within a liberal humanist ideology of individualism. This allows her to retrieve a sense of wholeness and control from the very continuity of alienation and isolation. The gender-specific reasons for such feelings are concealed beneath a notion of an inevitably alienated, inevitably isolated individual, and recast in terms of an ahistorical 'human condition'. The romantic pose of an isolated individual ranged against a society that cannot understand nor recognise a unique and transcendent subjectivity is the egotistical compensation for - and defence against - feelings of powerlessness, insignificance and alienation. For the diarist such a concept of selfhood is a form of control: an ideological control of a potentially disruptive subjectivity. Collusion in this control is a means of gaining coherence, continuity and singularity. In this framework the boundaries of one's relationship to the world are clearly delineated and fixed.

Diaries are often started at times when the self is thrown into crisis, when the continuity of a self experienced as secure, whole and understood in relationship is broken. Anais Nin began her diary on board a ship sailing to America, 'an alien land', having been uprooted from her much loved home and separated from her father. Elizabeth Barrett Browning began her diary when she was plunged into what appeared to her as 'unending uncertainty'. She was confronted with two major threats to her position of security in a stable world. Due to her father's financial difficulties, the family's future in their childhood home 'Hope End' was no longer secure, and alongside this, the inequities of her relationship with Hugh Boyd had given rise to doubts about his much valued affection for her. She had perceived a coolness in his manner toward her, and with the threat of departure and separation hanging over their friendship, her need for a clarification of his feelings becomes more intense, as does her sense of having no right to demand such clarification.

> ... Shall I ask Mr. Boyd if he _will_ go where we go, in the case of our going at all? It would be a comfort to me to know if he would make the endeavour; and yet after my past 'intrusions', I scarcely like asking. And yet (again) did he not tell me, that if I _had_ left Hope End, he 'would have been happier at Cheltenham than at Malvern, for one reason - because at Cheltenham there was nothing to remind him of my going to see him'. Must he not care a good deal for me, to feel _that_? And in the case of his caring _at all_ for me, must he not wish, for his own sake to live near me, wherever I am? I shall never get at any certainty by this interrogative system. Hope says one thing; and Fear, another, in reply. (Browning, pp. 1831-2).

Her past, present and future no longer participate in a secure continuum, but are susceptible to change over which she feels little control. In this state of potential loss, unconscious/conscious desires and fears disrupt the controlling mechanism of rational logic, revealing its inability to deduce a single, certain truth. The preoccupation with the loss of her family home and her insecurity about Boyd's feelings for her dominate the diary as she attempts to relocate herself amidst the confusion of a break with her past and a growing perception of ambiguity and uncertainty. The diary is a place where emotions are both expressed and rationalised as she seeks to regain access to a self no longer positioned securely in relationship, and hence only partially expressed there. The initial impulse of the diarist often consists of a desire to retrieve a lost wholeness of self, no longer experienced in relationship; a single sense of self held securely in a framework of single, fixed truths, in a time when words had no ambiguity, and communication held no doubts. She partly achieves this 'lost' singularity by naming the diary as 'a place of truth', an expression of a true core self; such is the appeal of romantic individualism.

However, relating to the diary in this way does not resolve contradictions; it merely renames them in a way that offers the illusion of control over a unified core self. Meanwhile the text of a diary threatens to explode this Cartesian myth at every turn of the page. The intimate and exclusive relationship set up as a means of reaching a stable 'true' self only leads to the inscription of a self in chaos, in a perpetual state of fragmentation and process. It is the distance of the autobiographer from her written self that achieves the greater unity and coherence. The text of a diary only plays out Brecht's assertion that 'the continuity of the ego is a myth; a man is an atom that constantly breaks up and forms anew' (Brecht, 1964, p. 15). The 'I' that is imprinted upon the page is constantly multiplying, dispersing through infinite possibilities as it moves through time. 'The secret chamber of the heart' contains no nugget of truth, only the revelation of this self in process; a self with no identifiable solitary core capable of resisting the dynamic interplay of relationships, or of transcending the conflictual, contradictory process of its many relational and ideological determinations.

Yet this is not problematic for the diarist. As I have shown such 'shapelessness' is often celebrated. A text that reveals such an absence of definition, form or fixity can be seen as immensely liberating. It is always becoming, asserting a self with infinite potential. It only becomes problematic when the exclusive relationship between writer and text is threatened. For the writing self sustains all that the written self would appear to belie. The act of writing, moving page by page through a book, allows some sense of linear development, and as I have indicated the diary - the material volume - is a form of unification and definition in itself, experienced as a means of containment, of self possession. Diarists won't just write on anything that is to hand; it has to be _in_ the diary. And beyond this, the 'lost' stability of a singular, fixed 'I' is retrieved in the 'I' who writes, endlessly. Habit becomes as Beckett says 'the shield of ego'. In the ongoing act of writing, a _constant state_ of formation, a constant process is maintained, and stability and continuity are gained whatever may be inscribed. Thus in the relationship between writer and written the diarist holds together a series of opposites. On the one hand she attains singularity, continuity, fixity, order, and on the other disorder, multiplicity and flux. And insofar as the writer and text are unified in a relationship experienced as exclusive, these opposites are unified, made whole.

In this way the diarist maintains a sense of control, of determining her own self, her own meaning, while acknowledging that meaning is open to transformation; she can both fix her own truth and make use of its relativity and susceptibility to change. She positions herself, in Barthes' sense, as both author and reader. In the previously quoted section from Emily Shore's diary Emily, as reader of her own text, has become aware of the gaps and silences within it. And though she regrets such absences they become present as she reads, releasing meanings that she may not have been aware of at the time of writing. She is in the process of 'disentangling', rather as an actual reader might be. But a reader who is other than herself breaks the Cartesian sense of wholeness and control that is achieved in the completely self-referential nature of her relationship with her diary. Such a reader will release meanings - even 'truths' - over which the diarist will have no control, separating the writer from her text, and either hurrying her off to the morgue or, worse still, holding up a now alien text as the mirror of its author's soul. To be read (whether 'disentangled' or 'deciphered') is to feel both concealed and exposed. The diarist may well adhere to the cultural estimation of the diary as a repository for a 'true self'.[1] But she does so within the confines of her exclusive relationship with her text; the idea of anyone else naming her text in this way is just another form of death. Leonard Woolf felt compelled to address this problem in his preface to Virginia Woolf's Diary:

> At the best and even unexpurgated, diaries give a distorted or one-sided portrait of the writer, because, as Virginia Woolf herself remarks somewhere in these diaries, one gets into the habit of recording one particular mood - irritation or misery, say - and of not writing one's diary when one is feeling the opposite. The portrait is therefore from the start unbalanced and, if someone then deliberately removes another characteristic, it may well become a mere caricature. (Woolf, 1953, p. 7).

And when the prospect of his biographer having access to his diary volumes arose, Shaftesbury remarked:

> They are of no value to anybody but myself; they have never been seen by anybody, and they never will be. They are a mass of contradictions; thoughts jotted down as they passed through my mind, and contradicted perhaps on the next page - records of passing events written on the spur of the moment and private details which no one could

understand but myself (Ponsonby, 1927, p. 196).

I suggest that Shaftesbury fears less that his 'private details' or contradictions will be incomprehensible, and more that they will be comprehended - but in terms not his own.

The diarist seems to recognise that author and reader do not present 'the symmetrical poles of an intersubjective process understood as communication' (Belsay, 1980, p. 140); that readers, like hearers, ascribe meaning to a writer's or speaker's words in a world where a one-to-one correspondence of words and meanings does not exist. It is partly this view of communication that prompts the diarist to privilege a private written self over a spoken self in interaction. Loss is a strong feature of diaries; loss of the past, loss of self, loss of control, but primarily loss of communication. Diaries in their unwillingness to communicate say a great deal about communication. They speak its redundancy, its absence and its pitfalls. Primarily they reveal a lack of faith in, and a concomitant fear of meaning not her own, or her potential powerlessness in interactions. In speech words seem to fall away into the uncertain realms of another's consciousness, and yet these words - spoken and no longer felt as under one's own control - are become part of the process of one's construction. In the diary she creates a relationship in which she can feel that the words she produces are under her exclusive control, and refer only and always back to herself. Thus the diarist <u>can</u> name the self constructed in this process as a 'true' self, separate and autonomous. Entering into communication with oneself in the diary allows access to absolutes no longer seen as fixed elsewhere. The incoherence and contradictions that are the material outpourings upon the page are contained within the Idealist boundaries of the relationship; absolute privacy equalling absolute self, the latter dependent upon the former. In this sense the diary is 'an inviolate island', but one constructed from within the recognition and revelation of perpetual violation, of that island constantly breaking up and forming anew. The diarist's struggle with subjectivity is similar to the way in which novelists have struggled with the twentieth century view of consciousness, seeking a form that will both control and express that consciousness. The diarist does feel that she achieves this. But while she identifies it as self expression, the quest continually to match her private experience in linguistic form, reveals the process of self formation.

Language has no transparency, even in the exclusive relationship the diarist constructs with it in her text, and therefore that relationship cannot produce a transcription of the self, but must participate in that self's creation. This, involving the validation of subjective experience and resistance to the totality of external definition, opens up the possibility of engaging more positively in one's own construction, overcoming perhaps what Christa Wolf has described as ´the difficulty of saying "I"´ (Wolf, 1982), and offering the possibility of transformation. ´Because´, as Susan Griffin writes, ´each time I write, each time the authentic words break through, I am changed. The old order that I was collapses and dies´ (Griffin, 1982, p. 232). Such transformation can break the dependency on the Idealist boundaries of the text, leading to a sense of self whose security is no longer based on exclusion or secrecy. The refuge of secrecy is a comment on the denial of such a sense of self in a patriarchal world where the prevalent notion of identity is one that is formed through fixed boundaries, and where women have little control over their representation. And yet for women that secrecy holds within it the possibility of turning the diary from a refuge into ´an odyssey from the inner to the outer world´ (as Anais Nin puts it). Nin´s diary was eventually published in her own lifetime and taking its place beside her fiction, served to challenge the rigid division between the ´real´ and the ´created´ divisions that she, like so many diarists, initially determined to draw. For it is only in the bringing together of the inner and outer worlds that the process of transformation can effectively challenge fixed boundaries and the fixed relations of power that govern our relationship to the ´self´.

NOTE

1. Palmer, the Rudgely poisoner made use of this notion of the diary. Having murdered his wife he wrote in his diary of his terrible grief, and on the day of her funeral: ´Saw the last of my dear wife for ever. How desolate life is!´ A week later he was angling for the insurance and living with the maid, which just goes to show the absurdity of endowing the diary with such status (see Ponsonby, 1927, p. 29).

REFERENCES

Barthes, Roland. (1977) Image-Music-Text, Fontana, London.
Belsay, Catharine (1980) Critical Practice, Methuen, London.
Brecht, Bertolt (1964) Brecht on Theatre, ed. John Willett, Eyre Methuen, London.
Browning, Elizabeth Barrett Unpublished Diary, 1831-2, ed. Phillip Kelley and Ronald Hudson, Ohio University Press, Athens, Ohio, 1969.
Capra, Fritjof (1982) The Turning Point, Flamingo, London.
Chodorow, Nancy(1979) ´Feminism and Difference: Gender, Relation and Difference in Psychoanalytic Perspective´, Socialist Review, 46.
Cixous, Hélène(1981) ´Castration or Decapitation?´ Signs. Journal of Women in Culture and Society, 7.
Eco, Umberto (1985) Reflections on the Name of the Rose, Secker and Warburg, London.
Griffin, Susan (1982) Made From This Earth, Women´s Press, London.
James, William The Varieties of Religious Experience: A Study in Human Nature (Gifford Lectures, 1901-2) from D. Bannister and F. Fansella (eds.), Inquiring Man, The Psychology of Personal Constructs (second edition, Penguin, Harmondsworth, 1971).
Lessing, Doris (1973) The Golden Notebook, Panther/Granada, London.
Nin, Anais (1973) The Journals of Anais Nin, vol. 1, Quartet, London.
Ponsonby, Arthur (1923) English Diaries, Methuen, London.
Ponsonby, Arthur (1927) More English Diaries, Methuen, London.
Sayre, Robert (1964) The Examined Self, Princeton University Press, New Jersey.
Tax, Meredith (1970) Woman and her Mind: The Story of Daily Life, A Bread and Roses publication, London.
Wolf, Christa (1982) The Quest for Christa T, Virago, London.
Woolf, Virginia Modern Fiction in vol. 2 of Collected Essays (London, 1966), originally published in The Common Reader (First Series).
Woolf, Virginia (1953) A Writer´s Diary, Hogarth Press, London.
Zaretsky, Eli (1976) Capitalism, The Family and Personal Life, Pluto Press, London.

TEN

LISTENING TO A SILENT PRESENCE: NOTES ON COLLABORATING OVER A TRANSLATION

Desmond Graham and Trude Schwab

Any act of translation involves at least a two-fold act of listening: listening to the author's text in one language and listening to oneself in another. In collaborating on a translation the complexity of this listening increases. The two translators have to listen to each other, listen to the author's text, and listen to themselves in their own languages and across languages. Quite possibly this will mean that collaborating over a translation may take more time. As the process of translation is in itself a matter of listening, carrying it out through a dialogue between collaborators might nonetheless prove a particularly appropriate method.

As the nature of the dialogue between collaborators will be affected by their degrees of linguistic competence, it is best to spell out the situation in our case. A is a native German speaker with many years' experience of living in England and is in effect bi-lingual. B is a native English speaker with some German and has lived in Germany on many occasions. The text translated was a selection of short stories by Ingeborg Bachmann.

Collaboration is basically a series of dialogues. The first dialogue takes place as translator A listens to the author's text to prepare a rough, comparatively literal draft. This draft serves as a working text on which the second dialogue takes place, that between the two collaborators. Within this dialogue which may entail a long period of discussion and re-working, the various forms of listening become the means of creating an independent text in the new language. The third dialogue takes place between this independent text and the native speaker of its language, B. The fourth dialogue is once again between the collaborators, with B reading the revised text to A, who listens to it while following the original language text. The independence of the translation as a new text can then be under-pinned by one or more further dialogues between that text and readers who have no knowledge of the original and their comments can be incorporated into the text during final revisions.

Most of the examples which follow are taken from Ingeborg Bachmann's story 'Der Schweisser' [Werke II, München 1978, pp. 59-75] ('The Welder') in which an uneducated welder in Vienna, through the chance discovery of a book under a coffee house table, becomes obsessed with reading and knowledge. He ceases to work, neglects his sick wife Rosi and his children and takes to his bed fanatically reading all day and night. His view of the world and even the language he speaks are transformed through this reading which brings with it deep insight, a sharp political awareness and finally despair. Many of his discoveries are revealed through conversations with the family doctor who fails to understand him. In our first example the doctor is in the man's bedroom, demanding why he has not visited Rosi who is dying in hospital:

> Der Doktor begann hin und herzugehen über Rosis blauen Läufer, der wie ein Steg durchs Zimmer führte, licht und selten benutzt (Der Schweisser, p. 67).

> The doctor started walking to and fro across Rosi's blue rug, which led across the room like a plank, light and scarcely used (Initial rough draft).

Discussion of this started with B picking up the repetition of 'across' and then wondering how exactly the rug led across the room 'like a plank'. 'How exactly did he walk across it, lost in thought, agitated, quickly or slowly; and wouldn't the bed be in the way?' A: 'The rug probably ran from the door to the window, a strip of carpeting'. B: 'A carpet-runner then! But how did the doctor move across it?' From various attempts at acting out the doctor's movements an expression was found which was implicit in the German, once the scene was envisaged: 'The doctor paced back and forth along Rosi's blue carpet runner'. The plank image, however, still seemed to lack precision and to make it more specific 'gangplank' was decided upon. One problem remained: What was the significance of 'light' in the phrase 'light and scarcely used'? B: 'It could mean light-weight, or could refer to the colour'. A: 'That ambiguity is not in the German word, 'licht'. Did you read it as 'leicht''? ''Licht' can convey only visual quality.' A then explained that the carpet-runner would be 'light' because it was 'scarcely used', and would therefore not be dirty: it was a reflection of Rosi's sense of homeliness, something looked after and cherished as a bright patch in an otherwise dark room, and probably in contrast to the flooring. Out of this conversation the phrase 'bright and hardly worn' emerged. The sentence as a whole now reading:

> The doctor began to pace back and forth along Rosi's blue

> carpet-runner, which crossed the room like a gangplank, bright and hardly worn.

At this point in the story the doctor addresses the welder:

> ´Sie sind wirklich verrückt. Warum lesen Sie bloss all das Zeug? Unsinn ist das, zu lesen. Ein Mensch, der im Leben steht... Ich stehe auch im Leben, wir stehen alle im Leben, und Sie lesen, sonst können Sie nichts, lesen, machen sich fertig. Das kommt doch von den Büchern, dass Sie sich fertig machen!´ (´Der Schweisser´, p.67ff.).
>
> ´You are absolutely mad. Why do you read all that stuff? Nonsense that is, to read. A person who is standing in life...I am standing in life, too, we are all standing in life, and you read, you can´t do anything else, just read and get yourself down. That is the result of the books, that you get yourself down!´ (Initial rough draft).

As a piece of direct speech the passage was discussed as a whole, starting with awkwardnesses of expression. B:´ What is meant by "a person who is standing in life..."´? A: ´This is a piece of literal translation to indicate that a problem is involved and not pre-empt a decision by offering a deceptively adequate phrase. The doctor is playing on a high-sounding empty phrase. A characteristic of his speech, which occurs again in the last expression in the passage, "sich fertig machen." Gradually a new draft took shape, with the readings: ´someone who has taken his place in life...´, and ´you ruin yourself...´. The next awkwardness to be tackled was: ´Nonsense that is, to read.´ A had retained the inversion to point where the emphasis lay in the German sentence. To reflect this emphasis the inversion was now dropped and an idiomatic expression was introduced to balance the sentence: ´It´s nonsense to read, that´s what it is.´ Wishing to sustain the idiomatic texture of the passage, ´you can´t do anything else´ was replaced by the unambiguous expression ´you aren´t good for anything else´, and the passage as a whole read:

> ´You are absolutely mad. Why do you read that stuff? It´s nonsense to read, that´s what it is. Someone who has taken his place in life...I´ve taken my place in life, too, we´ve all taken our place in life, and you read, you aren´t good for anything else, just read and ruin yourself. That´s what comes from reading books, you ruin yourself!´

The passage had involved elaborate discussion at the second

stage of dialogue so this version was set aside for re-working later. When it was discussed again with an ear to the doctor's way of speaking, the following refinements were found: 'I too have taken up my place in life, we've all taken up our place in life...' and 'just read and bring yourself to ruin. That's what reading books is doing to you....'

At the third stage of dialogue, listening to the text as a piece of direct speech in English without the German in mind, B moved further to the colloquial, replacing 'It's nonsense to read, that's what it is', with 'Reading's a load of rubbish, that's what it is.' B now read the text to A. Attending to the German text A realized that the opening idiom 'You are absolutely mad', reached by the attempt to be colloquial was in fact further from the German than necessary. In 'Sie sind wirklich verrückt', 'wirklich' had a perfectly acceptable literal equivalent in this context: 'You're really mad.' In turning from German to English idiom the listeners had slipped past what was specifically said and failed to notice, because the English idiom itself was seductively expressive. At the end of the passage, a similar inaccuracy had arisen. The German referred only to 'books' and not to 'reading books'. Again, listening in English had overtaken the act of translating. At the final stage, when a reader with no knowledge of the original listened to the English text a further improvement was suggested: 'you aren't good for anything else' would read better as 'you're good for nothing else'. This was discussed and incorporated into a last version:

> 'You're really mad. Why do you read all that stuff? Reading's a load of rubbish, that's what it is. Someone who has taken up his place in life...I too have taken up my place in life, we've all taken up our place in life, and you read, you're good for nothing else, just read and bring yourself to ruin. That's what books are doing to you, bringing you to ruin.'

The passage had been brought back closer to the German by listening to the English through the German text and by listening to it as an independent English text.

The degree of attentiveness involved in translating idioms is highlighted and intensified when it comes to translating slang expressions, cant phrases and proverbs. Here the accuracy of the listening will largely depend on awareness of such contextual factors as social setting, period, class, the speaker's or implied speaker's age group and degree of linguistic sophistication. The interaction of such factors is at the heart of a character's typical mode of speech. Expressions of this kind have therefore to be translated in a way which remains true to the character's individuality while bearing in mind the author's overall style. Here the literal is likely to be as much hindrance as help. In briefly illustrating this aspect of translating, it is necessary to introduce another kind of listening which occurs in nearly all kinds of translating: listening to dictionaries. This is an element within every stage of the translating process, and has its own complexity, as any one who works with a second language will know.

Near the end of 'The Welder' an extraordinary dialogue takes place in which the degree of misunderstanding between the doctor and the welder reaches breaking point. With increasing desperation the welder has tried to explain to the doctor the vision of society his reading has brought him. To this the doctor responds with a series of platitudes asserting the status quo and putting the welder in his place. In the end the process of dialogue has collapsed into an exchange of cliches, proverbs and cant phrases.

Translator A who was familiar with the German expressions used throughout the exchange could not come up with English equivalents for two of them and therefore turned to the dictionaries. For one expression, '<u>Rutschen Sie mir den Buckel herunter</u>', Muret/Sanders gave the following idiom: 'Go and take a running jump at yourself': hardly the language of a Viennese family doctor. Turning to Wildhagen various possibilities were found: 'I'll see you further ([slang] in hell) first; no, thanks; not I // go chase yourself'. 'I'll see you in hell first' was chosen as the expression most appropriate to character and context. Literal translation of the German expression ('You can slide down my back') would have had nearly as comic an effect as literal translation of the other expression '<u>Ich glaube, mich beisst was</u>': 'I think something is biting me'. For this, second expression, however, neither dictionary had an entry. Translation of this therefore depended entirely upon the dialogue between the collaborators. A explained the kind of situations in which such an expression would be used: B offered English set-phrases which A either knew and rejected or enquired further about. Eventually, 'I can't believe my ears' was agreed. Here are the expressions in context, the doctor speaking first:

> 'Kommt eine Zeit, kommt ein Rat.'
> ('Don't cross your bridges before you come to them.')
>
> 'Ich glaube, mich beisst was.'
> ('I can't believe my ears.')
>
> 'Ich geb keinen roten Heller für Sie.'
> ('I wouldn't give twopence for you.')
>
> 'Zu nachtschlafener Zeit und am hellichten Tag.'
> ('In the darkness of the night and the brightness

of the day.')

'Rutschen Sie mir den Buckel herunter.'
('I'll see you in hell first.')

'Sie haben die Weisheit wohl mit dem Löffel gefressen.'
('You seem to be a right pillar of wisdom.')

In translating set phrases such as these, the translator has little room for manoeuvre: in the second language he must find the appropriate set phrase. Most translation, however, involves a less restricted negotiation between numerous possibilities within which two broadly distinct activities can be recognized: deliberate listening and spontaneous response. In deliberate listening the translator works slowly and carefully to comprehend the exact nature of the original, taking into account such things as emphasis, diction, tone, register and style, choosing from a range of synonyms or potentially equivalent constructions in the second language. The limitations of this activity are that the translator remains highly conscious of the original language, keeps his ear attuned to it. This may result for example in over-elaborate phrasing, imprecise use of pronouns, insufficiently defined constructions, slightly unidiomatic usage and latent ambiguities in both syntax and wording. In contrast, the spontaneous response works through an immediate shift from the one language into the other, instantly activating the translator's capacity to hear within the second language. The virtues and shortcomings of this will be fairly obvious: especially in the translation of colloquial passages a happy phrase might be hit upon, expression may be more idiomatic, rhythms more effective, and tone better defined; beside this, nuances in the original may be lost, phrasing may be effective but inaccurate, and ambiguities may be overlooked. What the spontaneous response gains in reading better, it may lose in accuracy.

A simple example will reveal the spontaneous response at work. In the first draft, A translated '_Er lebte also in Ljubljana_' as 'He was living in Ljubljana then'. When discussing this, B asked 'Does this mean he lived in Ljubljana at that time in the past, or that Ljubljana was the particular place he was living in?' A replied, 'It means: "So he was living in Ljubljana"'. The ambiguity within 'then' which had been missed in making the draft was removed in A's spontaneous response to a question. The German word '_also_' has no temporal sense.

In this example literally questioning and listening enabled the translators to hear more accurately in both languages. Called upon to speak in English A spontaneously arrived at an unambiguous expression. In translating on the page the ambiguity had not been heard. This example also shows how collaborating can throw light on the process which takes place in any translating. The translator attempts to move towards an independent text which will reflect as accurately as possible the nature and spirit of the original. His progress towards this, however, may gain as much from the recognition of misunderstanding, the creative process of moving further from error or inadequacy, as from positive discoveries.

Working against misunderstanding and difference it is always the voice of the original that the translator is seeking to hear, hearing it often through its recalcitrant individuality as it challenges his attempts to provide a version. The following extract comes within a few lines of the point where the first example broke off. The welder, undeterred by the doctor's attack, attempts to present the new view from which he now sees things. He has just referred to how this work took him alongside the material displays of wealth in the shops of Vienna's First District. The German is followed by a near literal translation, so the reader without German may follow it:

> Aber sehen Sie, das war es nicht für mich, so neidisch war ich nie. Wir wohnen in Floridsdorf, Sie auch, Herr Doktor, drüber muss ich Ihnen wohl nichts sagen. Hier ist alles anders als es sonstwo wäre. Das Grün zum Beispiel von unseren Parks, die Luft, alles ist etwas zu kurz gekommen, den Strassen fehlt das, was eine Strasse schön macht, dem Park das, was einen Park romantisch macht. Gute Wohnungen haben wir in den Gemeindebauten, aber froh wird man nicht darin, an den Räumen ist zu wenig, an allem ist etwas zu wenig, an unsren Frauen auch, an der Rosi ist zu wenig, nicht dass sie keine gute Frau wäre, aber es ist bald zu wenig an ihr geworden wie an ihrem Armband zu wenig ist, an den Holzperlen und den dünnen goldenen Ohrringen mit den Vergissmeinnicht dran, an unsren Kindern ist zu wenig...

> But you see, that wasn't for me, I was never that envious. We live in Floridsdorf, you, too doctor, I presumably don't need to tell you anything about that. Everything is different here from what it might be anywhere else. The green, for example, of our parks, the air, everything somehow comes off badly, the streets have not got what makes a nice street, the park what makes a park romantic. We have good flats in the council blocks but you can't really thrive there, the rooms have too little, everything has too little, our wives too, Rosi has too little, not that she wasn't a good wife, but soon it became too little with her, just as there was too little with her bracelet, with the wooden beads and the thin gold earrings with the forget-me-nots, there is too little with our children...

Translation

In translating this passage each of the stages already described was gone through. Style was not so much considered at a particular point as taken into account throughout the discussion. Emphasizing this here, however, will mean slipping past many of the cruxes and details. In the German this passage is in a simple style reflecting the welder's speech, but at the same time it has a rhetorical patterning using repetition, contrast, enumeration and balance: an eloquence which comes from his reading. In seeking to understand this mode of speech, discussion focussed on the welder's attitude to his listener, the doctor: was he accusing or was he explaining things to him? Was he placing the doctor's position as one in contrast to that of the skilled labourer or was he seeing the two of them as sharing a district and its nature? The welder has found a new speech in which he is clear and forceful, giving and at the same time strict. And here the context of other styles in the story helps the translator towards definition. Beside the doctor's generalisations there is the welder's particularity, his determination to remain true to each part of his experience: the physical facts of it, his personal domestic conditions, the small possessions and family attachments, as well as his new found social and political consciousness. As he develops his case he focusses upon a simple expression, '_zu wenig_' (literally 'too little'), reiterating it and bringing it into unusual collocations such as '_an der Rosi ist zu wenig_'. Thus the welder is still using a simple vocabulary but the way in which he is using it reflects his new complexity of thought and argument. He is re-shaping the language at his disposal to express the pattern of his underprivileged existence.

Translation will therefore involve finding an expression adequate to the crucial phrase '_zu wenig_' and placing it within rhetorical patterns which hold true to the welder's new use of language. From discussing these issues, '_zu wenig_' was translated as 'lacking', and the passage as a whole read:

> But you see, that was not the thing for me, I was never that envious. We live in Floridsdorf, just as you do, doctor, I don't need to tell you about that. Here everything is different from what it would be anywhere else. The green of our parks, for instance, the air, everything somehow comes out badly, the streets just haven't got what it takes to make a nice street, the park, what it takes to make a park romantic. We've got decent enough flats in the housing estates, but one can't really thrive there, the rooms lack something, everything lacks something, our wives, too, Rosi lacks something, it's not that she wasn't a good wife, but soon there was something lacking, just as her bracelet is lacking something, the wooden beads and the thin gold earrings with the forget-me-nots, and our children lack

something...

To translate, listening has become a matter of hearing this welder speak in this situation, and hearing him speak what Bachmann is saying through his presence in the story.

The kinds of problem of listening involved in this passage are both extended by and assisted by that larger process of listening to a writer across a number of works. Translating a selection of stories therefore involves a further aspect of listening: listening across texts by the same author. Through that, something of the author's voice needs to be achieved, and seeking to hear it brings to the translators a further understanding of the nature of that voice.

Across the stories Bachmann is herself listening attentively to individual voices, in a world which actively or by default would distort or drown those voices in the generality of received ideas, commonplace attitudes and safe conformities. Her characters, always under threat from new situations or discoveries, are themselves re-learning experience through the process of being misunderstood, being unable to express themselves and redefining the way in which they use language. Language is at the centre of Bachmann's art and even the smallest elements within it can give a clue to her interpretation of experience. To identify the complexity of her understanding with a single phrase would naturally be excessive but it would not be untrue to the direction and the nature of that understanding. The welder's '*zu wenig*' keys us in to the irony within the title of a later story, '*Alles*' ('Everything'): our understanding of it deepens through the sound of barking which fills a lonely old woman's mind in '*Das Gebell*' ('The Barking'); it is at the centre of the seemingly successful journalist's forlorn and drifting quest in '*Drei Wege zum See*' ('Three Paths to the Lake'). At the same time it is the bleak understanding in that '*zu wenig*' which justifies the most attentive listening to details such as the doctor's 'pacing back and forth along Rosi's blue carpet-runner...like a gangplank...'.

The uniqueness of an author's voice, of course, also marks out the limitations inherent in translating. Even the best of translations can do no more than imperfectly echo the original, however powerfully the translation exists in its own right. There can therefore be no final translation of any work, for translating is an activity which must continue through each new listener. For this reason the critic of translation will always be aware of other possibilities, different readings: with generosity towards the wide margin of choice, however, any listener can take his creative part in the process: the negatives can again be turned to positives. Against the divisiveness inherent in differences of language, translation sets up an activity in which speakers of either or both languages can take their part. The translators listen to the original language and try to remain true to that, not only for their own benefit but because the reader of their translation may not be able to hear it; the translator listens to two languages for those readers who can only listen to one. The reader of a translation listens not only to the translators but listens to a silent presence beyond the translator, that of the author.

ELEVEN

THROWING THE BOOK: TOM STOPPARD AND THE POLITICS OF LISTENING

Neil Sammells

Words, according to C.W.E. Bigsby in a recent volume of the *Stratford-Upon-Avon Studies*, have become the very focus of contemporary English drama. A concern with 'the viscosity of language, its ambiguities, its availability as an instrument of social control' (Bigsby, 1981, p. 25) is shared by writers as different as the socialist Howard Brenton, a 'genuine anarchist' like Joe Orton, and Tom Stoppard, described by Ken Tynan as 'one of the two or three most prosperous and ubiquitously adulated playwrights at present bearing a British passport' (Tynan, 1981, p. 46). According to Bigsby, Stoppard stands centre-stage as a representative contemporary dramatist inasmuch as his plays are '*about* language' (Bigsby, 1981, p. 25). It would be more accurate to say that much of Stoppard's work is about *listening*. Indeed, an examination of Stoppard's obsession with our ways of listening and his demonstration of listening as a creative activity, will shed light not only on some of his most characteristic techniques and themes (such as his predilection for a dramatic dialogue constructed from the proliferation of puns, and what Bigsby calls his acknowledgment of the 'link between language and power' (Bigsby, 1981, p. 26)), it will also throw into relief a major development in his dramatic output: its hardening into a militant conservatism that is both political and linguistic.

In two early plays of Stoppard's, listening is examined in an essentially domestic context. The radio play *'M' is for Moon Among Other Things* (1964) gives the audience the chance to eavesdrop on a middle-aged couple, Alfred and Constance. While Alfred gnaws away at a recent social embarrassment inflicted upon him by his wife, Constance works her way diligently and silently, word for word, through the Universal Treasury of People, Places and Things, at the same time conducting an interior monologue on the subject of her wasted life. Alfred tunes in to the radio to be ambushed by the news of Marilyn Monroe's death and is plunged into a melancholy diatribe against the shallowness of the showbiz world: 'A girl like that, dying with a telephone in her hand - who did she have to call who would have done her any good?´ (Stoppard, 1983, p. 66). The irony is simple and slight: Alfred constructs a fantasy in which he saves Marilyn by answering her telephone call; meanwhile he remains unaware of his wife´s needs. The relationship, we surmise, is doomed by his failure to listen, to establish a dialogue with his wife. In *If You´re Glad, I´ll be Frank* (1966) the position is reversed and the play takes an incidental detail from *´M´ is for Moon Among Other Things* as its dramatic premise. Here it is the husband, Frank, who is desperately trying to establish contact with his wife. Gladys, unfortunately for him, is accessible only as the voice of the Speaking Clock. She remains contemptuously dismissive of the claims of the world outside her self-inflicted prison as Stoppard once again uses the telephone to explore isolation and, more particularly, a failure to listen.

Although in some ways little more than domesticated Ionesco, these two pieces are interesting inasmuch as they take their own form as their subject: they are plays about listening which entail a listening audience. In a sense, such self-consciousness is characteristic of Stoppard who is ever the artist as critic. His plays are often constructed from a critical engagement with the demands of established literary genre, whether it is Shakespearean Tragedy and Beckettian Absurdism as in *Rosencrantz and Guildenstern are Dead* (1966) or the less exalted form of the Le Carre spy-story as in *The Dog It Was That Died* (1983). By parodying the conventions of these forms, and their terms of existence, Stoppard is continually attempting to remind the audience of the ways in which they construct their literary meanings. In another radio play, *Artist Descending a Staircase* (1972), Stoppard examines the form of the whodunnit, which also comes under scrutiny in *After Magritte* (1970), *Jumpers* (1972) and, of course, *The Real Inspector Hound* (1968). More than this, however, the play takes much further the self-consciouness of the two earlier radio pieces: the audience is constantly made aware of its own attempts to create meanings in the act of listening, as it listens to, among other things, Martello and Beauchamp trying to interpret a loop of recorded tape as evidence of the murder of Donner, who for more years than they care to remember has completed this unholy trinity of superannuated artists.

Artist Descending a Staircase opens with a sequence of sounds which is to be interpreted by Martello and Beauchamp thus: Donner dozing, careful footsteps approach, Donner wakes and his droning stops in mid-beat, the footsteps freeze, Donner says ´Ah! there you are ...´, two quick steps follow and a Thump!, Donner cries out, crashes through the balustrade and falls heavily down the stairs. We then hear Martello and Beauchamp each leap to the conclusion that the other *has* to be guilty. ´I think this is where I came in´, muses Martello as the sequence of sounds starts again:

> Beauchamp. And this is where you hit him.
> (Tape: Thump!)
> Martello. I mean, it's going round again. The tape is going round in a loop.
> (Stoppard, 1973, p. 13)

Beauchamp interprets Martello's utterance in the light of his own certainty; in effect, as a listener he wrests meaning from the speaker and creates it anew. It is an important exchange, as we shall see, pointing back to After Magritte in which the 'viscosity of language' is a direct result of listeners appropriating the remarks of speakers in an attempt to make their own version of events prevail, and pointing forward to Stoppard's explicitly political plays about Eastern Bloc countries in which speakers are repeatedly dispossessed of their meaning by repressive authorities bent on listening in their own aggressive ways.

Beauchamp's certainty is, of course, matched by Martello's. 'There you are', announces Beauchamp as he switches off the tape. 'On the contrary, Beauchamp', comes the rejoinder, 'there you are. Unless we can agree on that, I can't even begin to help you clear up this mess' (p. 14). He claims to admire his companion's 'hopeless persistence' in protesting his innocence, 'But the tape-recorder speaks for itself. That is, of course, the point about tape-recorders. In this case it is eloquent, grandiloquent, not to say Grundigloquent' (p. 16). In fact, Artist Descending a Staircase hinges on a denial of Martello's point: far from 'speaking for itself' the meaning of the tape-recorded evidence is created by listeners - first Martello and Beauchamp and later the audience. The play also mounts an ironic response to Beauchamp and his claims for the significance of his 'tonal' art.

It transpires that Beauchamp had left the recorder running in the first place, trawling for the silences and unidentifiable sounds which comprise his artistic masterwork. In a flashback Beauchamp is heard defending his art to Donner who, in his dotage, has turned to Realism. 'If you played my tape on the radio', admits Beauchamp with pride, 'it would seem a meaningless noise, because it fulfils no expectations: people have been taught to expect certain kinds of insight but not others. The first duty of the artist is to capture the radio station' (p. 20). 'I refuse to discuss it', responds Donner, 'Horrible noise, anyway'. 'Only', insists Beauchamp, 'because people have not been taught what to listen for, or how to listen' (p. 21). His point is that there is nothing inherently significant in Realism; it is art for Everyman, 'only because every man is an initiate of that particular mystery' (p. 20). Beauchamp's 'tonal' art is, then, an attempt to deny that anything can speak for itself, a celebration of listening as a creative rather than purely 'receptive' activity.

The denouement of Artist Descending a Staircase is both a parodic estrangement of the whodunnit and a vindication of much of what Beauchamp has to say. The play ends by reproducing the sequence of sounds with which it began; this time, however, the audience is invited to interpret it thus: a fly drones, Beauchamp's footsteps approach ('Ah! There you are'), and the fatal thumping swat follows. So, perhaps Donner was not murdered but plummeted to his death while similarly engaged. As Beauchamp mutters, 'As flies to wanton boys are we to the Gods: they kill us for their sport' (p. 54). In other words, both Martello and Beauchamp are wrong in accusing each other and the audience has fallen into what Stoppard calls one of the 'ambushes' from which he constructs his plays (Stoppard, 1974, p.6). What the play demonstrates, then, is the listening audience's complicity in constructing both the original mystery and its solution.

Within this overall strategy against the audience Stoppard plants a number of smaller, incidental ambushes. As Beauchamp, Martello and Donner make their way through France on the eve of the Great War, we hear the clip-clop of Beauchamp's Tenth Horse and its skittering as he swats sundry flies. The punchline is the revelation that what we hear is just Beauchamp skilfully employing halved coconuts. He abandons his fictions as 'A squadron of cavalry gallops in quickly to occupy the foreground with a thunder of hooves; and recedes, leaving the men sober and stunned' (p. 45). Of course, this is just another fiction even if the technical means for producing the sound-effect are a little more sophisticated than those at Beauchamp's disposal. The point is clear: such reality as either incident can claim (and the same, of course, can be said of the entire play) is simply a construct of the audience's act of listening. Indeed, Stoppard keeps the creative 'blindness' of the audience in the very foreground by dexterous use of the blind girl Sophie. Her plight is exactly that of the audience: she must create her world and its meanings through the 'evidence' of sound alone. Her blindness and that of the audience are coextensive, both are prey to Beauchamp's 'tonal' art which confronts them with the spectacle of Lloyd George playing Clara Bow at ping-pong and Lenin struggling at chess with Jack Dempsey.

Not all of Stoppard's 'ambushes for the audience' are as successful as those in Artist Descending a Staircase. Ken Tynan points out that Travesties (1975), Stoppard's most exuberant exercise in theatrical self-consciousness and parody, starts with something of a damp squib. We see the Dadaist Tristan Tzara drawing words at random from a hat and reciting them in the form of a limerick which ends: 'Ill raced alas whispers kill later nut east./ Noon avuncular ill day

Clara!´ (Stoppard, 1975, p. 18). To French-speaking members of the audience the lines sound roughly the same as ´Il reste a la Suisse parce qu´il est un artist./ "Nous n´avons que l´art" il declara´. In English this means ´He lives in Switzerland because he´s an artist./ "We have only art", he declared´. ´No translation or explanation, however, is offered in the text´, complains Tynan, ´Nonspeakers of French are thus left in outer darkness, while French-speakers who have not read the published version are unaware that what they have just heard is a linguistic joke. The result is that nobody laughs´ (Tynan, 1981, p. 110). Tynan is probably right to suggest that this does not work as theatre, but the point, however clumsily handled, is an important one. The audience witnesses Tzara creating meaning and significance out of nothing and this process of ´making´ is paralleled by the audience´s listening. It is clear that Stoppard´s original intention in assembling this elaborate array of puns was to make the audience aware of the creative nature of their role as listeners as a prologue to the main concerns of the play: the way Henry Carr ´travesties´ the past, actively creating a spurious version of history which mirrors the various fabrications of the artists and politicians he has (or has not) met. Carr, Tzara, Joyce, Lenin and the audience are, the play declares, makers all.

The premise with which Travesties opens, that the creativity of listening can be demonstrated specifically in the ways we listen to language, is explored rather more successfully than in Tzara´s hat-trick by After Magritte. The play is constructed out of the various attempts to account for and explain two mysterious sights: the bizarre tableau with which the play opens (and which Inspector Foot regards as ´suspicious´) and the apparently unidentifiable witness who will prove the innocence of Harris et al. Harris and his wife are locked in debate about the ´bizarre and desperate figure´ (Stoppard, 1971, p. 34) they have seen in Ponsonby Place. Thelma recalls a footballer in strip and Harris a pyjama-clad figure carrying not a football but a tortoise. ´You must be blind´, insists Thelma. ´It was he who was blind´, comes the equable response (p. 14). ´I happened to see him with my own eyes´, continues Harris. ´We all saw - ´ counters Thelma. ´I am only telling you what I saw!´ (p. 19) repeats her husband, with mounting fury. Both are adamant that they are reporting only what they have seen; they are also equally incapable of recognising the degree to which they have themselves created the mystery as the initial visual impression becomes buried deeper and deeper beneath their insistence that every element should cohere and be related to a single explanatory factor. What they discover, in the course of their clash with Foot of the Yard, is that language is as difficult to interpret, as capable of transformation, as the evidence of their senses.

Stoppard´s point about puns, claims Clive James, ´isn´t

so much that the one sound contains multiple meanings, as that it has a different meaning in different places ... he is at his strongest when one precise meaning is transformed into another precise meaning with the context full-blown in each case' (James, 1975, p. 70). Such puns pullulate in the dialogue of After Magritte. Each speaker attempts to fix a viewpoint in language; the ambiguities which arise through the clash of contexts do so because each explanation of events is countered. In effect, meaning becomes the province of the listener rather than the speaker.

Foot, for instance, meets Harris' claim that there is a perfectly logical reason for everything apparently untoward in the house with the impassioned rejoinder: 'There is, and I mean to make it stick!' (p. 32). Foot is convinced that 'within the last hour in this room you performed without anaesthetic an illegal operation on a black nigger minstrel about five-foot-two or Pakistani' (p. 31), and reminding P.C. Holmes that 'What we're looking for is a darkie short of a leg or two' (p. 33), he meets each protestation to the contrary head-on, 'Is it all right for me to practice?' asks Mother:

> Foot. No, it is not all right! Ministry standards may be lax but we draw the line at Home Surgery to bring in the little luxuries of life.
> Mother. I only practice on the tuba.
> Foot. Tuba, femur, fibula - it takes more than a penchant for rubber gloves to get a licence nowadays.
> (p. 33)

Earlier, Thelma, insisting that the mysterious hopping witness was in fact a West Bromwich Albion footballer 'carrying under his arm, if not a football then something very similar like a wineskin or a pair of bagpipes', claims that what he had on his face 'was definitely shaving foam! [Pause] or possibly some kind of yashmak'. Harris, predictably will have none of this:

> Harris. The most -the very most -I am prepared to concede is that he may have been a sort of street arab making off with his lute - but young he was not and white-bearded he was!
> Thelma. His loot?
> Harris. (expansively) Or his mandolin - Who's to say?
> (p. 20)

Stoppard, equally predictably, will not let the pun rest. 'I don't see that the tortoise as such requires explanation', insists Harris as Foot indulges his obsession with his own success at 'deductions of a penetrating character', 'since the fellow was blind he needn't necessarily have known it was a tortoise. He might have picked it up in mistake for some other object such as a lute'. 'His loot?' pounces Foot. 'Or mandolin', comes the reply (p. 40).

As in Artist Descending a Staircase the whodunnit form of After Magritte is parodied and 'made strange' by the simple device of revealing that no crime has, in fact, been committed. Foot has set himself a non-existent problem to solve; in so doing the detective emerges not as the bringer of truth but as the agent of confusion. His insistent search for evidence to corroborate his hypothesis about the supposed double-crime (the robbery among the Victoria Palace Happy Minstrel Troupe and the unlicensed surgery at Mafeking Villas) has brought linguistic confusion to the play's dialogue, and his guilt is made explicit when we realise that it was he who was the bizarre figure who occasions so much dissension between Thelma and Harris.

Foot is the forerunner of the far more sinister Inspector in Stoppard's Dogg's Hamlet, Cahoot's Macbeth (1979), who attempts to truncate even further the cut-down version of Macbeth being performed by a small group of out-of-work, out-of-favour Czech actors before an equally out-of-favour audience; and both figures are descended from the menacing and sadistic Inspector Truscott of Joe Orton's Loot (1966). Indeed, in After Magritte Stoppard sketches the terrain over which will be fought the battle for language which is at the centre of his later plays about Communist Europe. In terms of the change in Stoppard's drama which sees a new emphasis on explicitly political subject-matter, Jumpers (1972), his first full-length stage-play since the precocious success of Rosencrantz and Guildenstern are Dead, occupies an important pivotal position. Significantly, in Jumpers, Stoppard examines the painful implications for the dissenter of the ways in which we listen.

Against the public background of a moon-landing and a Radical-Liberal victory at the polls (or was it a military coup?) Jumpers presents us with the private plight of the peripheral figure, in this case the professional philosopher George Moore. George is preparing a paper to be presented at the university symposium, a paper which argues the existence of God. Moore's 'philosophers' God' is not only a Creator but also the origin and guarantee of absolute values in aesthetics and in morality. George is hyperconscious of the fact that he is on the defensive. 'There is, presumably', he muses, 'a calendar date - a moment - when the onus of proof passed from the atheist to the believer, when, quite suddenly, secretly, the noes had it'. (Stoppard, 1972, p. 25). The orthodox philosophical mainstream against which he must swim is made up of 'Logical Positivists, mainly, with a linguistic analyst or two, a couple of Benthamite Utilitarians ... lapsed Kantians and empiricists generally ... and of course the usual Behaviourists ... a mixture', he adds, 'of the more philosophical members of the university gymnastics team and the more gymnastic members of the Philosophy School' (pp. 50-1). George declares it his intention to set British philosophy back forty years, 'which is roughly when it went off the rails' (p. 46). The paper he hopes to deliver is structured, accordingly, around a protracted critique of A. J. Ayer's Language, Truth and Logic which first transplanted the doctrines of Logical Positivism and the Vienna Circle from Teutonic to English soil in 1936. There is, says Jonathan Bennett in 'Philosophy and Mr. Stoppard' (Bennett, 1975, p. 5), no structural relationship between this academic philosophical material and the rest of the play; compared to the philosophical content of Rosencrantz and Guildenstern are Dead, which is solid, serious and functional, George's academic struggles are thin and uninteresting, serving Jumpers in only a marginal and decorative way. In fact, the binding element is Stoppard's interest in listening: George's confrontation with the central tenets of Logical Positivism functions as a focus for the playwright's exploration of the nature of freedom and criticism and his treatment of the implications for the dissenting voice of our ways of listening.

This can perhaps best be seen in George's disastrous encounter with that capstone of the Logical Positivist philosophy, the Verification Principle. Dotty (George's neurotic wife) provides the best introduction to the problem when she recites the Gospel according to Sir Archibald Jumper, the university Vice-Chancellor. 'Things and actions, you understand', she intones, 'can have any number of real and verifiable properties. But good and bad, better and worse, these are not real properties of things, they are just expressions of our feelings about them'. George's retort is predictably sceptical: 'Archie says' (p. 41). As presented by A. J. Ayer, the outcome of the supposition is that we can make significant statements about only those properties we can verify. A statement is only meaningful if we know what empirical observations would prove its truth or falsehood. If we cannot think of a method to prove or disprove a statement then it is of no significance, has no meaning, is, literally, nonsense. Although neither Ayer nor the Verification Principle are mentioned by name in Jumpers, this argument (or, rather, pre-empting of argument) is of particular and painful significance for George in his protracted consideration of the objectivity of moral judgments and the necessity of a divine First Cause. The consequence of what Ayer and Logical Positivism have to say with regard to both moral and aesthetic value-judgments is to deny that there can be any debate about them, that in speaking of them we can talk of anything but nonsense. Ayer's vision of 'ethics' is of a world emptied of meaning and hence of argument. 'In saying that a certain type of action is right or wrong', he explains, 'I am not making any factual statement, not even a statement about my own state of mind. I am merely expressing certain moral sentiments. And the man who is contradicting me is merely expressing his moral sentiments. So that there is plainly no sense in arguing which of us is in the right. For neither of us is asserting a genuine proposition' (Ayer, 1971, pp. 142-3).

In effect, George finds himself about to address an audience which simply refuses to listen, or, perhaps more accurately, listens only in the sense of actively emptying of meaning what he attempts to say. Indeed, George's consciousness of his audience's aggressively pre-emptive ways of listening disables him as a 'speaker'; he is betrayed into a series of comic defeats by the very words he attempts to use. 'Though my convictions are intact and my ideas coherent', he explains to Inspector Bones, 'I can't seem to find the words' (p. 46). An example of George's words betraying the thoughts they are supposed to express comes when he tries to claim, explicitly, the existence of God; in doing so he is acutely and painfully aware of Ayer's strictures against the mystic in Language, Truth and Logic: 'we know that if he really had acquired any information, he would be able to express it. He would be able to indicate in some way or other how the genuineness of his discovery might be empirically determined. The fact that he cannot reveal what he 'knows', or even himself devise an empirical test to validate his 'knowledge' shows that his state of mystical intuition is not a genuinely cognitive state' (Ayer, 1971, p. 157). 'How does one know what it is one believes' muses George, implicitly acknowledging the fact that the meaning of the verb 'to know' is the province of the listeners at the symposium 'when it is so difficult to know what it is one knows. I don't claim to know that God exists, I only claim that he does without my knowing it, and while I claim as much I do not claim to know as much; indeed I cannot know and God knows I cannot' (p. 71). George is similarly incommoded when arguing against Bertrand Russell's proposition that the series of proper fractions is an example of a sequence which does not have a first term and, by implication, first cause. 'But the fact is', counters George, lapsing into an absurdity which effectively negates the point he is striving to make, 'the first term is not an infinite fraction, but zero. God, so to speak, is nought' (p. 29). George has lost control of language, he attempts to use it in one way and it uses him in another.

George's linguistic incompetence is contrasted with the verbal gymnastics of the philosophical and political jumpers. Language jumps along with the rest of them. 'Are you telling me', George asks Dotty, incredulously, 'that the Radical Liberal spokesman for Agriculture has been made Archbishop of Canterbury?!!' 'Don't shout at me', she replies, 'I suppose if you think of him as a sort of ... shepherd, ministering to his flock ...' Dotty goes on to suggest that the old Archbishop uncoped himself. 'Dismantled himself, perhaps' (p. 38), suggests George, bitterly acknowledging the preeminence of the pun in the new world beyond the luxury confines of the Mayfair flat. The point is clear: George's philosophical enquiry is consigned to the category of 'metaphysical' nonsense, yet the puns make a kind of sense of their own. For those who know how to listen they are a linguistic sanction for that pragmatism in public life 'both here and on the moon' which so disturbs George and, indeed, Dotty, whether it prompts the new Government to rationalise the church or Astronauts Scott and Oates to struggle with each other for survival at the foot of their crippled spacecraft. Unlike the jumpers, George refuses to learn the new art of listening.

However, George's revolt is qualified by his propensity to draw a circle around philosophy. Despite his proud boast that were he given the Chair of Logic, it would 'apply itself occasionally to the activities of the human race' (p. 73), he is all too prone to thinking of himself as a philosopher first and a citizen second. He recalls, for instance, trying to discuss the Theory of Descriptions with Bertrand Russell (who, incidentally, was attempting to contact Chairman Mao through the local exchange with the wine-waiter from the Pagoda Garden hanging on to interpret); Dotty remembers George rambling on about 'language being the aniseed trail that draws the hounds of heaven when the metaphysical fox has gone to earth', and he is stung into defending himself. 'I was simply trying to bring his mind back to matters of universal import', he declares, 'and away from the day-to-day parochialism of international politics'. 'Universal <u>import</u>' gasps Dotty, 'You're living in dreamland!' (p. 31). Later, when Inspector Bones asks him what he was doing during the fatal party to celebrate the Radical Liberal victory, George says, 'I'm not interested in politics. I was trying to write my paper' (pp. 47-8). As a philosopher George is painfully aware that language has been appropriated by a collective interest, as a man he refuses to acknowledge the radical political consequences such an appropriation must entail. He remains, as Archie puts it, 'our tame believer, pointed out to visitors in much the same spirit as we point out the magnificent stained glass in what is now the gymnasium' (p. 63).

In <u>Jumpers</u>, then, we can indeed see Stoppard exploring what Bigsby calls the link between language and power; more particularly, however, the play focuses on <u>listening</u> as the exercise of power. The art of political listening is a self-sealing against criticism. In 'But for the Middle Classes', his review of Paul Johnson's <u>Enemies of Society</u> (1977), Stoppard applauds the author's hostility to 'closed-circuit systems which explain everything and are irrefutable only in the tactical sense that they avoid the possibility of refutation' (Stoppard, 1977, p. 677). It is, of course, precisely such closed-circuit thinking which Stoppard attacks in his critique of Logical Postivism in <u>Jumpers</u>; in 'But for the Middle Classes' Stoppard accuses Freudianism and Marxism of a similarly 'incredible intellectual arrogance' and goes on to declare that he shares, with Johnson, an allegiance to a Western Liberal Democracy favouring an intellectual elite and a progressive middle class dedicated to the pursuit of Christian moral values. In the plays which follow Jumpers and Travesties (and the canonisation of Stoppard on A Level syllabuses) he does not only go directly on to the attack against the 'closed-circuitry' of the Communist state, he also creates dissenting voices which (unlike George Moore) recognise the political nature of the art of listening. It is a development which signals Stoppard's switching of focus from the dissenter to the dissident.

The very title of Every Good Boy Deserves Favour (1977) announces that listening is going to be a primary concern. The analogy with music is clear: for the authorities, the dissident Alexander Ivanov presents them with a discordant note in an orchestrated society, a note they do not want to hear. As in Travesties, the play opens with a prologue which not only insists that listening is creative but which makes the audience aware of their own creative role as listeners. We see Alexander's cell-mate striking a triangle and the orchestra miming a performance. Very slowly the audience is allowed to hear what he can hear: the orchestra becomes audible and the triangle begins to fit into the context which makes sense of it. So Stoppard teaches the audience to listen in a certain way, to construct significance where there had seemed to be none. As in After Magritte and Jumpers the application of this lesson to our understanding of the ways in which we listen to language sanctions a proliferation of puns. In Every Good Boy Deserves Favour Stoppard does not just tack social comment onto linguistic clownery. His puns enact the politics of control.

The most significant pun occurs in an exchange between Alexander Ivanov and the Doctor, who insists on denying the claim that sane people are being locked up in mental institutions. 'I have a complaint', announces Alexander. 'Yes, I know' - comes the reply, 'pathological development of the personality with paranoid delusions' (Stoppard, 1978, p. 26). The Doctor's aggressive listening is neatly demonstrated as he throws Alexander in a deft example of linguistic judo. The dissident's problem is that the very cogency of his convictions will be enough to condemn both them and him; unlike George Moore, he can find the words but this is a world in which the speaker is in the power of the listener. The Doctor cites the parallel case of Pyotr Grigorenko 'of whom it has been stated by our leading psychiatrists at the Serbsky Institute, that his outwardly well adjusted behaviour and formally coherent utterances were indicative of a pathological development of the personality' (pp. 30-1). In other words, dissent is consigned to nonsense as effectively as George

Moore's metaphysical intuitions.

It is the very adroitness of the ways they listen which allows the authorities to save face when it becomes clear that Alexander Ivanov will not be broken and admit his insanity: the fact that his name is the same as his mad cell-mate with the imaginary orchestra allows Rozinsky to choose which of them to listen to. Alexander states, quite truthfully, that he does not have an orchestra, his cure is proclaimed and he is released without embarrassing the authorities by dying in their custody.

Professional Foul, the companion-piece to Every Good Boy Deserves Favour, was suggested by a trip Stoppard made to Russia in 1977 to collect signatures protesting against the Soviet treatment of dissidents. (Stoppard describes his Moscow trip in some detail in 'The Face at the Window' [Stoppard, 1977, p. 33].) He found himself the victim of a professional foul by the Soviet Customs Officers who simply stole the document. The visit to Moscow unlocked for Stoppard his first play about Czechoslovakia where he had been born and which his family had fled on the eve of the Nazi invasion (Ken Tynan, 1981 documents the deracinated childhood which followed in Show People). There are several 'professional fouls' in the piece: most notably the faked discovery of foreign currency in Pavel Hollar's dissident thesis in the boorish McKendrick's baggage. Significantly, a professional foul is also inflicted on a group of listeners: the Czech hosts empty the auditorium during Anderson's contentious paper (defending individual rights against collective, State rule) by sounding the fire alarm.

Professional Foul is, in many ways, about frustrated listening. One of the television play's most telling sequences is a series of close-ups at the philosophical colloquium Anderson uses as an excuse for his trip to see the England vs. Czechoslovakia football match. We see the bewildered reaction of the audience - and of the simultaneous translators they are listening to - as the lumbering American professor Stone gives a tortured analysis of the subtle distinction between 'The show ran well on Broadway' and 'Native Dancer ran well at Kentucky'. The scene is an explicit and comic distillation of Stoppard's insistence on the listener's complicity in the creation, and the absence, of meaning. Similarly comic is the scene when McKendrick, eager to ingratiate himself with his professional colleagues, confronts two of the English footballers after Anderson has explained that Crisp is a left-winger and Broadbent an opportunist in the centre: 'I hear you're doing some very interesting work in Newcastle. Great stuff. I like to think of myself as a bit of a left-winger at Stoke. Of course, my stuff is largely empirical ...' (pp. 59-60). Anderson winces, McKendrick prattles on about neo-Hegelians and Quinean neo-positivists and the two footballers find themselves as much in need of a simultaneous translation as the assembled philosophers at the colloquium.

However, the frustration of 'creative' listening is given a more poignant treatment in the scenes between Anderson and his ex-student, Hollar. Hollar tells Anderson that he is now earning his living as a cleaner:

> Anderson. (with intelligent interest) A cleaner? What is that?
> Hollar. (surprised) Cleaning. Washing. With a brush and a bucket. I am a cleaner at the bus station.
> Anderson. You wash buses?
> Hollar. No, not buses - the lavatories, the floors where people walk and so on.
> Anderson. Oh. I see. You're a cleaner. (p. 52).

The point is clear, as is the parallel with Stone's difficulty at the colloquium: the problem for Hollar is not how he uses the word, but how Anderson hears it.

In essence, Professional Foul presents us with Anderson's education through experience. Attempting to sidle out of the colloquium, Anderson is trapped into delivering an impromptu riposte to Stone. The importance of language, he insists in transit, is overrated: 'The essentials of a given situation speak for themselves and language is as capable of obscuring the truth as of revealing it' (p. 63). In the panic and the confusion of Hollar's flat, surrounded by police shouting abuse in a language he does not understand, Anderson finds his glib assurance put to the test. The situation speaks for itself because Anderson meets it with sharpened powers of listening: the scene is an ironic reversal of that in his hotel room when he had consistently misheard Hollar despite the fact that both were speaking the same language. His understanding of what takes place when the Czech police claim to find the foreign currency prompts not only his decision to change the paper he had agreed to read but also his smuggling of Hollar's thesis out of the country. Anderson learns two basic lessons: unlike George Moore he realises that his status as professional philosopher is no refuge from political realities and his recognition of the way he had initially failed to listen to Hollar teaches him that the dissident cannot simply speak for himself.

In Dogg's Hamlet, Cahoot's Macbeth (1979) dissent is not a solitary but a collective activity: the second half of the play centres on the attempts of a group of dissident actors to perform a truncated version of Macbeth which, for the assembled audience, in portraying a brutal and illegal seizure of power, is a reflection of what has happened in Czechoslovakia. For the dissidents the crowning of Malcolm is both an assertion of hope and an affirmation of faith in the efficacy of criticism. The proceedings are constantly interrupted by the Inspector who attempts to appropriate both the text and the performance by ending it at the crowning of Macbeth and lauding it with his own ominous banalities: 'Very good. Very good! And so nice to have a play with a happy ending for a change' (Stoppard, 1980, p. 58). The first half of the play, however, consists of Stoppard's attempt to teach his audience Dogg-language as they follow the struggles of the lorry-driver, Easy, to make sense of the strange world he has wandered into. In the end, Easy uses Dogg for the specific purpose of abusing the authoritarian headmaster of the boys' school. His arrival in the second half, as he blunders into the action and confuses himself with Banquo's ghost, gives the troupe the chance to use Dogg to finish their performance of _Macbeth_ in spite of the Inspector's intrusive presence.

The problem for the actors is that the Inspector, like the jumpers, can do with language what he will. 'I've got the penal code tattooed on my whistle', he assures Landovsky, 'and there's a lot about you in it. Section 98, subversion - anyone acting out of hostility to the state ... section 100, incitement, anyone acting out of hostility to the state ... I could nick you just for acting - and the sentence is double for an organised group, which I can make stick on Robinson Crusoe and his man any day of the week' (p. 61). The pun, for the Inspector, is an offensive tactic, a means of making us listen in a certain way: 'You know as well as I do that this performance of yours goes right against the spirit of normalization. When you clean out the stables, Cahoot, the muck is supposed to go into the gutter, not find its way back into the stalls' (p. 62). 'Words', he announces happily, 'can be your friend or your enemy, depending on who's throwing the book, so watch your language' (p. 59). _Dogg's Hamlet, Cahoot's Macbeth_ restates Stoppard's conviction that it also depends on who is listening, and how.

However, where the play departs from its two predecessors is in its construction of an alternative language capable of carrying the burden of dissent. The inventiveness of the Inspector, in other words, is matched by that of the dissidents. Cahoot starts to abuse the Inspector in Dogg, reminding Stoppard's audience that 'Afternoon, squire', means, in Dogg, 'Get stuffed you bastard'. The Inspector asks where Easy learnt Dogg: 'You don't learn it', replies Cahoot, 'you catch it' (p. 74). The riposte is a triumphant appropriation, and reapplication, of the formulaic identification of dissent with disease which is at the centre of _Every Good Boy Deserves Favour_. The performance of _Macbeth_, and that of Stoppard's own play, now speed to a climax. Dogg becomes a means of repelling the Inspector (his announcement that anything they say will be taken down and played back at the trial meets with the response 'Bicycles' Plank!' [p. 75]) and of completing _Macbeth_ before the Inspector realises what is happening. He is at a complete loss ('if it's not free expression, I don't know what it is!' [p. 75]) as language is wrested from his control.

In fact, it is now the Inspector who appears to be spouting nonsense: 'Wilco zebra over', he bellows into his walkie-talkie, 'Green Charlie Angels 15 out' (p. 76). In other words, it is Stoppard's audience who are now the aggressive listeners: by teaching them how to listen to Dogg-language Stoppard has implicated them in an act of collective and effective dissent. The play picks up where Professional Foul left off, turning to good effect the recognition that criticism cannot simply speak for itself.

'Actually', the Inspector tells 'Lady Macbeth', 'I thought you were better on the radio'. 'I haven't been on the radio.' 'You've been on mine', comes the nonchalant reply (p. 58). In Stoppard's version of Communist Europe 'official' ways of listening are both aggressive and furtive, awareness of which drives Hollar to drown with the sound of running water his conversation with Anderson in the hotel room. The implication that this is a perversion of what listening ought to be, is made explicit in his recent television play about the Polish Solidarity movement, Squaring the Circle (1984). The play is constructed from a series of disclaimers or denials, Stoppard's point being that we do not, and cannot, know for certain exactly what did happen in Poland during the months of crisis. The most obvious instance of such a disclaimer is provided by the two different versions we are given of the meeting in November 1981 of Walesa, Jaruzelski and Archbishop Glemp. In the first version Glemp backs the General, in the second he supports the union leader; the fact that neither can claim to be an objective record of the truth is underlined by the device of having the meeting played out as a game of cards. However, the most persistent way that Squaring the Circle contradicts itself is by having the Narrator consistently interrupted by a Polish Witness, who denies the version of events we are being given and passes less than flattering comments on the literary quality of the Narrator's efforts. In each instance the Narrator listens to what he is told and bows to superior wisdom. The point is clear: the Narrator's willingness to listen is a corrective to the repressive dogmatism of the Polish authorities; it is, in Squaring the Circle, Stoppard's index of liberalism.

However, the play also uses the device of disclaimer in a second, and more cunning way. We are, for instance, presented on one occasion with a powerful visual image: we see a line-up of the Party bosses reviewing a parade - they are dressed as gangsters and talk amongst themselves out of the corners of their mouths. Despite the Narrator's insistence that this is just a metaphor, the Witness protests that it is a distortion and his point is taken. Yet the effect is that Stoppard has it both ways: he couples reliance on a stereotype with the declaration that it is inadequate as genuine analysis. In his two most recent full-length stage-plays, Night and Day (1978) and The Real Thing (1982), Stoppard gives full rein to that propensity to oversimplify political issues which he seems rather embarrassed by in Squaring the Circle. In Every Good Boy Deserves Favour, Professional Foul and Dogg's Hamlet, Cahoot's Macbeth Stoppard is clearly on the attack, in Night and Day and The Real Thing he is as clearly on the defensive: both plays are apologies for the political status quo in Britain. Ironically, Stoppard's position is radically and decisively undermined by the fact that he espouses, in mounting this defence, a politics of listening identical to that which, in his plays about the Eastern Bloc, he has so forcibly condemned.

The setting of Night and Day may be Africa, but its subject is the British press. Stoppard's champion among his characters holed up in a luxury bungalow in the middle of an African civil war is Jacob Milne, the young freelance reporter seeking fame and fortune (having fallen foul of union intransigence in Grimsby) who consistently proclaims the importance of a press which is free. For Milne, the only guarantee of a free press is its economic freedom: it must remain a healthy arena for competing entrepreneurial interests. Milne is supported in his views by Ruth, the bored and frustrated wife of his host, who pretends to report the feelings of her son on the subject. The general consensus among the Lower Third, she claims, is that freedom is neutral: 'Free expression includes a state of affairs where any millionaire can have a national newspaper, if that's what it costs. A state of affairs, Allie says, where only a particular approved, licensed and supervised non-millionaire can have a newspaper is called, for example, Russia' (Stoppard, 1979, p. 84).

Milne's principal antagonist is the thick-skinned Australian journalist, Dick Wagner. As a union man Wagner represents the stifling pressures of collectivism, while Milne sets himself up as a thorn in the side of union solidarity. 'The Messenger isn't officially a closed shop, you see -', he says, explaining his metamorphosis into the Grimsby scab, 'they'd just got used to having a hundred per cent membership. I gave them a problem' (p. 38). Milne is the Western version of Stoppard's Soviet dissidents and, as such, is the guardian of the written and the spoken word against appropriation by collective interests. 'My God', he cries, accused by Wagner of betraying his fellow workers, 'you'd need a more supple language than that to describe an argument between two amoebas' (p. 37). He recalls that the House Trots at Grimsby spoke ordinary English on subjects like the death of the novel or the sex life of the editor's secretary, 'but as soon as they started trying to get me to join the strike it was as if their brains had been taken out and replaced by one of those little golf-ball things you get in electric typewriters ... "Betrayal" ... "Confrontation" ... "Management" ...' (p. 37). Milne's stewardship of ordinary

English is continued in his disparaging attack on the practices of junk-journalism, which 'is the evidence of a society that has got at least one thing right, that there should be nobody with the power to dictate where responsible journalism begins' (p. 61).

Milne's views on language are 'justified' not only by the obtuseness of his opponent, they are given tacit support by the form of Night and Day itself. Uncharacteristically for Stoppard, there are no verbal 'fireworks' in the play. The punning is partial, and it is Wagner who falls prey to it: lavatory graffiti in Dacca reads, 'Dick Wagner before he dicks you' (p. 25). That is to say, Stoppard uses the pun in the same way as the authorities he criticises in Every Good Boy Deserves Favour and Dogg's Hamlet, Cahoot's Macbeth: to 'throw' an opponent and encourage the audience to listen in a certain way. Similarly, the rare passages of pastiche in Night and Day serve to establish a hierarchy of discourse, not as in Travesties to cancel one discourse with another. Ruth, for instance, launches into a parody of travel-brochure cliches about the tourists' London: she recalls 'Covent Garden porters with baskets of fruit and veg piled on their heads, threading their way among the flower girls and the professors of linguistics', and 'The good old London bobby keeping a fatherly eye on the children feeding the beefeaters outside Buckingham Palace' (p. 43). The parody tricks out Ruth's resentment and frustrated anger, the disillusionment which Milne - the embodiment of positive values - is able to make good. Parodies of house-styles ('Sally Smith is a tea-lady in a Blackpool engineering works, but it was the way she filled those C-cups which got our cameraman all stirred up!' [p. 39]) are enlisted for the same purpose: to justify Milne's claims about the misuse of language, and to establish as privileged his specific viewpoint. The language of Night and Day then, differs from most of Stoppard's previous work in calling attention to itself as theme, not as form. Milne's 'ordinary English' is presented as a 'natural' standard from which all other discourses are deviations.

Night and Day won for Stoppard a vociferous new admirer in the form of John Barber, drama critic of the Daily Telegraph. Barber approved of both the matter and the manner of the play: Stoppard, he felt, had abandoned the fancy intellectual footwork of his earlier pieces to write 'a savagely serious drama about Fleet Street' (Barber, 1977, p. 10) which made all his other plays look like so many nursery games; he also applauded Stoppard's celebration of the loyalties a free press inspires. In other words, Barber felt perfectly at home with the play's assumptions about the nature of political criticism and the politics of literary form. Milne's conservatism combines the political and the linguistic inasmuch as it declares that contrary opinion is an abuse of speech. Similarly, the tenacity with which Night and Day observes the procedures of Naturalism suggests that a significant departure from them would constitute an abuse of literary form. The binding assumption is of a privileged discourse. What the play presents us with, then, in political, linguistic and literary terms, is a choice between sense and nonsense. In effect, Night and Day is a closed-circuit, which (like Stoppard's jumpers and his Marxists) attempts to avoid the possibility of refutation.

In a remark recorded by Ken Tynan, Stoppard made Milne's tactic explicitly his own. 'I don't lose any sleep if a policeman in Durham beats somebody up', he declared, 'because I know it's an exceptional case. It's a sheer perversion of speech to describe the society I live in as one that inflicts violence on the underprivileged. What worries me is not the bourgeois exception but the totalitarian norm. Of all the systems that are on offer, the one I don't want is the one that denies freedom of expression - no matter what its allegedly redeeming virtues may be. The only thing that would make me leave England would be control over free speech' (Tynan, 1981, p. 100). This articulates succinctly the politics of disengagement defining Night and Day. Stoppard's defence of the status quo is a two-fold retreat from complexity. First, it advocates a perspective in which the 'exceptional case' is reduced in importance. Second, it is a failure of the political and critical imagination to engage with real problems. Stoppard refers to political systems 'on offer', seeing political commitment as a choice between ready-made alternatives, rather than as their reworking. It is the same reliance on prefabricated options which allows Ruth to dismiss too close a scrutiny of the freedom of the press by pointing first to Fleet Street and then to Russia: the implication being that if you don't have one, you must have the other.

The Real Thing goes a step further than Night and Day: dissent from the status quo is regarded not as simply perverse but as fundamentally unreal. The play is Stoppard's most thoroughgoing attempt to dictate the ways in which we listen.

The steward of correct language usage in The Real Thing is the playwright Henry who is asked by his wife, Annie, to rework the autobiographical play written by a CND supporter gaoled after an anti-missile rally. 'I know it's raw', says Annie, 'but he's got something to say'. 'He's got something to say', comes Henry's response. 'It happens to be something extremely silly and bigoted. But leaving that aside, there is still the problem that he can't write. He can burn things down, but he can't write' (Stoppard, 1983, p. 50). To make his point Henry brandishes a cricket bat: 'This thing here, which looks like a wooden club, is actually several pieces of particular wood cunningly put together in a certain way so that the whole thing is sprung, like a dance floor'. What Henry is trying to do 'is write cricket bats, so that when you throw up an idea and give it a knock, it might ... travel'. His objection to Brodie's play is that 'what we've got here is a lump of wood of roughly the same shape trying to be a cricket bat, and if you hit a ball with it, the ball will travel about ten feet and you will drop the bat and dance about shouting "Ouch!" with your hands stuck into your armpits' (p. 53). The difference between the two, Henry insists, is not simply a matter of preference but one of absolute quality: 'This isn't better because someone says it's better, or because there's a conspiracy by the MCC to keep cudgels out of Lords. It's better because it's better' (p. 53). The problem with Brodie's play, as far as Henry is concerned, is that form and content destroy each other: the 'rawness' of the form, he claims, is inseparable from the inanity of the ideas. Both, in effect, are a perversion of discourse. Henry's cricket bat demonstrates not just the necessity of saying things correctly, but of saying the correct things.

Brodie, says Henry, warming to his task, is a 'lout with language'. 'I can't help somebody', he continues, 'who thinks, or thinks he thinks, that editing a newspaper is censorship, or that throwing bricks is a demonstration while building tower blocks is social violence, or that unpalatable statement is provocation while disrupting the speaker is the exercise of free speech' (p. 55). Brodie's problem is not just that he can't put words together ('traditionally considered advantageous for a writer' [p. 52]); his lack of linguistic facility is inextricably bound up with the nature of his ideas. Brodie does violence upon discourse: 'Words don't deserve that kind of malarkey. They're innocent, neutral, precise, standing for this, describing that, meaning the other, so that if you look after them', counsels Henry, 'you can build bridges across incomprehension and chaos' (p. 55). The central point is clear: the 'rawness' of Brodie's expression is the index of its untruth. If he really knew how to use the words he does, he could never think the things he thinks he thinks.

Finally, Brodie is dismissed by Henry's appeal to an unquestioned reality which exposes the fraudulence of his ideas. The cricket bat is replaced by a coffee mug as a didactic tool: 'I turn it, and it has no handle. I tilt it, and it has no cavity. But there is something real here which is always a mug with a handle, I suppose' (p. 54). Although prepared to put his trust in the world of objects, Henry will not countenance the reality of politics. 'Public postures', he had claimed earlier, 'have the configuration of private derangement' (p. 34) and _The Real Thing_ moves towards a climax in which Henry's point is proved. The _real_ story behind Private Brodie's desecration of the Cenotaph has little enough to do with the siting of nuclear missiles: he was simply out to impress Annie. Annie's work on the Justice for

Brodie Committee is likewise exposed: as a political act it has the configuration of her personal atonement of guilt for Brodie's arrest. 'You should have told me ...' suggests Henry, recalling his problems with Brodie's dramatised autobiography. 'That one I would have known how to write' (p. 84).

Henry also feels the need to protect language against the 'persuasive nonsense' of his precociously sophisticated sixteen year old daughter. Debbie's 'That's what free love is free of - propaganda', prompts her father to describe it as 'Sophistry in a phrase so neat that you can't see the loose end that would unravel it. It's flawless but wrong. A perfect dud' (p. 68). Debbie does not 'knock the corners off words', like Brodie; she makes them perform, jump into line. However, Stoppard's principal target is not Debbie's dexterity but Brodie's 'loutish' and restricted way with language, his use of the cudgel rather than the cricket bat. This is made clear by the form of The Real Thing itself which is a self-conscious demonstration of elaborated discourse and, as such, an example of the very standards violated by Brodie and his ilk.

Michael Billington in the Guardian, claimed that by means of 'fly Pirandellian games' The Real Thing 'questions the nature of reality' (Billington, 1982, p. 9). These are precisely the wrong terms in which to describe the point of the play's formal intricacy. In fact, the 'Pirandellian games' perform exactly the same function as the straightforward Naturalism of Night and Day. They demonstrate the real thing, privileged literary discourse. The play blends its own action with scenes from Strindberg's Miss Julie and John Ford's 'Tis Pity She's a Whore, a door slam recalls A Doll's House and a stained handkerchief Othello. The Real Thing ranges itself alongside 'fine writing', a touchstone of literary excellence shared by author and audience alike. Those scenes in which the audience gradually become aware that they are watching not a theatrical representation of real life but excerpts from Henry's House of Cards and his reworking of Brodie's play serve the same purpose: to measure the distance between 'good stuff and rubbish' (p. 65). Basically, then, the intricacy or tricksiness of The Real Thing is its own point: it parades the elaborateness which 'places' Brodie's dissent and, in so doing, proudly displays a shared range of cultural experience, ushering the audience into complicity with the author.

In effect, by opposing its own elaborated form to Brodie's 'restricted' code, The Real Thing draws a sharp line between sense and nonsense, and puts Brodie firmly on the wrong side of it. The audience is encouraged to 'listen' to Brodie only in the paradoxical sense of creating an absence of meaning in what he has to say - in the same way as his opponents disable George in Jumpers. Of course, the success of the tactic depends on the assumption that listening is not as intrusive as this suggests: Brodie is convicted of talking nonsense because he flouts rules governing meaning which are passed off as absolute rather than determined by class, or other, interests in which the audience might share. The audience, then, actively upholds the fiction that, as listeners, they are *in*active.

In *Squaring the Circle* Stoppard shows the creativity of listening in its most positive aspect, finding its expression in an active responsiveness: he presents us with a Narrator who, whatever his failings, admits contrary opinion and is, by implication, a 'good' listener. In this respect, the play reiterates a point made in different ways by *Professional Foul* and *Dogg's Hamlet, Cahoot's Macbeth*: the 'speaker' needs a listener who can actively contribute to the message. In both plays dissidents are deprived of such listeners until the involvement of 'outsiders': in the former, Professor Anderson and, in the latter, the audience, which has been taught Dogg-language. The implication of this, of course, is that 'good', responsive listening is an index of the Western Liberal Democracy which Stoppard explicitly supports. The problem with *The Real Thing*, of course, is that, in defending that society against its enemies within, Stoppard promotes a politics of listening which, in the way it consigns dissent to nonsense, is identical to the aggressive tactics employed by the Communist authorities in his own plays. *The Real Thing*, in effect, is precisely that kind of closed-circuit which, in its Marxist forms, Stoppard so abhors. It seals itself against criticism and is, to use Stoppard's own terms, irrefutable only in the tactical sense that it avoids the possibility of refutation. In a sense, then, the play sponsors two ways of listening: it defines what the audience must actively listen *for*, and what can, and what cannot, be listened to, or responded to.

James Saunders, a playwright as extravagantly praised during the sixties as Stoppard is now, says of his former friend's politics: 'He's basically a displaced person. Therefore, he doesn't want to stick his neck out. He feels grateful to Britain, because he sees himself as a guest here, and that makes it hard for him to criticize Britain. Probably the most damaging thing that could be said about him is that he's made no enemies' (Tynan, 1981, p.71). In the light of *The Real Thing* Saunders's opinion needs to be revised: the most damaging thing that can be said about Stoppard is that, in his recent work, he promotes a conservative message by adopting tactics he had previously condemned and, in so doing, espouses a political outlook which, by putting the lie to his myth of liberal responsiveness, is at best self-contradictory and banal and, at worst, cynical and dishonest.

REFERENCES

Ayer, A.J. (1971) Language, Truth and Logic, Penguin, Harmondsworth.

Barber, John, Review in Daily Telegraph (4 July, 1977), p. 10.

Bennett, J. (1975) 'Philosophy and Mr. Stoppard', Philosophy, 50, pp. 5-18.

Bigsby, C.W.E. (1981) 'The Language of Crisis in British Theatre: The Drama of Cultural Pathology' in C.W.E. Bigsby (ed.), Contemporary English Drama, Arnold, London.

Billington, Michael, Review in Guardian (17 November, 1982), p. 9.

James, C. (1975) 'Count Zero Splits the Infinite', Encounter, 45, pp. 68-76.

Stoppard, T. (1971) After Magritte, Faber, London.

Stoppard, T. (1972) Jumpers, Faber, London.

Stoppard, T. (1973) Artist Descending a Staircase and Where Are They Now?, Faber, London.

Stoppard, T. (1974) Interview in Theatre Quarterly, 14, pp. 3-17.

Stoppard, T. (1975) Travesties, Faber, London.

Stoppard, T. 'But for the Middle Classes', Times Literary Supplement (3 June, 1971), p. 677.

Stoppard, T. 'The Face at the Window', Sunday Times (27 February, 1977), p. 33.

Stoppard, T. (1978) Every Good Boy Deserves Favour and Professional Foul, Faber, London.

Stoppard, T. (1979) Night and Day, second edition, Faber, London.

Stoppard, T. (1980) Dogg's Hamlet, Cahoot's Macbeth, Faber, London.

Stoppard, T. (1983) The Dog It Was that Died and other Plays. Faber, London.

Tynan, K. (1981) Show People, Virgin, London.

TWELVE

THE DOGMA OF AUTHENTICITY IN THE EXPERIENCE OF POPULAR MUSIC

Michael Pickering

> The first duty in life is to be as artificial as possible. What the second duty is no one has yet discovered (Oscar Wilde).

The neglect of the role of the listener has led to many inadequacies in the study of popular song and music. Where characterisations have been made of the audiences of popular music, they have often been built upon a priori categories and assumptions, so that what is then said of the process of reception is deeply coloured by certain expectations and preconceptions about the 'mass' nature of the music, or of popular cultural 'effects'. Conclusions made about the cultural and ideological consequences of popular music are commonly made by reading these off from a study of the text or sound, and this practice is informed much more by pre-existent ideas about the kinds of music that are to be approved and denigrated than it is by knowledge of specific audience uses and meanings, in definite and concrete circumstances. What I shall argue in this paper is that the discourse of the experience of popular music remains too often locked into a duality of thought that permits no synthesis or transcendence, and whose opposite elements are complementary to each other, existing in a necessary antithesis.

At one end of the typical spectrum there is the 'authentic' moment where the listening is an affirmative expression of individuality, of one's own unique and real self. At the other is the moment where the experience of listening to music is a standardised response to the existence of a product made for the sake of profit, a mere unit of bought time in an unvariegated flow of consumption. This denies individual selfhood, debases the aesthetic experience, impoverishes the cultural process. The 'realness' of sound or expression or 'meaning' is commonly established by reference to its ideologically defined opposites of 'commercialism' or 'noise'. Over and over again, in a variety of positions, the success of this strategy relies upon the two mutually dependent tendencies of idealisation and rhetorical condemnation. Critical practice oscillates between these two tendencies. The conservative approach poses the 'authentic' experience in terms of that which is constructed as 'high' cultural achievement and appreciation, opposed in its original conception to the vulgarisation and homogenisation of reception. The idealisation here is of the individual's discriminating response to a 'great tradition' of Western 'classical' and 'folk' musics, and the concomitantly extravagant disparagement is of the consumption of products exhibiting common or baser tastes and values, necessitating little exercise of the critical faculties, and promoting petty bourgeois or proletarian values. The establishment of a literary, artistic and musical canon as superior to all else in the realm of cultural activity enabled the condemnation of 'debased' mass tastes and cultural proclivities to be made from an Olympian summit. This led to paralysing dichotomies in the critical vocabulary from which we are still not entirely free in the way we sometimes conceive the whole field of musical activity and its assimilation. Enshrined in the incestuous categories of classical/popular, serious/light, civilised/barbaric, art/entertainment, etc., is an evaluative conception of what should be involved in the audience sphere, and this has in the past excluded such things as erotic dancing to hot 'jungle' rhythms, the use of music as 'aural wallpaper', or subcultural participation grounded among other things in a fierce identification with particular bands, performers or generic sounds.

The radical response to this has commonly taken either one of two unsatisfactory directions. Romantic populism embraces that which is rejected from the domain of high culture, in a movement which may suggest an inverse snobbery as well as declaring an anti-establishment stance. The mass audience culture it celebrates is here idealised, and authenticity is found in a eulogised general rather than individual experience. The critique of a mass culture of the commodity is dismissed as intellectualist, and therefore irrelevant to an exalted but amorphous 'people'. In the case of 'traditional' song and music, it is the 'folk' who become a similarly asociological and unhistorical category, and the serious study of popular song and music performed by amateurs in local milieux is rejected as academic and irrelevant to 'pure' appreciation. Those tendencies do not of course always manifest themselves in quite the extremist and simplistic ways in which I have isolated them here. But I characterise them thus in order to indicate the direction in which they point and the mode in which they operate. Romantic populism reacts by taking a diametrically opposite position to mass culture criticism, which it denigrates but does not supplant precisely because the movement involves only a conscientious attempt to avoid overt prejudice against the 'popular'. Folk primitivism exhibits the same ideological closure in a different aesthetic quarter. It perpetuates an elitism of folk over mass in scorning out of hand the enjoyment and use of mass cultural products, and in idealising a 'popular' culture constructed in the mould of high aesthetic criteria.

In the traditions of Marxist cultural analysis and critical theory, cultural 'pessimists' have argued - ironically enough, along with a Leavisite type of approach - against the unlikelihood of anything good or progressive coming out of popular music which is commercially produced and marketed. Where one approach may focus predominantly on questions of aesthetic value and cultural standards, the other focuses more on questions of ideological control and subjugation. In either case, audiences are allowed no space actively to interpret or resist what is commercially made available, and what is made available accurately and comprehensively reflects the values of a dominant culture, conceived as either philistine or hegemonic. The 'false consciousness' view of the popular audience, following positions laid down by Adorno, Horkheimer, Marcuse and others, overestimates the extent to which mass culture means ideological domination and cultural homogeneity. The very real threat of these tendencies produces alarmist diagnoses - the work of Seabrook is a case in point - that contain much truth but skew it too strongly in one direction. The mass culture critique, whether developed from the point of view of Tory exclusivism, socially concerned liberalism or anti-capitalist negativism, either promotes a form of cultural apartheid or patronisingly assumes an educative stance in relation to the less civilised or cheapened tastes of a monolithic common people.

The danger of romantic populism is the abandonment of any serious critical impulse in relation to the object of espousal, but it can allow gains to be made over mass culture critiques in encouraging the relativisation of the prescriptive and purist criteria of folk or art aesthetics. The ways we think about and respond to classical music should thus be seen as inappropriate to popular music, which requires an understanding of the different dispositions and competences it commands. The songs and music liked and enjoyed by a large number of people, in most cases produced originally for commercial reasons, should also be recognised as not _ipso facto_ culturally or musically inferior. And the inflated value of high cultural criteria needs to be understood, in an extended perspective, as supportive of the possession of cultural capital within an unequal social order. What mass culture critiques commonly ignore are the politics of representation in popular song and music, and the dynamic aesthetics of their reception. We should not simply assume the conspiratorial intentionality of those who market the goods; the synonymity of purpose of singers and musicians, and the corporate economic enterprises for whom they work; or the dumb passivity of those who consume. We should also be aware of the range and variety of texts and sounds, among which evaluative responses are made, as well as of contradictions within cultural forms which audiences have to negotiate.

Seeing this does not mean that we should adopt a heroic conception of a truly popular culture and music already in existence, out there on the periphery among a discriminating and authentic working class, defined in contradistinction to the two opposed art and mass musics. Whether our focus is urban street culture or backwoods rural vernacular, it would be wrong to imagine that there is anything wholly and autonomously popular in song and music that can be defined outside the conflict and struggle over what is to be institutionally constructed and established as 'popular'. The 'mass' versus 'art' and the 'pop' versus 'folk' aesthetic polarities are manifestations of that struggle in the West, but the use of 'art' and 'folk' as aesthetically ennobled opposites presupposes that the cultural processes and artefacts associated with them are separate or separable from the economic framework of a capitalist social formation, and the asymmetrical relations of power and subordination which support it. In a commercialised world of entertainment and leisure, the <u>sine qua non</u> of popular music is to promote the economic success of corporate business structures. Yet all music today is given definition by this commanding fact and by the social relations it demands. Song and music are distinct from commercial processes only in the artificial situation of state patronage, or at an amateur level where few financial considerations impinge. It is precisely these areas of musical activity which have been most commonly elevated, and in the popular sphere, most distorted. The development of a 'folk' construct during the latter part of the nineteenth century created an idealised conception of popular music with which to condemn an increasing commoditisation of culture, but even at the amateur level which was its regressive preoccupation, this produced a view of musical practice among working people that was largely bunkum.

The influence of this disabling conception has stretched across the whole of the succeeding century. Its emergence is of course inseparable from the historical semantics of the term 'popular', as well as being connected with the very difficult problems associated with the term 'tradition'. In more concrete terms, the folk/popular distinction was, as well as being an enabling device in the construction of a 'national' music and culture, a response to the entrepreneurial and business impact on song production and performance, in the sheet music industry, and in the culture of the music halls and concert halls. In his inaugural address at the inception of the Folk Song Society in England, Parry attacked the tastes of an 'unregenerate public' for music made with a 'commercial intention out of snippets of musical slang'. 'Folk' songs by comparison had 'no sham, no got-up glitter, and no vulgarity'; they were, he declared elsewhere, 'characterised by the purest beauty, by a simplicity, sincerity, tenderness, playfulness, innocent gaiety, healthy vigour' (Parry, 1899, p.3; 1924, p. 112). The aesthetics of folk music were thus conceived, in the same image as those of high culture, as free from commercial imperatives and influences, and thus authentic and good. The idea of a folk music led to the construction of an established canon, and this, although hierarchically ranked, was regarded as the purest distillate of popular musical expression.Its fine achievements, along with those of art music, have commonly been seen from the point of view of advocates of one or the other (or both) as under threat by the music that is disseminated by large-scale, industrialised media of communication. But by comparison with the music appropriated by the late Victorian and Edwardian bourgeois collectors, there was little real interest in the 'folk' audience as people. They were patronisingly regarded as simple-minded, having 'for the most part ... false ideas, or none at all', and little sense of the beauty or value of the songs and music they performed (Parry, 1899, p. 3).

Yet insult was combined with injury to our historical knowledge of the realities of popular music audiences. An exaggerated divide developed between town and country populations, and this fed on an English ideology of ruralism which celebrated a mythical 'organic folk community' of a pre-industrial, pre-urban 'golden age'. A veritable orthodoxy of social and cultural homogeneity grew up with regard to the interrelationship of 'folk' performers and audiences. This was of course ironic in relation to the alleged homogenising effects of mass culture, but it also obscured the location of popular audiences in the social class structure, and gave succour to a Tory anti-commercialism that idealised the past as a means of condemning contemporary social ills. The contrast in the survivalist perspective was always with a 'sham' music hall culture which was destroying the 'genuine' musical culture of an English 'peasant folk' (Sharp and Marson, 1904-9, p. 57). <u>The Strand</u>, for instance, spoke in March 1892 of how the 'rustic mind delights in parading and flaunting shoddy of the music hall in preference to its own substantial if less gaudy homespun'. The folk music movement of the early twentieth century sought to purge such 'shoddy' from people's culture and to reform and elevate popular tastes with the civilising agent of a fabricated and idealised 'nationalised' song tradition. The movement misleadingly stressed as characteristic of village song and music the qualities of orality of transmission; spontaneity of expression and communication; longevity in tradition; stability of repertory content, song meanings and values; communal uniformity of response and understanding; and autochthonous, non-commercial vocal artistry. It is these qualities which, in varying combination, were said to be the benchmarks of authenticity in the content and experience of popular music. The pursuit of this idealised authenticity distorted what working people actually sang and listened to, which of course included far more than the exalted content of folk song collections.

It is only recently that historical study has begun to show how the songs and acts of the music halls and concert halls, despite their commercial contexts of performance, did address (albeit selectively) the realities of life for its predominantly working class audiences. These audiences were not simply dictated to by the music business. Though music hall culture existed to serve capital, capital did not have complete control. As Peter Bailey has put it, music halls were 'uniquely live' and although the entertainment was sold to its customers,

> ... there was a sense in which the sale was being renegotiated throughout the performance. It was this telescoped, immediate and reciprocal relationship between the producer and consumer which made the halls unique. As the social complexion of the music hall public changed with increased lower-middle class patronage, and as other larger social forces widened and deepened the impress of conformity, large numbers of the audience may have been willing converts to more stable patterns of performance and a passive spectator role. But for much of the Victorian period consumer power in the halls was assertive and effective, and greatly complicated strategies of proprietorial control and artistic embourgeoisement (Bailey, 1982, p. 204).[1]

But the politically reactionary 'folk' optic has not only distorted what we know about - and how we understand - the song and music of working people in the nineteeenth century. It has also had a prejudicial effect on the discussion and analysis of what popular music means to its listeners today because of its uncritical adoption by socialist intellectuals and activists of the present century.

The cultural nationalism which inspired the first 'folk' song revival has also informed the anti-Americanism of the second, leftist movement of the post-war period. 'Folk' song has continued to be idealised as the genuine and most valuable form of popular musical expression, and this has been accompanied by an elitist sense that it is this music which has to be reimplanted in people's cultural consciousness. The romanticism has long been apparent. The Proletarian's

Musicians' Association of Moscow in 1929 characterised folk music as 'the true expression of the working class', and radiating out from its Bolshevik and Stalinist origins, the idealisation of folk music soon became the major device utilised by the left in Britain and America for attacking swing, and then rock, and for attempting to mobilise workers politically (Buxton, 1983, pp.93-106). The reformatory impulse characterises both brands of revivalism, though obviously with a different end in view. A. L. Lloyd, the doyen of English folk song advocates on the left, was just as critical as Sharp of the 'insubstantial world of the modern commercial hit' and just as eulogistic of the allegedly communal 'home-made lyrics of the working people' (Lloyd, 1969, p. 410). In fact, as Harker has recently shown, 'the links between Lloyd's and Sharp's ideas are stronger than the differences'. Lloyd worked within a materialistic perspective (albeit rather mechanically), pursued folk song into the industrial heartlands, and saw the 'folk' as transformed into the working class. But otherwise he 'not only perpetuated Sharp's "folksong" consensus', but also 'allowed its contradictions to take a serious toll on his marxism' (Harker, 1985, pp.231, 246).

Raymond Williams pointed out over a quarter century ago that there are no masses, 'only ways of seeing people as masses' (Williams, 1977, p. 289). Similarly, there are no folk, only ways of talking about people as such. Yet, in song and music, the assessment of authenticity of expression and experience has not moved out of the long shadow of these ways of seeing and thinking. The paradigmatic division between folk and mass audiences, and the ideas associated with this, continues, however diffusely at times, to inform the discrimination between two allegedly opposed, and qualitatively split, types of listener. Rock in the 'sixties and 'seventies has been distinguished in this way from pop, just as folk song was pitted against music hall pieces and is today contrasted with 'the mumbled withdrawals or frantic despair of the pops' (Harker, p. 251). Belz's description of 'rock as folk art - a voice <u>of</u> the people' (original emphasis) - depends upon the conceptual opposites derived from folk ideology; performers such as Frank Sinatra, Perry Como and Andy Williams are described as 'not fundamentally concerned with artistic creation', unlike rock musicians. Yet with rock, 'as with any folk idiom, a consciousness of art is unnecessary for grasping the full impact of a particular work' (Belz, 1967, 130-42 and 1972 p. 7). Rock is an art, but because it is folk art its practitioners and its audiences do not self-consciously perform it or appreciate it as 'Art' and are therefore not concerned with aesthetic questions. Aesthetic criteria are, on the contrary, present in the activity of listening to rock, and they only go unnoticed because they are taken for granted, working as the implicit assumptions on which judgments and choices are made.

As Frith has shown, in a fine essay, this account of the essential integrity of rock as opposed to middle-of-the-road pop records regards rock as an authentic representation of a community, a truly popular form of music like 'folk' that integrates performer and audience. Rock shakes it but doesn't fake it. The promotion of rock in the 'sixties as a communal expression of the counter-culture drew, ironically enough, on the folk aesthetics of the dominant culture. The notion of the organic community lived on symbolically in the rock account of its youth audience, while the folk construct of non-massification continued to sustain a romanticised conception of popular musical artistry and creative involvement alongside a mass culture view of atomised individuals, isolated from the bonds of locality, community and kinship, and divorced from those wholesome tastes and habits that would otherwise be there if it were not for industrialisation, geographical mobility, processed culture, consumerism and such. The disposition of authenticity in rock was individually conceived, a true expression of self that conveniently erased the problem of the performer's celebrity status. Paradoxically, appreciation of this was then said to symbolise community - this is 'our music' that the Man can't bust. It was the 'real' voice of a generation, just as in the left appreciation of 'folk' what is heard is the 'real' voice of the working class. The lack of differentiation between performer and audience was fantasised, and the commercial context which did bind them together was ignored. Rock ideology inherited the contradictions of 'folk' and spawned some of its own as it developed a sentimentalised conception of the adolescent working class experience of music. Rock in this conception has idealised working class street culture and incorporated it into a more privileged social world. It has provided an alternative experience - or at least the sense of it - to the tensions and frustrations of bourgeois competitiveness and deferral of reward, to a suburban pattern of ordinariness, to the constraints of living in 'straight society'. It has given 'an illicit, immediate sense of solidarity and danger, an unbourgeois innocence of caution, an uncalculated directness and honesty'. As Frith goes on to say: 'What is on offer is the fantasy community of risk - such a use of music has a long history: in the 1920s and 1930s, middle class adolescents were, for similar reasons, drawn to jazz' (Frith, 1981, pp. 159-68). The rock experience in this conception has drawn its feeling of liminal release from associations with the music's black origins. These work on an exciting sense of cultural (if not racial) difference that also has a long history, stretching back beyond jazz and ragtime to the widespread appeal of nineteenth century 'nigger' minstrelsy to the middle classes of Britain and America (Pickering, 1986; Bratton, 1981, pp. 127-42; Toll,

1974).

But the ideology of rock refuses to acknowledge the use value for capital of the very music it promotes. The aesthetic criteria of authenticity and sincerity that separate rock and pop flies in the face of the actual structural forces that propel popular music production, including those that generate and maintain its star system and consumerist ideology (as manifest in the ever-changing charts). Conferral of the status of art and authenticity on the industry's rock product protects the music, and the experience of its assimilation, from association with the profit motive and the commercial transactions involved in its manufacture and distribution. Meanwhile, we continue to buy, as circumstances force us to, and the existing capital relation remains inviolate. The accompanying aesthetic injunction against imitation also stimulates the continual flow of products that is necessary for the success of any capitalist enterprise. Such success is characteristically premised not on production according to human need or desire, or to foster human creative activity and harmony, but production fuelled by calculation of the exchange value of the resulting commodity. Because song and music means so much to us in our lives, we tend to interpret this as cultural harlotry, and the ideology of art helps us, in rarefied intervals of wishfulness and aspiration, to make more 'meaning' out of music than that existent in an exchange relation. But the quest for authenticity of personal feeling and awareness, to which identification with the performers of popular music often contributes, is in the end an evasion of the realities of existing <u>social</u> relations. The anti-quotidian emphasis in a star's charismatic personality distracts attention from our own ordinary interests and needs - these are suspended by absorption in the star's fetishised public image. 'Authenticity' is seen to depend on degree of self-disclosure - assessed by sincerity of feeling, depth of involvement, commitment, integrity and expression of 'character' - and our close identification of and with these qualities in the experience of the music as a whole generates a sense of community, a sense of belonging, of homing in on 'the heart of a heartless world'. As Buxton has put it, the 'breakdown of traditional social relations due to urbanisation and mass production left identity in a void, which consumerism filled as <u>the</u> basic social relation' (Buxton, 1983, p. 97). It is through consumerism now - the marketed emotions, the star commodity - that the quest for alternative individual and group identities is so often made. Dull, alienating work leads to identification of leisure as freedom, the space where one's 'authentic' self can be realised, yet the effort is conducted in conditions and via products which are structured by the demands of capitalist production. Stars give succour to a contemporary sense of insecurity about personal identity and self by providing consumerist role models and seductive illusions of other possibilities, other ways of life or self-expression beyond the material constraints of our own that are sensed as somehow more real, more authentic. Stars traffic in hope.

The reified sensation of community in rock ideology, and rock's subterranean appropriation of the aesthetics of folk, have of course been challenged at various times by left-wing folk ideologues. MacColl, for instance, has spoken of pop music as 'a defiant relinquishment of responsibility towards this society'. Rock here is lumped together with pop. The 'folk' music of jazz and blues is seen as having become commercially exploited in rock culture, the effort of the second Folk Revival as diluted into folksy sweetness in the record industry's attempts at imitation. The 'whole of the pop song industry', according to Parker, 'is based on the exploitation of folklore, of grass roots musical and poetic forms ...' for the sake of profit and 'the induced self-gratification of an audience'. The Folk Revival by contrast withstands 'the blandishments of commercialism' and any 'assertion of the contemporary relevance of traditional song to repertoire, singing style, and instrumentation' is said to constitute 'a threat to commercial popular music'. Parker notes the working class orientation of early rock and skiffle, and also cursorily acknowledges how some rock music 'with a distinct intellectual content' has an appeal for 'a progressive minority', as distinct from the mass audience appeal of 'essentially mindless pop'. But rock, it is said, cannot be identified 'with "art" in any meaningful sense of the word' and rock protest is illusory. Pop/rock is anti-community and manipulative, 'a master tool of social control' (Parker, 1975, pp. 134-67). This is familiar Adornian territory, but staked out here under a folk banner and along lines made conventional since the 'thirties by C.P. cultural policy.

Rosselson similarly despairs of the ability of pop or rock to mobilise its audiences politically, primarily because of commercialism, while the popular music of lived cultures that 'bubbles up, as it were, from below', becomes as processed as the Tin Pan Alley type of product. Rosselson also concedes the 'common identity' between performers and audiences in early rock 'n' roll, but dismisses its later developments as ersatz, a consumerist 'teenage rebel package'. Skiffle for Rosselson posed more of a genuine challenge to the dominant culture in Britain, and 'by demystifying technique and breaking down the great divide between performers and audience, it offered just a blurred glimpse of a situation where the music is not the property of an elite but a shared experience in which everyone, in a sense, is a participant'. The U.S.A. folk protest movement of the 'sixties was 'a genuine response', but was defused and became trendy and personalised; the West Coast counter-culture was initially subversive but the dream became assimilated by big business. Seeing industry and business as polar opposites of 'genuine culture' is a seductively simple but nevertheless deceptive way of conceptualising the dynamics of popular music. In rejecting rock as 'incapable of saying anything valuable about the world in which most people live, love and work', Rosselson turns to folk clubs and the folk idiom as the only viable alternatives to the music industry, and to rock or pop, because, among other things, performers and audiences are not divided, audience participation is encouraged, and songs in the folk idiom have the potential to make 'a community of the already converted' (Rosselson, 1979, pp. 40-5).

Herman and Hoare (Gardner, 1979, pp. 51-60) have offered a valuable critique of Rosselson's position on popular music. The brunt of what they say is that those on the left cannot afford to hide from the realities of capitalism's inimical effects on artistic creativity in a 'blind cultural archaism', in a folk bunker mentality. This point is neatly encapsulated in a statement by Enzensberger: 'fear of handling shit is a luxury a sewerman cannot necessarily afford' (Enzensberger, 1976, p. 27). But their rejoinder is also to be applauded for its clearer sense of the dialectical nature of cultural commodities, and of the way social context mediates the process of consumption. They understand that 'the old nature of song as popular expression rooted in the experience of the oppressed classes' has not been utterly destroyed by the commoditisation of culture, and that a song's meanings and significances 'are not immutable, independent of context'. Commercial values have been enormously influential in popular music for well over a century, but they do not totally determine the nature of the product or its uses. The consumer is of course far from 'sovereign' in a situation where the 'private ownership of economic resources entitles the owners to whatever surplus the resources yield', and where 'maximisation of the surplus is the main motor of economic enterprise' and 'the quality and direction of output are governed by market potentialities which reflect the prevailing distribution of income and wealth' (Westergaard and Resler, 1977, p. 249). But the values songs and music have in everyday social relationships and milieux are what make them, as commodities, contradictory in nature. Capitalist cultural products are not inevitably and straightforwardly the kind of social cement certain marxists have believed, precisely because of the dialectic at their heart. Moreover, capital's primary necessity is to reproduce itself: that is the logic of its accumulation. This means that profit can be made from works that are ideologically opposed to the kind of social relations and organisation it engenders. Hence the revolutionary texts of Marx in Penguin, or 'Anarchy in the U.K.' in the charts. As Richard Dyer has pointed out, 'it is because of this dangerous, anarchic tendency of capitalism that ideological institutions - the church, the state, education, the family, etc. - are necessary' (Dyer, 1979, pp. 20-3). It is the moral entrepreneurs and guardians who censor or condemn what seems to them obscene or subversive. Frankie says, 'Make Money'.

It would be easy to exaggerate or romanticise the oppositional potential of subversively listening to or using popular music, but songs and music can be appropriated in different ways from those intended, and meanings can be realised in different ways in particular subcultural and minority group contexts which are contrary to those privileged in the original text or sound. Hoggart, for instance, in his celebrated study of working class culture, noted that 'After the Ball is Over' was 'taken over by the people' and 'taken over on their own terms', and so it was 'not for them as poor a thing as it might have been' (Hoggart, 1969, p. 162). Many other examples could be given, in what would have to be a more empirical study, but if there is any authenticity in reception it is here, in the creation of cultural proximity. This is the process whereby a song or piece of music (or any other cultural product) is assimilated into a particular subculture or social group, so that its meanings are realised in accord with people's situated consciousness and position in society. Musical commodities which are condemned out of hand in the mass, folk and rock conceptions of the popular audience thus become, in specific enabling contexts, creatively used and resignified. The same can be true of the technology of commercial popular music.

This has proved time and again to have creative possibilities not realised in original or prevailing commercial usages, both for performers and audiences. What did a cheap Woolworth's guitar do for punk if not 'demystify technique'. And why can't the cheap synthesiser, courtesy of the microchip' be seen as the 'modern equivalent of the old tea-chest and a piece of string' (Goodwin, 1985, p. 26)? The transistor, television, cassette-recorders, videos and walkmans have radically extended and transformed our modes of listening to popular music. What aid is 'folk' retreatism to becoming critically reflexive about these changes? The nativist disapprobation melodramatically exaggerates the real worries they provoke, and in doing so pejoratively dismisses the real pleasures and possibilities they nevertheless offer. Rock ideologues of the 'sixties surprisingly inherited this 'folk' suspicion of music technology, if in an attenuated form, presumably because its pastoral undertones proved compatible with hippy ruralism. It is not that this distrust, as well as anti-commercialism, do not have any political credibility for radical critique, but that they can be badly mishandled, and need to be revalued from an audience point of view. The technological mediation of music constructs and facilitates its own realities of experience and use. It is on those grounds that the question of authenticity must be posed, and in terms that are appropriate to the particular contexts in which the experience of popular music is lived.

'Authenticity' is a relative concept which is generally used in absolutist terms. I have tried to show that in the discourse of popular music, the rigid demarcation of audience experience between manipulation and corruption, and what would otherwise be authentic and genuinely expressive of popular sentiments and ideas, produces an ideological circularity of presentation and argument. The general lack of investigation of situated processes of reception and of the specific and changing social conditions in which they occur, has served to encourage the perpetuation of this self-confirming style of thinking. It is ideological in nature in that it naturalises the existing structure of social relations involved in the transmission of popular music. It distinguishes between user and consumer by fetishising the symbolic value of selective cultural commodities, as if this can be divorced from the relations of exchange, and thus has the indirect effect of vindicating popular music's entanglement in those relations. The rock and folk ideologies not only echo the elitism of Leavisite approaches to mass culture, but also rationalise existing productive relations and goals by idealising their own specific idiom, by giving it exclusive rights to authenticity of expression and experience. And in doing so both insult the masses (or the working class, who are on the reverse side of that euphemistic epithet). Time and again the formulaic differentiation between authentic and commerical works as a way of placing others, socially and culturally, a shorthand device for categorically separating the masses from ourselves, in a way which obscures the real inequalities of opportunity and resources.

It is no coincidence that this ideological segregation of authentic individual expression and appreciation from its alleged denial in a standardised product and usage is predominantly of middle class origin and reproduction. Sound empirical work on the stratified use of popular music among the general range of audiences in Britain is lamentably sparse; the sociological research which has been conducted has largely concentrated on youth. The results of these studies reveal (among many other things) that those having (or aspiring to) middle class status, with a proven track record of academic success and good future prospects, conceive of the popular music they cleave to within a value framework that stresses the 'uniqueness of each person's response', discrimination and authenticity of individual choice, and the community of shared musical taste. These qualities are opposed, predictably enough, to mass taste and 'the evils of commercialism' (Murdock and Phelps, 1973; Frith, 1983, ch. 9; Murdock and McCron, 1973, pp. 690-1; Troyna, 1979, pp. 406-14).[2] Commitment to music exhibiting these exalted aesthetic features is also generally most intense among rebels and drop-outs, middle class youth rejecting success and thus seeking alternative sources of identity more 'authentic' than that offered by their own class culture. As in the wider discourse of popular music, the artist is pitted against the industry, the individual listener who is informed and intelligent against the mindless mass audience. The same formula applies in the music as imaginary entry into working class culture or adolescence. The fundamental duality of thought focused on in this paper once more manifests itself on the one hand in the derision of the working class audience as credulous, unaware of being exploited, fickle and herd-like in reaction, debased in taste and manners, and on the other hand in the veneration of working class culture as a source of vitality, danger, liberation, innovation, sincerity and authenticity (romantically conceived). Though it is now a well-worn truism, it is perhaps worth reiterating the point that when the middle class regard the working class it is usually only the positive or negative images of themselves which they see.

Musical taste is more often than not defined in terms of peer-group culture, particularly for British youth but generally, as well, among a wide range of social groups and networks. It is within these contexts that the habitual mode of thought discussed in this chapter - revolving around the twin processes of idealisation and rhetorical condemnation - is most resonantly deployed, as a way of engaging in social participation and of defining the boundaries of group identity. This can in itself have its rewards, but it also commands a heavy price: exclusion from a variety of musical forms, idioms and genres that may otherwise afford considerable satisfaction and pleasure, if only the portcullis of prejudice could be raised. This is true of all kinds of music and all kinds of individuals and groupings. Its roots lie in the manifold ways in which divisions of class, gender and race, emanating out of an unequal social order, are felt and lived, as the aforementioned sociological studies of pop media use among adolescent school students have demonstrated. But the assertions of authenticity which so often follow, predominantly in middle class groups, find nourishment in the rootlessness and instability that is fundamental to the experience of modernity.

People often use music as a means of self-validation. Particular singers, musicians, songs, idioms or genres are more hotly attacked and ardently defended than most other kinds of artists, or other forms of cultural performance, precisely because of this high degree of personal identification. Such subjective investment means that we authenticate ourselves by the music we identify ourselves with, and musical taste thus becomes valorised in what is essentially a puritanical mode of self-justification. Whereas music preferences and antipathies are generally group-specific, the notion of authentic musical expression and experience as immanent in an abstract individual realm retains the most active emphasis. Consider Ian Kemp's formulation: 'Music', he says, 'has authentic meaning and value only to the individual. No one can claim to know what that might be for anyone else' (Kemp, 1978, pp. 117-34). Tendentially at least, this amounts to a kind of solipsism of musical aesthetics. It is however, part of a much broader historical structure of attitude and outlook which sustains, in the modern era, an accelerated sense of individualisation. This sense is an integral feature of the specific personality structure of our kind of complex, highly diversified and divided society. 'In more developed societies', as Norbert Elias has it, 'people see themselves broadly as fundamentally independent individual beings, as windowless monads, as isolated "subjects", to whom the whole world including all other people, stands in the relationship of an "external world"' (Elias, 1985, p. 52). If individuality is viewed as existing in isolation from others, then on that basis friendship and intimacy must be seen as dependent upon the disclosure of self as a unique source of meaning. The refusal of 'meaning' and 'value' as social categories, as matters of communal interdependence, encourages a false sense of division between self and outside world, and obscures even the self-evident truths of social and cultural praxis. 'Community' is then thought of in idealised or fictitious forms. This can indeed engender the pathological tendencies of a culture of narcissism, and what Sennet calls 'destructive Gemeinschaft'; the star system and the myth of folk community in rockism are obvious examples of these tendencies (Lasch, 1980; Sennett, 1977; Bocock, 1980, pp. 91-121).

The obsession with intimate self-revelation, and the equation of authentic self-disclosure and social bonding, combine to evade critical confrontation with the simultaneously exhilarating and dislocating experience of turmoil that is integral to modern life. We move today within the context of environments and within modes of experience whose structural dynamics are predicated upon the constant change, disruption and renewal that are demanded by capitalist economic development. Our sensibilities are moulded by the social forces thus unleashed, so that against the expansion of ideas and possibilities, the liberation from restrictions and tradition, the increase in material comforts and technological equipment, we experience the contradictory effects of modern life in feelings of disorientation and social alienation, loneliness and longing for stability and community, disgust at the consumerist exploitation of hopes, dreams and desires; most seriously of all perhaps, we suffer from a sense of the disintegration of the integrity of self (Berman, 1983; Anderson and Berman, 1984). One of the commonest strategies for dealing with such distinctively modern feelings is to imagine that inauthenticity resides in the prevailing social relations which engender them, and the road to what is real is to be pursued through a process of self-cultivation. In this stress upon individual experience as the locus of validity and truth, the reality of culture-as-commodity and its accompanying relations is easily lost from view.

An imaginary performer/audience community acts as a complementary adjunct of individualistic conceptions of authenticity of experience. It provides a self-regarding fantasy of unity in a radically disunited world where only 'our music' is valid and true, and produced or performed in good faith. As Benjamin first pointed out, the conception of authenticity as confined to the original and therefore unique work of art has been displaced and rendered archaic by the development of mechanical reproduction (Benjamin, 1970, pp. 215-53). Authenticity of artefact or product can no longer be proved. It is therefore sought in the process of cultural production (its creative moments) and the experience of cultural reception and response (its critical or discerning moments). There is no way of knowing objectively when these moments are authentic, since they are relative to culture, gender, class and period. Yet we continually insist upon our own privileged access to knowing exactly what's real and what is not in song, singing and musical performance. Instead of grappling with the ambiguities and contradictions of modern life and its diversity of cultural forms and experiences, twentieth century response to the tensions and conflicts thus engendered tend to lurch 'far more toward rigid polarities and flat totalizations':

> Modernity is either embraced with a blind and uncritical enthusiasm, or else condemned with a neo-Olympian remoteness and contempt; in either case, it is conceived as a closed monolith, incapable of being shaped or changed by modern men (sic). Open visions of modern life have been supplanted by closed ones, Both/And by Either/Or (Berman, 1983, p. 24).

Within such a closed either/or vision, 'authentic' cultural expression and experience have perforce to be conceived along romantic lines as constitutive of an essentially other, inviolate world, distinguishable from and counter to the politics and philosophy of the marketplace. What these orientations amount to are ways of evading the social and economic, a crucial effect of which is to provide a justification for existing capitalist practice in the sphere of cultural and musical expression. And out of them comes that over-neat equation of high quantity of product with low quality of reception. It is the unique piece of music which has value, not that which is produced and distributed on a large scale. The effect is to dehumanise and decontextualise actual use and assimilation of those pieces of song and music widely disseminated by the media of cultural communication and, within specific groups and contexts, consensually identified as commercial or cacophonous, reserving an embattled space for free and active choice of those idealised performances singled out as original, unique, authentic, beautiful and true. This space is illusory when conceived as independent of market and class relations. Popular agency is delimited by these relations but not utterly curtailed, as can be witnessed in the volatility of the market for popular music, the appropriation of music technology, the creation of cultural proximity and the resignification of text or sound. Yet it is for the most part the emphasis on a self-confirming and cultural worth of music, its individualist (rock) or communal (folk) 'authenticity', which permits the commercial imperatives of the industrial structures in which popular music is produced to be successfully occluded. Commercialism means the imposed standardisation of value. The romantic ideology of 'real' self expression, and of the unique listener, does not challenge this underlying logic of commercialism, since such features can always be found somewhere or imagined to exist. More importantly, capitalist enterprise in the popular music field requires that such qualities be encouraged precisely in order to conceal and offset its own innate rationalist tendency to standardise, a tendency which encourages the onset of creative stagnation and, as public interest wanes, leads to sluggish sales and economic decline. That is the necessary paradox behind innovation, and not the finally victorious artist wresting control of his or her creativity from a mercenary music business.

Many of the prevalent categories and conceptions used to evaluate popular music are therefore informed by the contradictions in and between its cultural production, transmission, use and assimilation, but as I have tried to indicate in this paper, they do not transcend those contradictions. Instead, they replicate them in romantic ideas of art and the artist which are readily incorporated by the culture industry for its opposite ends. In Marx's words: 'The bourgeois viewpoint has never advanced beyond the antithesis between itself and the romantic viewpoint; and the latter will accompany it as its legitimate antithesis up to its blessed end' (Marx, 1973, p. 162).

NOTES

1. Bailey gives an intriguing example of the activeness and creativity of music hall audiences. 'Spotting foreign visitors in the London halls at the time of the 1862 Exhibition -"the Mossoos with the big heads" - was a great sport. When George Sims and his middle-class party descended upon the East End halls in the late 'eighties, they were greeted with the chant of "Hottentots", a neat and carnivalesque inversion of the imagery of the social explorers.'

2. This list of research on adolescent music is of necessity selective, and any more comprehensive bibliographical reference would of course need to refer to the substantial body of work now existing on youth subcultural analysis.

REFERENCES

Abbs, P. (ed.) (1975) The Black Rainbow, Heinemann, London.
Anderson and Berman, (1984) New Left Review, no. 144 (March-April).
Bailey, P. (1982) 'Custom, Capital and Culture in the Victorian Music Hall' in R. Storch (ed.) Popular Culture and Custom in Nineteenth Century England, Croom Helm, London.
Belz, C. (1967) 'Popular Music and the Folk Tradition', Journal of American Folklore, 80, pp. 130-42.
Belz, C. (1972) The Story of Rock, Oxford University Press, New York.
Benjamin, W. (1970) 'The Work of Art in the Age of Mechanical Reproduction' in Illuminations, Cape, London, pp. 215-53.
Berman, M. (1983) All that's Solid Melts into Air, Verso, London.
Bocock, R. et al. (eds.) (1980) An Introduction to Modern Sociology, Harvester, Brighton.
Bratton, J. (ed.) (1986) The Victorian Music Hall: Performance and Style, Open University, Milton Keynes.
Bratton, J. (1981) 'English Ethiopians: British Audiences and Black Face Acts, 1835-1865', Yearbook of English Studies, pp. 127-42.
Buxton, D. (1983) 'Rock Music, the Star-System and the Rise of Consumerism', Telos, no. 57, pp. 93-106.
Dyer, R. (1979) 'In Defence of Disco', Gay Left, no. 8, Summer, pp. 20-3.
Elias, N. (1985) The Loneliness of the Dying, Blackwell, Oxford.
Enzensberger, H.M. (1976) Raids and Reconstructions, Pluto, London.
Frith, S. (1983) '"The magic that can set you free": The Ideology of Folk and the Myth of the Rock Community' in R. Middleton and D. Horn (eds.) Popular Music, Cambridge University Press, Cambridge.
Frith, S. (1983) Sound Effects, Constable, London.
Gardner, C. (ed.) (1979) Media, Politics and Culture Macmillan, London.
Goodwin, A. (1985) 'Interview with Daniel Miller', Marxism Today, (August), pp. 26-28.
Harker, D. (1985) Fakesong, Open University, Milton Keynes.
Herman, G. and Hoare, I. (1979) 'The Struggle for Song: a Reply to Leon Rosselson' in C. Gardner (ed.) Media Politics and Culture, Macmillan, London. pp. 51-60.
Hoggart, R. (1969) The Uses of Literacy (Penguin, Harmondsworth.
Kemp, I. (1978) 'Music and the Forbidden Corner', University of Leeds Review, 21, pp. 117-34.
Lasch, C. (1980) The Culture of Narcissism, Abacus, London.

Lloyd, A.L. (1969) Folk Song in England, Panther, London.
Marx, K. (1973) Grundrisse, Penguin, Harmondsworth.
Middleton, R. and Horn, D. (eds.) (1981) Popular Music, Cambridge University Press, Cambridge.
Murdock, G. and McCron, R. 'Scoobies, Skins and Contemporary Pop', New Society, no. 547 (March, 1973), pp. 690-1).
Murdock, G. and Phelps, G. (1973) Mass Media and the Secondary School, Macmillan, London.
Parker, C. (1975) 'Pop Song, the Manipulated Ritual' in P. Abbs (ed.) The Black Rainbow, Heinemann, London.
Parry, C. Hubert (1899) 'Inaugural Address', Journal of the Folk Song Society, no. 1, p. 3.
Parry, C. Hubert (1924) Style in Musical Art, Macmillan, London.
Pickering, M. (1986) 'White Skin, Black Masks: "Nigger" Minstrelsy in Victorian England' in J. Bratton (ed.) The Victorian Music Hall: Performance and Style, Open University, Milton Keynes.
Rosselson, L. (1979) 'Pop Music: Mobiliser or Opiate?' in C. Gardner (ed.) Media, Politics and Culture, Macmillan, London.
Sennett, R. (1977) The Fall of Public Man, Cambridge University Press, Cambridge.
Sharp, C. and Marson, C. (1904-9) Folk Songs from Somerset Simkin, London, vol i.
Storch, R. (ed.) (1982) Popular Culture and Custom in Nineteenth Century England, Croom Helm, London.
Toll, R. (1974) Blacking Up: The Minstrel Show in Nineteenth Century America, Oxford University Press, New York and London.
Troyna, B. (1979) 'Differential Commitment to Ethnic Identity by Black Youths in Britain', New Community, vii, pp. 406-14.
Westergaard, J. and Resler, H. (1977) Class in a Capitalist Society, Penguin, Harmondsworth, p. 249.
Williams, R. (1977) Culture and Society, Penguin, Harmondsworth.